J U N G L E K E E P E R

JUNGLEKEEPER

WHAT IT TAKES TO CHANGE THE WORLD

PAUL ROSOLIE

CONVERGENT

NEW YORK

Convergent

An imprint of Random House

A division of Penguin Random House LLC

1745 Broadway, New York, NY 10019

convergentbooks.com

penguinrandomhouse.com

LIBRARY OF CONGRESS CATALOGING-IN-PUBLICATION DATA

Names: Rosolie, Paul author

Title: Junglekeeper / Paul Rosolie.

Description: New York, NY : Convergent, [2026]

Identifiers: LCCN 2025031642 (print) | LCCN 2025031643 (ebook) |
ISBN 9780593980392 hardcover | ISBN 9780593980408 ebook

Subjects: LCSH: Rosolie, Paul—Travel—Madre de Dios River Valley (Peru and Bolivia) | Rosolie, Paul—Travel—Amazon River Region | Durand, Juan Julio | Junglekeepers (Organization) | Nature conservation—Madre de Dios River Valley (Peru and Bolivia) | Nature conservation—Amazon River Region | Conservationists—Biography | Madre de Dios River Valley (Peru and Bolivia) — Environmental conditions | Amazon River Region—Environmental conditions

Classification: LCC F3451.M2 R668 2026 (print) | LCC F3451.M2 (ebook)

LC record available at https://lccn.loc.gov/2025031642

LC ebook record available at https://lccn.loc.gov/2025031643

Printed in the United States of America on acid-free paper

1st Printing

FIRST EDITION

BOOK TEAM: PRODUCTION EDITOR: Loren Noveck •
MANAGING EDITOR: Allison Fox • PRODUCTION MANAGER: Sarah Feightner •
COPY EDITOR: Liz Carbonell • PROOFREADERS: Barbara Jatkola, Zora O'Neill,
and Katie Powers

Book design by Barbara M. Bachman

Title page image by Stephane Thomas and
background image by Adobestock/tannujannu

The authorized representative in the EU for product safety and compliance is Penguin Random House Ireland, Morrison Chambers, 32 Nassau Street, Dublin D02 YH68, Ireland. https://eu-contact.penguin.ie

To the great jungle and
the wild heartbeats
who have given me so much.
Long live Amazonia.

CONTENTS

===

INTRODUCTION

FAR OUT ON THE WESTERN EDGE OF THE AMAZON RAINFOREST, deep in the Peruvian jungle, a pair of loggers plunged their chain saws into the buttressed roots of an ancient ironwood tree. It took them over an hour to guide the blades through expert cuts before the fibers of the tree's core began popping and creaking. An ironwood, or shihuahuaco, of this size is a giant among giants, an emergent sentinel that reaches heights of 160 feet, towering over the rest of the canopy.

This particular tree had started its life as a tiny sapling in the great jungle, a story that began before the Spanish reached Peru, long before the United States was even a dream, at a time when Leonardo da Vinci was still honing his talents in a faraway part of the world. Through the Renaissance, the First and Second World Wars, and the birth of our grandparents, this tree was out there, slowly charging upward, anonymous. Just one pillar among the billions of others. But on this day in August 2024, when the two loggers worked, this witness of the centuries came crashing down through the canopy with such cataclysmic power that it shook the earth.

The shockwave rippled through the jungle.

Somewhere in the leafy distance, a clan of Mashco Piro people stopped in their tracks, listening. They were barefoot and naked, part of the last nomadic "uncontacted" tribes living in the most geographically inaccessible reaches of Amazonia. Just like the ancient tree, theirs was a story that had for centuries existed far from the happenings of the world, guarded by hundreds of miles of rainforest. A kind of natural time capsule of deep jungle, untouched and grown wild since the dawn of time. These were people whose ancestors had always lived far from the rest of the world, so much so that the Mashco not only exist without modern technology, but have never seen a wheel. They don't shape metal or even have access to stone. While the world modernized, they'd maintained a hunter-gatherer lifestyle far out in the Amazon. But the distant droning of chain saws and the sound of great trees falling meant all that was about to change.

The Mashco Piro stalked through the forest, ducking vines with lithe barefoot steps, drawing closer to where the loggers worked.

The tribes are known to use botanical compounds as insect repellent and war paint, to stain their naked bodies and create a kind of camouflage that allows them to all but vanish into the forest. They also employ animal sounds—the calls of capuchin monkeys and tinamous—to disguise communication, so they can surround their enemies, totally undetected.

With the chain saw fitted into a metal frame, the loggers were working to mill the tree trunk into boards. The frame allowed them to cut clean planks to make the wood easier to haul out to the river, where they would float it down for almost a week before reaching the first town with a road. The screaming chain saw's racing teeth and the flurry of sawdust demanded their strength and focus and rendered them all but deaf. Neither of them would leave the jungle.

Just out of sight, in the shadowed obscurity of the leaves, the tribe watched. They were naked save for threads of plant fiber that held their penises up against their bodies. Each man carried arrows that were nearly seven feet long and almost weightless. Each of these arrows, which most of us would call spears, was fitted with a bamboo tip as long as a machete. The bows that shot these were taller than a man and crafted of black palm wood. They are weapons capable of piercing a spider monkey mid-swing on a tree branch at a hundred feet. But that wouldn't matter here. This was up close. Personal. Powerful bows flexed as strong arms pulled the strings, took aim, and shot.

Perhaps it went just like that. Perhaps it didn't. What we know for certain is that the bodies of the loggers weren't found until days later, when thundering military helicopters came ripping over the canopy, searching for a scar from downed trees in the otherwise endless jungle. Commandos in camouflage and combat helmets carrying automatic weapons investigated the scene. The bodies were bloated and had been fed on by jungle animals and picked at by vultures. There were maggots flowing from their eyes and mouths. But other than a show of force and due diligence, collecting the bodies and flying off, there was nothing that the commandos could do—clashes between illegal loggers and the last uncontacted tribes are regrettably common in the Peruvian region of Madre de Dios.

The lore and wonder surrounding the uncontacted tribes of the Amazon are haunting. The stories are numerous and are often whispered around backcountry campfires. For decades the government of Peru tried to convince the public that the tribes were nothing more than a legend that locals told to keep the loggers from going into the sacred parts of the forest. It's not very logical to imagine, after all, that a tribe of naked warriors has managed to stay in the shadows for the last several centuries and is still out there hiding.

But those of us who live out in the wild know better.

We are careful to heed the subtle signs the tribes leave— a trail you may not cross, or a stream that is off-limits. They

guard the last, deepest corners of the jungle with lethal determination and a simple, resounding single message: Stay out.

The loggers they killed in August 2024 hadn't respected this
request. By October of the same year, I would be running at full
speed, heart pounding, taking cover behind trees. The tribes of
Amazonia would stalk out of the mythical realm they had always inhabited in my mind—streaked with war paint, their
bows and arrows ready—and prove they are very real, full of
questions, and capable of a kind of warfare that is almost unseen
in our modern world.

≡

I first traveled to this brutal backcountry in 2006, when I was
just eighteen years old. It was my dream to see the wildest place
on Earth, and so I signed up as one of several volunteers on an
expedition that was set to travel by river for two days, deep into
the jungle, to a remote research station outpost where we would
collect data on threatened species.

It was supposed to last just a few weeks.

Almost twenty years later, as I write these words, the jungle
is my home—and protecting it has become my life's purpose.

The original expedition was led by Juan Julio Durand, a
local conservationist from a nearby Ese Eja Indigenous community, who goes by JJ. He and his partner, Emma, a British biologist, had followed their dreams and started a tiny research base
camp. They called it Las Piedras Biodiversity Station. It was so
remote that the only way to get there was by boat. You had to
travel for days on end, camping along the way. Piled on the boat
with you were all the supplies you would live on for the next
few weeks: Rice. Beans. Eggs. And lots of batteries for the night.
At the research station there was no light, no electricity, no
communication with the outside world—we really were on our
own.

For as long as I can remember, it had been my dream to see the Amazon. I had no way of knowing JJ and I would hit it off and I'd eventually be unofficially adopted by his Indigenous family. Or that I was about to be thrown down the Amazonian rabbit hole to depths I couldn't have imagined (though it's probably more accurate to say I flung myself).

But this isn't a story about the early days when I fell in love with the jungle. That was the easy part. No, this is about what happened next, what I learned about the responsibility that came with that love and all the implications and understanding it brought me. It's about the events that would change the trajectory of my life and reshape the destiny of a river.

Since 1970, we've lost more than 50 percent of the wildlife on Earth. Not 50 percent of the species, but the overall number of wild animals across the globe has decreased by over half in just a few decades. It is the direct result of human activity. For that reason I've spent my adult life running toward seventy-foot flames in the Amazon Rainforest, trying to save what animals I could. While trying to document the destruction around the world, I've rescued singed monkeys, wrestled giant anacondas, and been charged by rhinos. In India, I've tracked the last remaining tigers on Earth and lived with herds of elephants who have nowhere left to go. Seeing these and other threats to the natural world has fueled my sense of urgency.

Given all the death and destruction I've witnessed, it would be easy to slip into the popular antihuman narrative that we are a plague on the planet—the oceans are rising, the climate is changing, the pandas are dying, and there's nothing that can be done. But my career in conservation has given me a glimpse into an alternate narrative. I've met people who are proving more and more that something *can* be done. I'm talking about real heroes. People who have dedicated their lives to redeeming the evil that is capable of being waged by the human soul. People who are guarding the flame amidst the storm, proving every day what so many have forgotten: There is still hope.

While so much of the Amazon is being destroyed, today we are on the brink of establishing one of the largest protected areas of rainforest on Earth. What started twenty years ago as a dream between me and my Native friends in the Amazon became a multimillion-dollar international movement to protect more than 100,000 acres of pristine habitat: millions of wild heartbeats, entire Indigenous communities, and untold numbers of new species and undiscovered medicines.

They say the master has failed more times than the beginner has even tried. As you are about to read, it wasn't a linear path, nor an easy, clean, or particularly pleasant one. I've been bitten by crocodiles and snakes and tigers, and have gotten run over by boats. I've almost died from infections and been stranded for weeks in deep jungle. My body is a Jackson Pollock painting of old flesh wounds, but these are a warm summer breeze compared to things that left real scars along the way. Following your dreams, it turns out, often requires cutting away most of what constitutes a normal life, parts of you that stitches can't fix. Protecting the wild isn't a job, it's a calling, and I'm no example to follow.

One of the most important things I've learned is that if you can survive enough failures, close calls, tragedies, and do-overs . . . you gain enough familiarity with the hits to start to see the punches coming. You gradually come to know the wrong path, and knowing which way *not* to go is one step closer to the right direction. The wild will either kill you or teach you to find a bearing—and that's why I'm writing this book.

It comes out of the quest to attain the child's dream of being an adventurer—to share the surreal wonder of exploring some of the deepest jungle on Earth, the last truly unknown corners of the Amazon. I want readers to glimpse the animal mind, and understand what it takes to protect species on a professional level. And what it really means to follow your dreams at all costs.

This book is the story of how a dream can turn into a mission and how that mission can turn into a quest—one that might lead you down through the jungle and into the glowing, hallowed hidden space where the truest of human treasures exists: purpose.

The pages ahead are a journey that is both spiritual and physical. Spiritual because I had to lose my mind to find my path, and because the people and creatures I encountered allowed me into their world in profound ways. Through these experiences, I've learned with shocking clarity just how intimately humans depend on the living environment around us. Physical because, sometimes, these adventures came incredibly close to costing me my life. Above all, I've learned that literally anything is possible, and that life is about more than just yourself, your country, or your kind.

I write these words, the truth of my experience, as a kind of promise: There really is adventure out there waiting for you, and so much good in this world that needs doing. The cynics will try to convince you that we live in the end of days. They are wrong.

This is just the beginning.

—*Paul Rosolie*

LAS PIEDRAS
BIODIVERSITY
STATION

JUNGLEKEEPER

THE RIVERS IN
OUR VEINS

≡

THERE WAS ONCE A LITTLE FOREST STREAM ABOUT AN HOUR'S boat drive from the research station. It slithered beneath the canopy like a little blue snake—from a bird's-eye view it was invisible. A hard-to-access, seldom-visited capillary of the great Amazon River. You already know what this place looks like in your mind: a hidden, vine-draped jungleland, shadowed by umbrella leaves, dappled with butterflies, and humming with wild beauty. That's the spot JJ and I used to love to explore.

We'd head out in the morning with a boat and fishhooks, machetes and no shoes. Well, sometimes we brought shoes, but when we did, we left them in the boat, the way one leaves shoes outside before entering a temple.

The stream was small, never more than thirty feet across, often as little as ten, and not very deep. Most of the way up we could walk it like a path. Sure, there were pools at the bends, but we stayed away from those, knowing that's where the largest crocs, the longest anacondas, and all the stingrays were hiding. For the most part we could see the streambed as we went. White sand. Soft on the feet. The water was cool and swift and full of little fish eager to swarm-feed on our dead skin if we gave them the chance. The tree branches met overhead like the ceiling of a great emerald-green cathedral.

We tried to formulate a theory as to why the trees here were so exceptionally tall, even for Amazonia. There were towering buttress-rooted Spanish cedars and pillar-straight quinillas with crocodile-skin bark, gargantuan kapok trees, manchinga, remo caspi, and gnarled matapalos. This was true old growth. In between the giants were myriad saplings striving upward and competing for light. Branches held bromeliads the size of small elephants. Vines interlaced the canopy, and up in the loftiest branches, cacti and orchids bloomed where butterflies and rare bees doted over their high-altitude habitat. This was true primary forest. A jungle that had never been cut. An ecosystem in its most abundant and diverse iteration, a constant state of biological climax.

ONE NOVEMBER DAY, we were picking our way along the stream and stopping to look at small wonders. We were barefoot and shirtless and each had a machete so sharp it could sing. There was no reason for snacks or water bottles on an all-day hike: JJ would find all the food we needed along the way, and the water of this stream was so clear and clean, we could drink any time we pleased.

JJ told me how his father, Santiago, was once searching deep in the jungle for vines to harvest for ayahuasca, when he found an anaconda in a stream not unlike the one we were walking in. The giant snake had almost finished swallowing an entire tapir (an animal roughly the size of a small cow).

JJ told many stories as we went. Every so often we would pause for a teaching moment in the present. Like when JJ spotted jaguar tracks on the beach beside us.

"Lookadis!" JJ said, motioning with his machete.

"Big one," I said.

JJ smiled condescendingly. "No. Look. Mira."

I studied the sand and tried to imagine what JJ saw. He can put his mind inside another animal and tell you what it wants and where it is going.

There were two jaguar prints, front paws, just by the water's edge, deeper at the toes.

"That's where he leaned forward to drink," I said.

That earned me a smile.

By then I knew I was being tested, so I knelt. Close by was a thick log of jaguar scat covered in butterflies and bees and green flies. I guessed it to be about a day old. The tracks around the scat were clearly older than the ones by the water's edge. Gradually the scene was coming into focus. The dry tracks and fly-buzzing scat were from yesterday. I could also see where the big cat drank yesterday—those imprints had settled and had bits of leaf material in them. Then there were the newer tracks, still moist, from perhaps moments before we had come around the bend. So from what I could discern, the jaguar had been visiting this beach regularly in the last twenty-four hours.

"Es macho, no?" I asked.

JJ nodded. "Sí. . . . Qué más? What else?"

"He was here yesterday . . . and today . . . like, just now . . . two days in a row . . ." I trailed off, thinking. Jaguars are usually marchers. They never stay in one place long. It seemed strange for one to be pacing around this spot. I was trying to imagine why the cat had been returning to this part of the stream.

JJ lifted the jaguar shit and broke it in half, removing some red fur. He asked me what it was. I said venado (red brocket deer) and he nodded in a way that told me he would have been pissed if I'd gotten it wrong. The presence of teeth in the scat was fascinating. Usually we picture a predator eating the flesh off the skeleton of an animal, not devouring the meat and bone all at once. Did the jaguar eat the deer's face, teeth and all? There were several hard seeds in the scat as well. Neither of us took much notice, but I remember thinking it was odd. Hair, bone, teeth, and seeds all set into the fecal material.

Now that he had my guesses, JJ gave me the report. Without speaking, he used a finger to indicate where the cat had come out of the jungle, shit, and then drunk (yesterday). Then where it came out from the same spot today, and chose a slightly different site to drink. Finally, he grabbed me by the shoulder so we were cheek to cheek and he pointed up into the foliage where two king vultures were nervously crouched on a branch. But their attention wasn't actually on us—which was strange. They were looking instead at something a little way off, just where the jaguar tracks had gone into the bush.

Finally I got it. My jaw dropped and a satisfied smile spread over JJ's face. He whispered, "Let's go quietly. The jaguar, he doesn't like to be disturbed while he is eating." We tiptoed away, checking over our shoulders, peering through the shadows for a glimpse of the golden eyes that were surely watching us as we went.

This was life with JJ. I would have seen the tracks, taken a photo, and kept walking. But JJ-level tracking meant interpreting an animal's movements, its thoughts, preferences, and current position. Each grain of sand, each behavioral detail was filed away into his vast archive of natural-history data, which he had been building for more than thirty years, since he was a barefoot Ese Eja child beside his father and the other men of the village. The vastness of his knowledge gradually came into focus for me as I watched him identify which nuts on the forest floor would have a grub inside to use as fishing bait. Which vines at which time of year were right for making a broom. Or medicine. All the different trees and their woods of various densities and for various uses. The animals, their tracks and scat and habits. If someone had an ear infection, JJ ground up fungus and cured it. If you had a fever, a skin infection, a toothache, there was a sap that could cure you. He had a sixth sense for the forest. Where I saw a mess of green jungle, one large confusing thing, he saw a completely different reality. Each vine, flower, animal print, bone, fossil . . . it all had meaning that was indecipherable to me.

This was because he had grown up with the people of the jungle. The Indigenous men and women of the Madre de Dios region. People to whom working indoors was a purely anecdotal concept—like telling a wild lion about zoos. The men of the Madre de Dios were outdoorsmen: loggers, miners, fishermen, trackers. They were men who had no idea what a perfect credit score meant, but knew it couldn't save your life in a storm. These were men who took pride in the calluses on their feet. Who didn't own sunglasses, but squinted into the sun's glare. They had never used sunscreen, but knew which mud was smooth on the skin. For them, good manners, clean clothing, a knife and a fork—these were the concerns of tamer animals.

The funny thing is, you can't just ask JJ to tell you what he knows. I've tried it. It doesn't work. He just giggles, or changes the topic. Where to even start? You truly have to spend the time, walk with him, and watch how the jungle pulls his attention, what he gravitates to and what catches his curiosity. That's when you begin to get a glimpse. And it's nothing to him. I was pretty floored by the jaguar lesson; JJ was on to his other favorite topic: English and Spanish. He had recently learned somewhere about collective nouns for animals.

"Ay. What is it called when they make other names for animals?"

"What?"

"Elephants don't make a parade?"

"Ohhhh, yes, I know a few of these."

"Like what? Which ones?"

A murder of crows.
A swarm of bees.
A caravan of camels.
A quiver of cobras.

JJ smiled and checked to see if I was tricking him. "What are others?"

I couldn't think of many. I told him that giraffes are a tower. Penguins are a congress.

We paused on either side of a spot where the banks were hard and the stream narrow, and below the rushing water a tremendous stingray with blue spots was floating magically over the sand. We watched in silence.

"What do they call a group of rayas?"

I told him I didn't know.

"How about humans?"

I shrugged.

We were rounding a bend in the river where a monstrous old tree had fallen. It was one of the 150-foot-tall giants wrapped in a strangler fig, probably 700 years old, with a trunk thicker than a minivan. The way it fell made a bridge far above our heads. Its immensity made us feel small, like we were in some dinosaur-jungleland. It felt surreal. There were orchids and bromeliads still growing from its crevices. And the vines it had torn down when it toppled were trailing in the water. JJ said the jaguars and ocelots must love a tree like that, a natural cat bridge.

At one spot in the stream there were so many butterflies that we could hear their wings. They made a startling din. We both stood in awe. There were yellows and whites and greens and purples—metalmarks, morphos, numberwings, and asteropes. Thousands of them all puddling on the ground, their proboscises lapping against the clay. I stepped forward slowly, eager to take a photo, but at that moment several thousand wings took to the air. Suddenly we were engulfed in a swirling vortex of kaleidoscopic lepidopteran color—the sunlight filtered through wings casting rainbow hues all over us. We raised our arms and exchanged a look of mad wonder.

IT TAKES AGES TO understand a forest. My journals from those early days are a mess of discoveries and crisscrossed arrows. Like I was trying to draw the connections I saw in the ecosystem we explored.

On one page, a single day on the stream, JJ and I found tracks from capybaras, tapirs, agoutis, ocelots, jaguars, pumas, deer, peccaries, caimans, jabiru storks, sun bitterns, tayras, and neotropical otters. We saw the stingray, untold numbers of fish, and I dare not try to count the butterflies. All I could grasp was that I saw butterflies that day that I had never seen before. The stream was simply a mecca of flora and fauna. A riot of life. A stunning example of a world untouched by human time. A place where the complex ensemble of the Amazonian orchestra was in full, beautiful harmony.

Absorbing this hyperdiverse ground-level view of the Amazon began to intertwine with the endless reading and research I was doing on its ecosystem as a whole, and the results gradually changed my perspective on reality.

It works like this. Zoom upward and out above our heads and past the treetops, high enough into the atmosphere where you can see it all. Not just the stream we walked, but the Amazon Rainforest itself, the dominating green patch that is the defining feature of the South American continent. Of the some 400 billion trees that make up the great jungle, each one is a hydrological volcano of moisture—like a biotic machine misting evaporated water into the air.

During photosynthesis, the pores on leaves open wide, and a large tree in the Amazon can release up to a thousand liters of water into the air per day. The great rainforest exhales twenty billion tons of water (or twenty trillion liters) each day. Boiling even one liter of water until it evaporates into the air requires significant energy, so lifting twenty trillion liters off the ground is an act of bio-biblical proportions, but one that the tropical sun performs effortlessly each day. In this way the forest is a natural pump that draws water into the air above the Amazon Rainforest, creating a river of airborne moisture. It is the rain from this sky-river that makes it possible for the Amazon to exist. The great basin produces its own weather system.

But even the vast accumulation of moisture in the air doesn't form rain on its own. Rain requires "seeds," something particulate to cling to, to catalyze the moisture in the air to form into droplets. For this we look to the biogenic volatile organic compounds that are released by the plants of Amazonia. Because of the high chemical reactivity of many of these compounds (like butane, isoprene, ethylene, and others), and their mass emission rates from forests, they can be powerfully influential in the chemical composition of the atmosphere. They mediate the relationship between the biosphere and atmosphere.

There are other types of particulate debris in the air above Amazonia, including sands from the Sahara, blown across the Atlantic Ocean from Africa and suspended high above the jungle. Rich in nutrients, vital to life. Mixing with bits of pollen and salt and dust and whatever other microscopic debris might be swirling around.

As the water released by the trees condenses into clouds, marching across the green infinity of the basin, it lowers the air pressure, which creates the winds that drive the sky-river of rain clouds. We don't think of weather as a living system, but trees around the globe pumping moisture into the air produce 90 percent of the water that reaches the atmosphere over the continents. The air above the Amazon is thick with clouds.

Fluffy in the sky, white against the vivid blue—but made up of water droplets and ice crystals. A cumulus cloud one cubic kilometer in size could weigh upward of *five hundred tons*. The ten-mile-tall cumulonimbus giants that float above us on any given day represent millions of tons of airborne water.

Descending from this lofty perspective—down through the clouds and the leaves of the canopy and understory all the way to the earth—can change the meaning of everything.

Leaf-cutter ants are endlessly ferrying bits of leaf matter. Bees are pollinating flowers. Birds and monkeys are eating fruit and transporting seeds through the trees. On the ground and in the branches, the work is being done by the animals, like nocturnal bats carrying ironwood seeds. Kapok trees shed their cottony seeds to float on the wind like great dandelions. Tiny green orchid bees are an essential part of the pollination process of Brazil nut trees, some of the tallest, most emergent structures of the forest. There are fifteen thousand species of tree in the Amazon, each with its own complex reproductive process, inextricably linked to the other organisms around it. The billions of individual trees are intricately woven, created, curated, gardened, and laced with vines and mycelia, by the vast diversity of floral and faunal conveyors. The animals make the forest. The forest makes the animals. It all makes the weather. The world we live in.

There is even evidence to suggest that some thick-shelled seeds benefit from the wear and tear of being processed through the guts of various animals. Peccaries and tapirs are major seed dispersers, with the latter reported to spread as many as eighty varieties of seeds within their home range. Many seeds are hard and cannot germinate without being soaked or scratched. Tumbling through the gut of a herbivore is sometimes necessary.

Then there is the further complexity that many herbivorous animals have small home ranges and are often themselves quite small. When a predator eats a prey animal, like a jaguar consuming a deer, it is sometimes possible for the seeds consumed by the prey to enter the jaguar's digestive system. Predators often cover larger distances in their home territories, thereby dispersing seeds at far greater ranges.

A howler monkey with a stomach full of seeds after snacking on some ficus fruit is snatched by a harpy eagle—and those seeds just got aerial transport to another part of the forest. This secondary seed disbursement is referred to as diploendozoochory. First formally described by Charles Darwin himself in 1859, the phenomenon has been little studied despite its potentially vast implications in ecosystems across the globe.

The seeds in the jaguar scat!

No wonder so many angiosperms—flowering trees and plants—put so much energy into producing delicious fruits laden with seeds. They hold back, keeping them small and bitter and green until they are ready, and then fill them with nutrient sugars, their skins an advertisement of bright colors.

There are examples of fruit-bearing plants that will alter the color of their fruits based on the seed dispersers they are trying to appeal to. One study contrasting plants in Uganda and Madagascar discovered that the plants in Uganda, on the mainland of Africa, make their fruit color appeal to the eyes of monkeys, apes, and birds, which have tricolor vision, like humans. On the island of Madagascar, the same species indicate that their fruit is ready to eat by giving it a yellowish hue, a color more visible to lemurs, which are red-green color-blind.

It took me years in the field to realize how little I knew.

Walking the stream each day, we could see these little processes playing out. Parrots in a fruit tree noisily knocking bits of seedy ficus fruit to the forest floor. Peccaries feasting on the parrots' mess and running off with guts full of seeds. Silver-scaled stream fish rushing to snatch bits of the same fruit. The kingfisher perched on a branch, poised to strike at the fish as they glimmered in the flow of the stream. The caiman basking in the sun, waiting for one of the birds to mistake it for a rock. The leafy loads of tapir dung that were so often in the stream, full of seeds carried on the currents, whisked past the stingrays and stones, leaves and bones, and out into the great river beyond.

I had never considered it directly, but I had always thought of animals living in forests, not *creating* them. And similarly for humans. This was reshaping how I saw everything. City people talk about visiting nature as if they are somehow outside it, a fish in water deciding to go to the beach. We don't think of the relationship between rain and forests, between our farms and our food. In the jungle, the laws of nature, the rules of the game, are all observable and clear: Everything makes sense.

That stream became my spiritual refuge. We spent days reveling in the surreal, Lothlórien-level beauty of it. This realm of infinite complexity restructured how I saw the world. There were no Coke cans. There was no sign of anything human. The air was wild and crisp and still. We spent days hiking and fishing— balancing on logs, wondering at snakes. Tracking big cats, studying the birds. There were places where little waterfalls fell into pools deep enough to plunge into. And there beneath the rushing water, immersed in cool sensation, we were transformed.

One day, we had walked long and had been swimming. Far above the stream, up above the canopy, it was a scalding-hot day. But in the dark hallways beneath the great jungle, it was cool and shaded, with only some sun reaching the forest floor. So when we emerged from the water to sit on the hard clay banks, we made sure to find the spots warmed by sunbeams. I had just sat in one when JJ's eyes widened. He looked at me like God himself was standing behind me.

With the air of a man divulging a great secret, JJ gripped me by the wrist and the elbow and lifted my arm into the sunlight, where it was possible to see the mist rising off my own skin. Then he knelt, cupped his hands, and drank from the stream. When he stood, he stepped into the light himself, bare-chested, arms spread, palms upward, and eyes closed to let the sun wash over him. The solar heat lifted a plume of vaporized particulate moisture off of him, igniting him so that he glowed. Stream to hands to mouth to veins to sky.

A sacrament is the outward and visible sign of an inward spiritual grace. We spent much of that day silent, contemplating all we had seen. It was as if we had witnessed something divine, as though we had peeled back the curtain to expose the gears of the game, the raw code of the universe.

It was late afternoon by the time we made it back to the boat. At the mouth of the stream, clear water swirled, mixing with the silty golden current of the main river. The sky was leaden. By the time we got the motor going and began chugging downriver, a heavy rain was falling. Squinting in the rush, we exchanged a smile. With one hand steering, JJ reached down and scooped some water out of the river and into his mouth. Then, mouth open, tongue out, he caught raindrops, drinking the sky. The rain intensified to a blinding downpour that demanded our attention. Two minuscule homo sapiens in a tiny boat motoring down a tributary in the Amazon.

We had many days of profound adventures on that stream. It was there I first saw a harpy eagle drinking. It was there I came face-to-face with tapirs. Sometimes we'd use our machetes to hunt thick white fish or toothy wasaco (wolffish). Sometimes we'd drop hooks baited with bits of bugs we'd found. In the evening he'd fit these strange fish onto larger hooks, and the next morning we would often find giant catfish caught on our lines. Years passed in this way, with the stream as the center of our world, the church—the place of mariposas and symphonic birdsong, where the nights throbbed with frogs and crickets and the world was lush—and the canopy a towering ceiling of lofty leaves.

=====

Then one day they burned it down. We arrived in the boat as we always did. Machetes and no shoes. But this time what we found was a hellscape. The great trees lay dying, their charred bodies smoking, their lifeless arms spread across the black earth. Every leaf, every butterfly, every flower, all the otters and birds and jaguars and ants . . . The sacred cycle broken. The cacophony silenced. Entire worlds gone. I stood beside JJ in the burning wreckage and for a long time we said nothing.

A swarm of flies.

A murder of crows.

A hell of humans.

THE RAREST SPECIES

≡

IN THE MONTHS THAT FOLLOWED THE BURNING OF OUR SACRED stream, the Loreto—as we would come to call it later—a kind of eclipse began in both our lives. We had come to love the place so much that the shock of losing it would reverberate through us for years. Seeing that stream turned to ash was, emotionally, of a caliber comparable to having your house burned down. Or losing a loved one. Something you love deeply is gone from the world. A place of complexity and wonder and joy and memories—deleted from reality. Grief broke over us like a wave. The currents of mourning upwelling in our hearts were intensified by the knowledge that this was just the beginning.

In order to understand what happened next, it is first important to know that the relationship JJ and I had formed was the result of a strange series of events. Two life trajectories that are starkly different and yet remarkably similar. Although I started my life in New York City, with parents living in Brooklyn, somehow I had found my way to a part of remote Amazonia that was far beyond the beaten tourist trail, beyond where even the most daring scientists and researchers were willing to go. This in itself is no easy feat, and the credit is in no way mine, but instead goes to the incalculable luck of meeting the right person at the right time. The old saying "It's not *what* you know, it's *who* you know" was never truer.

You see, one does not simply walk out into the Amazon jungle. Even if you buy a ticket to Lima, Peru, and then choose one of a half dozen jungle towns accessible by airline—Pucallpa, Iquitos, Puerto Maldonado—and catch a taxi to the edge of the jungle, your options are limited.

Either you end up at a five-star resort with polite guides who speak bad English and keep you on marked trails, or you risk it and go with whichever local guides you find on the street.

Israeli traveler Yossi Ghinsberg tried the latter option and joined a few other would-be adventurers to raft the Tuichi River in Bolivia. They found a guide who took them out, and things went so badly that the raft went over a waterfall and they all got separated. Yossi barely survived and had such an ordeal during the three weeks he was lost that he later wrote a book about it. He came face-to-face with a jaguar, tore his anus apart on a stick (slipped, mud), and was finally rescued by local communities who had been mobilized by the one surviving member of the expedition. The other two and the "guide" were never found.

So it was not lost on me how incredibly lucky I had been in meeting JJ. But it would be almost twenty years until I truly understood the magnitude of the lottery I had won. He was a naturalist and explorer of such rustic and refined caliber that I have never seen his equal.

Indigenous, scientist, adventurer—in order to understand this strange alloy, one has to consider the complexity of the landscape that shaped him.

For one born in a modern city—Singapore, Tokyo, New York—especially high up in an apartment in a glass-paneled building, life takes place in an environment that is built for humans by humans. It's a kind of metal, glass, and concrete hive. Even suburbia is heavily curated. These highly populated areas are the culmination of thousands of years of civilization and technology: mining and farming and complex systems that make urban life possible. There are doctors and hospitals and police and schools, zoning laws and traffic signals. Temperature control indoors, and level sidewalks outdoors; the media, the economy, the architecture, the crosswalks.

JJ's LIFE BEGAN IN a tiny clearing where a palm-thatched hut nestled deep in the jungle that stretched from horizon to horizon. A barefoot baby on red Amazonian clay, walking amongst the chickens and dogs. The Indigenous villages of rural Amazonia are often small farming settlements carved from the jungle, heavily dependent on the surrounding forest for sustenance. Their fish come from the river and are caught by going fishing. Their meat is shot by bow and arrow or rifle and is procured by hiking through the jungle. Their water comes from putting buckets at the edges of the roof to collect the rain, or from knowing a good spring. It's a different world, and in 1974 when JJ joined it, born at home with the chickens and the woodsmoke, it was the song of the jungle birds that he first heard, the raw earth his new feet touched.

It's a life so wild that it's hard to understand. Plenty of people around the globe live close to the earth, but the western Amazon takes it to another level.

The Peruvian Madre de Dios is nestled in the southeast corner of the country, Brazil to the east and Bolivia to the south. When I first arrived it was a region accessible only by a long, perilous, unpaved, and often avalanched-out road from the nearest "real" city, which was Cusco, high in the mountains. But unlike Cusco, the Inca city, Puerto Maldonado was a lowland jungle town, a place far from everything and familiar to few—think of a steaming jungle with a drumbeat pulse.

Puerto Maldonado sits at the sharp confluence where the Tambopata's bulky current washes into the larger Madre de Dios—Mother of God—River. The Tambopata is a river that originates in the Andes. It's born from glaciers that loom more than two vertical miles above the jungle. These glaciers cling to the jagged peaks of the Andes—Tambopata's uppermost tributaries. These are the tiny east-flowing veins of crystal current that make up its headwaters, flowing down from the mountain rim of cloud forest that makes up the western limit of Amazonia.

At seventeen thousand feet, high above the tree line, there is little oxygen and almost no life. You may spot the odd Andean condor, or the rare herd of alpaca, or vicuña, their wild cousins. Pumas (yes, the same animals we call mountain lions that roam the American Rockies) stalk the sharp cliffs, where ancient high-altitude glaciers guard caves of sapphire-colored ice. Each day when the equatorial sun beats down on these ice fields, the caves pour streams of an ethereal blue that trickle down the mountains, creating the uppermost source of the southern Amazon basin.

Theoretically, if you threw a tennis ball into one of these streams, it would be carried several thousand miles across South America until it charged out the mouth of the Amazon River delta and into the Atlantic.

The Madre de Dios region is the uppermost reaches of the Amazonian river system. A place so far from everything that it has remained virtually unexplored, a place almost forgotten by time.

In the 1970s, astronauts had already gone to the moon and the first rudimentary computers were becoming available to the consumer market. Led Zeppelin, Queen, and the Eagles were all in their musical heyday. In 1974, the year JJ was born, Nixon was stepping down as president, Muhammad Ali was fighting George Foreman (rumble in a different jungle), and in Africa a young Jane Goodall was crouched in the forest with her clipboard amongst a family of chimpanzees—researching her findings that would redefine our species. The world was full of hustle—planes, trains, automobiles.

But in the village where JJ was born, it was like a prior century. There was no communication technology that would allow them to access the outside world. The jungle spread for hundreds of miles in every direction like a silent guardian.

JJ didn't have shoes until he was thirteen years old, even though he would, every day, walk with his siblings for over an hour through the jungle to the community of Infierno, where they would attend school.

A child in a community like Infierno knows by the time they are three how to use a knife to remove the scales from a piranha. They know how to make and tend a fire. Walking the jungle barefoot, they are in daily contact with a variety of small horrors: wasps and bullet ants and a host of thorns and other assailants that force them to be alert. The resounding pain of a bullet ant sting is a lesson you only need to learn once. And there are worse things in the jungle, with bites and stings you don't recover from: bushmasters, stingrays, jaguars. Living far from medical help, you don't want to get injured. When you do, the options are grim.

The adults in the community are people who hunt each day for their food. For JJ, the jungle was a wild supermarket. Spix's guan, a kind of large forest bird, was a family favorite. As were howler monkeys and spider monkeys. Rodents called pacas (the size of an obese beagle) could be hunted by slinking around the jungle at night with a bow and arrow. And if all else failed, every house in the community had a stump out back on which to whack a chicken's head off. The kids knew how to pour boiling water on a chicken and remove the feathers too.

JJ grew up hustling behind his father and uncles and brothers, who were all expert trackers. The Ese Eja Indigenous jungle men knew where herds of peccaries came to eat palm seeds. They knew which special nooks in the river contained large fish. And their wild apothecary was the source of most of the remedies they had access to.

In this world of mud and blood and rain and leaves, JJ grew up in intimate tactile contact with nature. When he stepped on a thorn, his mother would treat it with sap from the sangre de drago—the dragon's blood tree. When he had an ear infection, they'd use mushrooms from the forest called dead man's fingers. Fevers were treated with caña caña, which has aspirin-like properties. The local shaman, it was said, could treat infertility and impotence, and aid in the healing of broken bones. There was even a plant that could numb someone before giving them stitches. Whatever ails you in the jungle, there is a sap for that.

JJ's older brothers were highly skilled jungle men by the time they were in their midteens, and they made their contribution to the family by going out with fishhooks, guns, and bows and arrows, and returning with a menagerie of wildlife that made up their diet. Some days, JJ's brother Chikki would come home with two howler monkeys he had shot while camping alone in the jungle. Other days, Elias would bring home a giant zungaro negro—a catfish that can weigh a few hundred pounds. Sometimes on their way home from school the siblings would come across a yellow-footed tortoise. This too would be cooked up, added to the rice and yuca and plantains. After school they'd all go fishing and catch piranhas or wasaco or pico de pato (a kind of shovel-nosed catfish).

JJ's father, Don Santiago, as I knew him, was a local legend.

Santiago had helped to unite the clans of warring Ese Eja tribes that were scattered around the Tambopata River, and aided in helping them formalize into a government-recognized Indigenous territory. He helped get them titled land, which would be theirs forever. He was able to accomplish this because of the experience and connections and reputation he'd earned during the time he had spent as a policeman in Puerto Maldonado, doing drug busts and working with law enforcement. Whether he was in uniform as an officer or bare-chested as a logger out in the jungle, Santiago Durand's name was known throughout the region as someone with above-average grit, valor, and ability.

After spending his formative years using a pole to push boats up the Tambopata, Santiago was remarkably strong. He was one of those lean guys with sunken cheeks and huge hands, squinty eyes from years on the river, and a wrinkled face. Each year, he took his sons on family hunting trips in the jungle for weeks at a time, deep into Ese Eja territory in search of fish to salt and peccaries to shoot. All the boys in one long dugout canoe with a small motor, winding through trackless jungle for days on days, stopping only to make camp and then go deeper. They were a family of explorers. It was in this way that JJ learned that the farther you go from civilization, the more animals there are.

Life in the jungle was harsh, and life as Santiago's son was no easier. Despite his deep respect for his father, JJ often found himself reluctant to skin howler monkeys, crack open tortoises, sit for days or weeks on boats, or help to cut down trees. This lifestyle sustained their family, but JJ was also noticing a worrying trend that flowed opposite to the currents in his heart. Each year there were fewer and fewer animals in the community. They would have to travel farther and farther away by boat each time they wanted to hunt. The fish that used to fill the rivers were gone. The herds of peccaries that used to march through the jungle had vanished. While the community had once lived with bows and arrows and handmade nets, now they had shotguns and industrially made nets that could span a river.

There were other technological changes flooding the region as well. The Alan García government was struggling with popularity in Peru and so, as a sign of good faith, began giving small grants to rural people. Santiago and his sons used a grant to buy their first-ever chain saw.

They were working on cutting down a tree with their new tool when tragedy struck. One of the older boys who had learned how to use the chain saw was finishing off a cut, and everyone ran for cover. But the large tree swung on a vine and pulled down several others, and soon it seemed like the whole jungle was falling. There were trees coming down everywhere, branches swinging through the air—one of which landed on JJ's brother Pico, sixteen at the time, and crushed him.

At first, they hoped he would get better. The village shaman tried to cure him with local remedies, but there was skeletal damage, broken bones, intense internal destruction that they could not see. JJ watched his brother lying in bed in agony, unsure if he would live or die. They were all waiting for him to show signs of recovery that never came.

It was then that Santiago began killing cows.

They would sell the meat to make some money. It was clear with every passing hour that Pico's health was declining. To get real help, they would have to get him to Puerto Maldonado (a six-hour boat ride), onto a plane, and then to the capital, Lima, where there were modern doctors and medical facilities capable of handling the severity of his condition.

It would take most of the family's assets and savings to save Pico, if it was even possible. With Santiago gone to Lima with Pico, JJ's mom in Puerto Maldonado with the younger boys, and most of the older boys out in the jungle working hard felling trees for timber or hunting for food, thirteen-year-old JJ was told to watch the farm and the animals and was given a machete to keep back the jungle.

For the first week no one came. After the second week he took to climbing a tall tree each evening to look out over the river. By the third week he began to wonder if his family would ever return, and if his brother had lived or died. It was two months before anyone came to get him.

A year later Pico returned. He was alive, in high spirits, but with a right leg that was destroyed from an infection he had sustained while in the hospital. He would have a severe limp and health complications the rest of his life.

WHEN JJ WAS FIFTEEN, he was bathing in the river with his brothers and they spotted something floating down out of the jungle. It was a balsa-wood raft with several emaciated teenage boys. They were sunburned, bug-bitten, and starving. They said they had been floating through the wild for two weeks. When Santiago interviewed the boys, he found out that they were all refugees, child soldiers who'd been forced into working for a branch of the Shining Path, the quintessential South American rebel terrorist group, with all the usual mayhem—guns, drugs, human trafficking, and lots of camouflage. They were big enough as an organization that they made Peru known as a dangerous country for foreigners at the time. One of the boys, Alex, explained that they had been taught to use weapons, to fight. They'd been taught that blood is good. "If blood comes out it's good, it means you are taking action."

Alex told his harrowing story to Santiago and asked him if it would be all right to work on his farm in exchange for food and a place to stay. Santiago agreed. And while the other boys spent some time there and moved on, over the next few years Alex fell in with the Durand clan and became like part of the family.

Eventually Santiago formally adopted him, making him brother number nineteen.

By the time JJ was in his midteens he was fed up with seeing the big trees cut down. He was sick of killing wildlife for food. He liked the animals and was saddened by the rate at which he saw them declining. As he once put it, "The only thing we got from cutting the forest was hurting people. Bad things happened."

There was a period when he was in the Peruvian Army, which was compulsory for all young men at the time. He did not enjoy marching or rules, or when he was shot in the leg during an incident when the police were fighting the military (yes, you read that correctly).

When JJ returned to Tambopata, he got a job at an ecotourism lodge.

At the time, JJ had hardly seen foreigners and was fascinated by them. They spoke other languages, had fancy things. One day while cleaning out a tourist's room, he found a pair of boots that the people had simply left behind. These he took. He also found a strange kind of perfume he decided to sneak a sample of. JJ pepper-sprayed himself in both armpits and went screaming out of the room.

But he learned fast how to guide these exotic visitors and began using his Indigenous knowledge as a foundation on which to build a breathtaking wealth of scientific knowledge. He worked beside birders, ornithologists, and mammologists and began practicing his English. He learned what foreigners struggled with in the jungle and how to care for people who wanted an adventurous vacation. But he always liked working with the scientists. JJ is, at his core, incredibly, insatiably curious; he loves to learn. He gradually learned hundreds of birds by their calls, both their common and scientific names. Because of his upbringing, the jungle was his world, and so where others struggled, JJ flourished. For him, guiding some birders on a walk through the jungle and then returning for a warm meal prepared by chefs was luxury.

Then he met Emma, a young, blond British biologist. They fell in love, and it wasn't long before they hatched the idea to start their own research station. They wanted it to be somewhere really out there. So in 1999 they used their savings and the spark of their new romance to launch half a year's worth of exploring the jungle. They went to Manu National Park and up the Tambopata River and to the Heath River and the Colorado and far up another tributary where few had the guts to go: Las Piedras.

JJ's brothers, who had all worked in Las Piedras during the mahogany boom of the '90s, had told them the stories. The uncontacted tribes, the massive current, the deadly whirlpools, and the fact that there was virtually no one there, forever. For infinity. It was wide open. And so JJ and Emma spent six months exploring. Finally they chose their small spot in the middle of nowhere, as far from the world as they could go in two ten-hour days of driving a boat. It was ambitious verging on reckless, but they both clawed toward their dream of having the most authentic, remote, and devoutly sustainable research site in the Amazon: Las Piedras Biodiversity Station.

MADE IN
BROOKLYN

THE QUEST FOR TRUTH IS ONLY USEFUL

IF YOU'RE PREPARED TO TAKE ACTION

ON WHAT YOU FIND.

—UNKNOWN

I LOVED DAYS AT THE BRONX ZOO WITH MY MOM AND DAD and sister, Michelle. It was magical. Observing animals was foundational to my young mind. Seeing a gorilla in real life, being able to wave to him, and see him wave back. There is no substitute for the marvel of real experience. That power and intelligence, so much like our own. The zoo had penguins, bears, and all kinds of animals I enjoyed, but most important, it had JungleWorld.

I loved how hot and steamy it was, and that they had designed enclosures that accurately simulated the atmosphere of a real jungle. The feeling of wonder as you walked through the darkness, the vines, searching for animals. It was all simply my favorite thing. There was a feeling I got—like every bad sensation melted away, like I was plugged into some positive energy source. Like I was home. I was enchanted by these amazing other creatures, other forms, other iterations of life. Were there really parts of the world like this? Where these creatures just existed? It made me feel like the world was brimming with magic.

But even as a child my love for wild things was tinged with grief. The people who made JungleWorld did a really good job. Almost too good. As you leave, you see videos of men with chain saws cutting tall rainforest trees. There's even a life-sized cross section of a felled tree (an order of magnitude bigger than any tree I'd seen in real life). There's real footage from Africa of logging trucks hauling ancient trees. The gorillas' home is being destroyed. These nightmare videos play on a loop. The sound of chain saws. Football fields per day are going down. There are statistics that say that elephants could vanish in our lifetime or that rhinos will be hunted to extinction. Soon this could all be gone. Soon the most amazing things that exist will be gone forever.

I remember crying to my mother before bedtime. We had just read that Lonesome George was the last Pinta Island tortoise in the Galápagos. He was the only one of his kind, which meant that when he died, the subspecies would be gone. A millions-of-years-old story would be over. The idea of extinction haunted me.

I was drawn like a magnet to animals of all kinds. Mom and Dad took Michelle and me to the woods all the time. Our home videos are of me at six years old leading Michelle, three and still wobbly on the rocks, barefoot through the streams. We were explorers in the dancing, dappled-green shadows of the sycamores. We were on missions to find the crayfish and frogs, salamanders under logs.

My family are third-generation Italian Americans, New Yorkers through and through. People who took pride in being from Brooklyn. Most of my early memories are from 10th Avenue and 82nd Street in Dyker Heights. Sunday dinners at Grandma's house with all the aunts, uncles, and cousins. A few years after I was born, my parents moved to the New Jersey suburbs, and suddenly we had a backyard, trees, dogs, and it was a few minutes' drive to some truly remarkable forest.

On any given day when I was young, my mom would have me in the backyard blindfolded while she spun me around. She would challenge me to touch the bark of the various trees and identify them by the texture. Which one was a birch? Which one was the dogwood? Which one was the oak? Maple? I grew up listening to cicadas throbbing in the summer air and the oak leaves rustling outside the window. During the day, the light we played under was dappled by the leaves of those trees. On the weekends the streams sparkled with adventure.

If nature was paradise, school was hell. The first time I did first grade, a simple math sheet was placed in front of me. There may have been twenty different mathematical equations that we would be timed to complete. That first time, I fidgeted and drew a picture because I hadn't yet learned how to add or subtract. The second time, I got a stern talking-to from the teacher, and kids were starting to laugh. By the third time, I knew how this racket worked.

The timer was set, the room went quiet, everyone was working. I had no idea what to do. I didn't understand how to answer any of the questions. As the minutes ticked by I began to sweat, shake, I knew I'd be made fun of, I knew I'd be in trouble. The other children would laugh when they realized that I was confused and frustrated. I ran out the door into the hallway, and I still remember hitting the exterior doors (that metal bar), bursting out into the sunlight, and running into the forest and sitting under tall oaks and maples, where it was safe. Needless to say, the teacher called my parents.

But Ed and Lenore Rosolie were no ordinary set of parents. They knew they were raising a child who vibrated on a different frequency, and they did everything and anything to adapt. One of the best things my parents did, starting around when I was in fifth grade, was to save up a little money and send me to summer camp. It was in the Catskills and it was a special program called Wood Wise. There I was able to be around other kids who loved the woods, though none of them ever breathed them and needed them the way I did. More important, though, were the instructors: "adults" (probably in their early twenties) who were experienced outdoors people. They knew how to take us on hikes that would challenge us, teach us about different species, and instruct us on basic camping techniques. How to manage your food, hydration, pack weight, energy levels, tent setup, and so much more—a world of learning that happens only through experience. I learned the "sacred socks" principle: Always have a waterproof core bag hidden down in your pack, with a set of socks, underwear, shirt, and pants that are 100 percent dry. It's a sanity saver when you've been wet for days and are at your wits' end, to finally crawl into a dry sleeping bag in dry clothes.

By the time I was entering my teens, I had begun developing my wilderness craft and had read books like *The North Runner, Papillon,* and *The Call of the Wild;* I had grown up on movies like *White Fang* and *Legends of the Fall.* That was enough inspiration for me to take my worship of the wilderness seriously. I had also read about Native American vision quests and Aboriginal walkabouts, and so at a young age I was going out into the woods with my dog and a knife, on a mission to camp on my own. My golden retriever, Bugsy, and I would find the wildest places we could, deep in the woods, far from any trail, on the side of a mountain: no tent, one steak, a single match to build a fire.

When you spend time in a forest, you learn to move differently. Things come into focus and you become attuned to a kind of green-world lucid state. I've always felt strongly that we are connected to nature in ways that have yet to be discovered—

ways far more complex than the obvious reliance on oxygen, sunlight, vitamins, minerals, and the Earth itself. Time in the forest made me look on society as a massive disruption in our connection to nature, and I suspected that at least some of my feelings of depression, anxiety, and disassociation might be a symptom of a larger societal problem: that we as a species are fish perpetually out of water. In the nascent, still-desperate stages of these half-drawn conclusions, I only knew that my brain became bearable when I was deep in the woods. That I could feel the animal instincts in me, that my bare feet on the rocks and leaves made me feel connected to the Earth like I was being directly charged by an invisible force. When I learned to drive, I once saw a deer freshly struck by a car and brought it home to practice processing my own meat. I was desperate for an ever-greater connection to the mountains and streams and the animals they held. Haven't you ever just wanted to leave it all and live in a cabin in the woods?

Even as I was spending so much time in the forests, it bothered me that the woods I explored, as beautiful as they were, were not the original growth. The United States lost over 95 percent of its original forest cover when Europeans colonized the land. The Industrial Revolution saw vast slabs of the continent's forests fed to iron fires. The woods of New Jersey and upstate New York are beautiful: poplars and oaks, maples and birches. But the trees are small; old growth is a thing of the past. I dreamed of what it must have been like for the Mohicans and the Lenape, existing in a world where nature was still pure and vibrant— when you could still drink from the streams. These questions haunted me and colored my life. I spent years feeling like my life was a postapocalyptic nightmare. The natural world was dying and nobody cared.

I won't drag you through how dismal life was for me at school, but suffice to say I was hardly ever not in detention or getting suspended. I even got into physical fights with teachers. Years of being picked on by kids and being told by teachers that I was a loser were making me into a bad person. I was getting angry. Long-term angry. You can only be told you suck so many times before you start to believe it. Only so many teachers can tell you you're going to work at a gas station if your grades don't improve. Those test scores start to make you wonder if there really is something wrong with you.

To combat this, when I was fourteen my mom helped me bend the truth on a particular program that you had to be seventeen to participate in. This one was called the Trip Leader Candidate Program. It was going to be a multiweek expedition through the Adirondacks. Bigger mountains, real wilderness. Higher stakes. For the program, we had to plan our own logistics, budget what food we could carry on our backs or in canoes for weeks at a stretch, and learn to read topographical maps. This was expedition school. The consequences were real: If we planned wrongly, we would starve out there. Things *would* go wrong. We would have to call for help. The Adirondack Park is more than double the size of Yellowstone and Yosemite combined. It has moose, bear, and virtually unlimited lakes and mountains to explore.

Spending weeks out in this new caliber of wilderness taught me valuable things. When I had started hiking years earlier, sometimes I would be so hungry or thirsty that I would fall to the ground, throw off my pack, and begin drinking and eating. But the trip leader would never do that. The guide, the expedition leader, would always help others and make sure the whole team was okay before tending to their own needs. Trail etiquette dictates that the person who is in charge, or at least the person with the most experience, is the one to eat and drink last. It's a type of unspoken code that took me a while to understand.

But like everything else, if you get punched enough times, fail frequently enough, it becomes possible to adapt. The summertime expeditions became so important that I would train for them in the off-season (aka normal life, during the school year). I joined the cross-country team in the fall and in the spring I played lacrosse. All because I wanted to increase my cardio and endurance. The following summer at camp, when the hike pushed me beyond my limits and we finally stopped, I didn't fall on the ground. I didn't guzzle water. I had learned how to budget. I'd been through this before—I knew I'd be okay. I'd also built up some strength and resilience. That temperance and understanding made it possible for me to help some of the newer kids, one of whom was sprawled out on the ground, panting, one shoe off, promising he could go no farther. He hadn't yet discovered that he could continue.

I learned a few crucial lessons. That reality I faced when I was in school and detention was just one bad room: There was a whole world out there and a lot of it was exciting. That was a revelation worth holding on to—a glowing thing I carried with me that kept me going. I thrived out on the trail and in the wilderness, on the side of the mountain and in the thunderstorm. The more intense conditions got, the more I seemed to turn on and engage. The closer to disaster we came, the more focused and alive I felt. The reputation you have at school isn't the one you keep your whole life. At camp I wasn't a loser. At camp they didn't know I was underage. In the wild, being able to hike for a long time and keep your cool when things got tough was something that the guides respected, and that pretty blond nineteen-year-olds found impressive enough to enthusiastically, albeit unknowingly, relieve you of your virginity.

The woods don't care if you are rich or poor, who your parents are or what your grades are or your credit score is. The woods are where the Old Ways still rule. It's the first place I got to help other people, where I began to truly learn things, and even excel. Have you ever felt it? The need to leave everything and strike off into the forest? The trees are patient, immortal friends. No matter what is happening in life, the forest is a timeless refuge where the moss and rocks and streams and the wind are waiting for you. To spend a day hopping the rocks of a stream. To lie on your stomach and watch the moss. To turn onto your back and look up at the trees—watch the wind whisper through the leaves.

At school, I was always envious while reading books about people like Winston Churchill, who had gone to war when he was my age. Or Teddy Roosevelt and what he had done out west. Jane Goodall had been barely out of her teens when she first went to Africa. People had led such exciting lives. There was adventure out there. But it always seemed like it was fifty years ago. I was terrified that I had been born in the wrong time.

Once, when I was lamenting how much I hated sitting all day in school and doing homework, a friend's mom said something like "You don't like sitting at your desk in school? Wait till you grow up, then it's a desk for the rest of your life—just add in bills and a boss, you'll see." I didn't have any defense for this. She scared the shit out of me. Was this all life was going to be? Everything felt like a downward spiral toward darkness.

My parents deserve all the credit. They're the ones who suggested that I just drop out of high school after sophomore year. They're the ones who got me proper meetings with a psychologist. It turned out I wasn't entirely stupid. My IQ qualified me for the American Mensa society. But I was dyslexic, and I processed information differently than other people. That's why I hadn't been able to do the math sheets in first grade. That's why I could never get through the reading assignments in middle school—there was a reason!

They said that if I went to college, the structure would be different. Classes were only part of the day. Work was done on your own time. There was no detention. It might be something I would enjoy more. Plus Ramapo College was literally across the street from the Ramapo Mountains, my favorite place to camp.

When junior year of high school started, I simply didn't go. The administration would call the house, and my mom and I just watched the phone ring, laughing.

Soon I was attending college classes. It was like punching through the wall of a prison and seeing light on the other side. It wasn't long until I had gotten it in my head that I was going to use the winter break between semesters to launch my first grand dream: seeing the wildest place on Earth.

It's worthwhile to mention that I thought the Amazon Rainforest was only in Brazil. So I fixated all my efforts on getting to Brazil. I was crushed when absolutely none of them worked. Six months went by and there was no research position. Nothing and no one legitimate would take me. Not at seventeen years old with no experience. Even the professors at college told me that only grad students got to go do cool fieldwork in tropical countries. I wasn't even supposed to be out of high school yet!

As a throwaway, I sent a half-hearted email to some folks who had a terrible little website whose design looked like it had come from the '70s. Bad as it was, I had a feeling its lackluster quality was a sign of authenticity. These people were really out there and didn't have the time to care what their website looked like. Turned out that was exactly the case. A month later, a woman named Emma wrote back and said they could take me on as a research volunteer for twenty-five dollars a day for room and board. She warned, however, that the place they operated out of was so remote that getting there was a serious undertaking. There was no connection to the outside world, we'd have to carry in and carry out, and it was truly dangerous. They compared it to going to Antarctica or Everest.

When you run out into the world after a dream, you might not even know what you really want, or need. I thought I needed to go to Brazil. I fought hard to get to Brazil. It wasn't happening. But when you reach your first brick wall or closed door, it doesn't mean it's the end of the dream—sometimes the universe is dutifully barring you from straying from your path, the one you must ultimately take.

If I hadn't suffered the way I had in school, I never would have built up the anger and wild hunger to drop out and jet off into the world with laser focus on my dream. No pressure, no diamond. And sure, I had to fight my parents ("There's no way you are going to the Amazon Rainforest alone!"), and I had to shut my eyes and jump. Thank God I didn't get what I thought I wanted, because what I got instead was what I had always needed so badly—the call to my own life.

Flying over the Andes and into the Amazon, I was pressed against the window of the plane with my heart backflipping in my ribs. The two-day boat ride up the Las Piedras River was a crescendo into a fantastically remote reality that my young New Yorker mind could barely comprehend. When I first saw leaf-cutter ants in real life, I fell to my belly in awe. Macaws were flying across the sky. The trees were enormous, with branches the size of the largest oaks at home. They were covered with vines, bromeliads, moss, monkeys, lizards, and snakes. It was almost more than I could take.

In my wildest dreams, the farthest I'd ever gotten was reaching the jungle. I never imagined I'd be inducted, suited up, handed a sword, and asked to fight.

My first few years in the Amazon, from 2006 to 2008, were pure exploration, a beautiful age of innocence. JJ and I became fast friends and went on every adventure we could. At the time we met, he was thirty-two and I was eighteen. I think each of us found in the other the kind of friend we'd always wanted. For the first time there was someone as eager to explore a stream as I was, and even more impressive, he was willing to suffer to do it. Walk all day with no tent, get stuck outside and then sit in the rain all night, and trudge back in the morning? No problem. In those days we were writing a contract, testing each other out. Constantly pushing the limits. I admired his knowledge, how he walked barefoot, how he was more comfortable in the jungle than most people are in their own homes. I admired his mission to protect the forest, and was perplexed by his insistence that the destruction would come. It seemed so far away, so vast; it felt like nothing could touch us.

As I went through college, whenever I wasn't attending a semester, I was in the jungle. Sometimes being in the jungle meant I didn't make it home in time for the semester (like the time I adopted and raised a giant anteater named Lulu). I was a fish thrown into water for the first time, a cicada emerging from a seventeen-year larval stage to something capable of flight. When you can attain wild freedom, it is a powerful narcotic. It's the same adrenaline-filled elixir that drives people to spend their lives chasing waves or climbing mountains. There's a simplicity to raw wild. The forest was thick and crawling with life— teeming, cheering, howling, and packed with deep unknowable things.

In those early days I quickly learned that the jungle is its own interactive godlike reality. It's a superorganism that often feels like it is aware—it has a kind of consciousness, different moods. Getting to know its secrets, its rules and boundaries, was thrilling. It felt like I had peeled back the layers and was tapping into the mains.

That's why I started this book with the story of the stream

that JJ and I used to explore and how horrified we were when we saw it burned. The horrors of the future were looming on the horizon, the thing we loved was being destroyed, and we were faced with the question that would come to define our lives: Do we run? Or is there some reality where there is a way to make a stand and fight? I don't think we had any idea of the magnitude of what we were up against, and that's probably a good thing. Had we known what the fight was going to cost, or the horrors we were about to see, I'm certain we would have run. But we had no idea. We were just two friends living far out in the Amazon, wholly unaware that the battle before us would define our lives.

HOW TO KILL
A MOCKINGBIRD

TAKING A CLOSE LOOK AT WHAT'S AROUND US,

THERE IS SOME SORT OF A HARMONY.

IT IS THE HARMONY OF OVERWHELMING AND

COLLECTIVE MURDER.

—WERNER HERZOG, *BURDEN OF DREAMS*

JJ AND I SPENT SEVERAL DAYS WAITING FOR A BOAT, OR ANY sign of other humans. That rainy season it felt like the sky was trying to kill us. It would rain half the day and most of the night with big heavy raindrops that pelted the canopy and the roofs of the station. I imagined the monkeys huddled together in the trees, cold birds on branches just waiting.

Emma and JJ were breaking up and undoing their lives and all they had built, which meant JJ and I were in limbo. It was looking like they would have to sell most of the almost six thousand acres of jungle they owned and protected, including the station. All the work they had done and all the dreams they had built were being dismantled.

We had guided a group and, after they went home, were living at the station without a boat. For a week or so this was okay. We went on adventures, but things were changing. The good times were over, we could feel it in the air. The tomatoes ran

out or turned black, the onions began to dry up, the rice bag ran
low. Eggs were long gone. The only thing we still had was salt.
There was no power at the station in those days. We didn't even
have a generator. We were completely on our own. The only
way to contact the outside world was an old CB radio that we
could plug into a car battery that charged off a solar panel on
one of the roofs.

When supplies ran low, JJ began calling Puerto. If we wanted
to live out in the jungle, we needed rice and beans and basic
necessities from town. But sending a boat in with food was expensive, and no one seemed willing to endure the weeklong
round trip it would take to run provisions into the jungle. Most
of the time we called out into the blind static distance, we got
no response: "Charlie dos! Charlie dos, this is Loreto, do you
copy?" Static. We were cosmically alone.

Our nearest neighbors were over an hour downstream from
us. JJ's friend Satuko was an older guy who had lived there with
his family, a wife and two sons, long before JJ had even come to
the river. Satuko wasn't Native, but he had finished whatever
career he had had and moved to the jungle to raise a family far
from civilization. His boys, Willi and Paul, grew up going to
Puerto only once or twice a year for supplies and to sell Brazil
nuts.

"Satuko will have food," JJ said with his hands on his hips.

We were standing by the river as we had done for days, waiting.

The night before, the sky had dumped biblical amounts of
rain on the jungle. Large trees had fallen in the night. The palm
thatching on the roof had taken heavy fire. Every stream had
burst its banks and overflowed into the jungle. The river had
risen almost twenty feet before sunrise. We stood at the bank in
silence for a long time. Then JJ saw something that made his
eyes narrow.

It was an especially large tree coming around the bend from upriver.

"Let's take it."

"What?"

"Vámonos!"

We shed whatever we didn't need, kicking off shoes. I left my camera and extra clothes in a dry bag and dove into the river.

The river was full of debris, as it always was when it was rising. Sticks and leaves and animals and entire trees came with the flood. Logs and jungle shrapnel of thorns and detritus swirled by in the thick, churning current. In the dry season the Las Piedras was small and slow; you could just about walk across. Now it was another thing altogether, a dangerous, intimidating monster, thirty feet deep and a hundred meters wide, charging through the landscape.

Swimming as fast as we could, JJ with a machete between his teeth, we made our way out into the current. The tree was massive. I don't remember what kind because in those days I was still learning my basics. What is certain is that this one was large enough that it was almost unbelievable. The branches stretched twenty feet over the water's surface, the trunk was two-thirds the girth of a school bus. It was like an ocean liner. We climbed on and our presence had no effect on the balance. It didn't roll or dip like a normal-sized log—it just kept going on its powerful journey downriver. Like it didn't even know we were there.

"Lookadis! Dat's a good one!" JJ laughed and patted the tree, pleased with his choice. We were barefoot and walked back and forth, up and down the long trunk. From roots to its lowest branches the tree was over sixty feet long. It was so big we felt like insects. He whacked the machete home where a branch had broken, and stood like a proud pirate at the helm of his ship, watching the world go by. These were the barefoot machete days.

I climbed up one of the tall branches, like a crow's nest.

"Con cuidado!" JJ said. Be careful.

"Aye, Captain!" I said and jumped into the river, then swam back to the trunk. JJ did the same, kicking his legs as he fell the twenty feet and splashed in. After the initial fun, however, we were just . . . riding. Time passed, and the dark sky scraped over the canopy. The sound of the river alone was intimidating. The whirlpools at the bends were more than thirty feet in diameter. The river was angry and dangerous. We sat side by side on the log as it barreled downstream, the walls of jungle towering above us.

"This is real jungle," I said, marveling at the raw beauty we passed.

"Ay, Paul, how do you say 'selva' in English?"

I asked him what he meant. "Selva?"

He confirmed that "selva" was "jungle" and "bosque" meant "forest."

I shrugged.

"'Selva lluvioso' is 'rain-jungle' not 'rainforest'? What is the proppa term?" I enjoyed every morsel of JJ's British-flavored Spanglish. He went on to explain that he had learned that, scientifically speaking, there were various types of forest. He pontificated that, of the forest types he knew, there was tropical deciduous forest, tropical dry deciduous forest, temperate rainforest, tropical rainforest, scrub forest, savannah . . . so what really then is jungle? La Selva? "Esta es la selva real, no? So dis is proppa jungle?"

I was enjoying his curious enthusiasm for this kind of knowledge. It was a good question. What do we mean when we say "jungle"? There is no ecological designation for the word. Temperate deciduous forest, what I had grown up with in New York, goes through four seasons: spring, summer, fall, and winter. Each distinct. Of the various kinds of tropical forest, to the best of my knowledge, nothing was officially recognized as jungle.

We agreed that "jungle" was more a common term—like "black panther." Mountain lions are called panthers in some localities. All big cats belong to the panther family, but of the two species that we refer to when we think of black panthers, neither fits into any official taxonomic puzzle. A black leopard (*Panthera pardus*) is a leopard that is melanistic, meaning it has high melanin and so appears almost black, like the opposite of albino. Leopards, though, live in Africa and Asia. Now, jaguars (*Panthera onca*) come in "black panther" as well, and they are found in the Americas. But like the leopards, a black jaguar is just a rare, melanistic version of the standard model with yellow and white and black spots. So a black panther isn't really a scientifically described species, it's just a common name, a thing people say.

We spoke of jungles and lions and jaguars as we floated. A journal entry of mine from around that time says:

The glowing eyes in the shadows just beyond the firelight. It's "Dr. Livingston, I presume?" It's where the Wild Things still are. It's the borderland between what we know for certain, and the shadows of our dreams at the periphery of reality, where the ancient drumbeat still makes its way through our bare feet and into our bones like some seismic metronomic pulse of the planet; the whispers of truths long forgotten.

Our tree came charging down a long straightaway, passed a high cliff, and then turned south. "Here is!" JJ said, and stood with excitement. We'd have to make the swim to exactly where we needed to land: the little break in the jungle where Satuko's boat was tied.

We jumped in and swam like mad. We hit our mark and walked in along a trail for some time. When we reached the little thatched hut we found chickens and not much else. JJ hooted like an owl and stood with his hands on his hips, waiting. A hoot replied from the jungle.

That was the day we met Satuko's son Paul. I thought it was interesting that he had heard us coming and hid in the jungle. He had come out only when he'd seen our faces and knew we were friend and not foe.

Paul was handsome, with long pin-straight hair. We shook hands and he and JJ fell into conversation. He was the first other person we'd seen in almost two weeks. I followed enough to glean that JJ was explaining the rain and how we'd come and asking about food. There were some boiled plantains with salt that he offered to us (and which we ate greedily). But for more than that, he said, we were out of luck. The rest of the family had gone to Puerto to get supplies. With the river this full they wouldn't be able to make the return journey. It could be weeks till they came back. He too was running low on food, but a life in the jungle had made it so this was nothing special. Paul was quiet, reserved, the product of being brought up in the wild, waiting for boats and for fish to bite.

"Tienes anzuelos?" JJ asked. You got hooks?

That much Paul had. And a little bit of gasoline.

Soon we were on his boat, weaving between logs and chunks of wood and zipping along the outskirts of whirlpools that threatened to pull the whole boat down. We fished at a few different spots, but all we had for bait was the plantains. Also the river, when it's high, is not the greatest place to fish. Dry season? Different story. Throw your hook in anywhere and something will bite it, but in the charging flood levels of the rainy season, the fish are all hiding. At least that's what JJ said. By afternoon no one had gotten so much as a nibble. Sitting on the boat, we were getting eaten alive by sand flies and growing ever hungrier and more frustrated, when a wicked grin spread over JJ's face. He spoke a few words to Paul and we made for the mouth of a stream.

"Lookadis," JJ said, adopting his teaching posture.

"Show me," I said, leaning in. By then I knew when something good was coming.

"Okay, do you see any bait? What can we use?" I looked around. Nuts, seeds, sticks, leaves, wood. Nothing a fish would want. I'd learned that because the water was opaque, most of the fish have poor eyesight. You can't just throw in a metal spinner the way you can in a clear New York stream and hope a trout sees it. Out here you had to tempt the piranhas and catfish with real calories, something juicy and stinky. We needed a fat grub, a grasshopper, or a slice of old smelly meat. "The fish are like us, they want protein," JJ said. "So what are you gonna do?"

"What am I gonna do?" I laughed. I was delirious from hunger and beginning to go mad from the bugs.

JJ smiled and gave a wink to Paul. "Candamo!" he said, and grabbed the machete. He placed one foot on his knee and felt around his heel. "Ooooooh ya." He looked up to make sure I was watching closely. Then he placed the blade of the machete against his heel, where the thick callus from walking barefoot made a white horseshoe. He sank the blade in and began to saw. I cringed and recoiled as the blade made its way into his flesh. Soon JJ produced a two-inch-long slug of soggy callus. "Dat's one!" Then he did the other foot.

We baited the hooks with fresh JJ meat and concentrated on the mouth of the stream. Within two throws Paul pulled up a little shiny fish. This they both instantly cut into smaller pieces and shared them between the two hooks. They redoubled their efforts. Ten minutes later JJ got an even more encouraging pull. This one was a bagre, a kind of catfish about a foot long that, I was warned when it came flopping into the boat, had venomous spikes on its pectoral fins. JJ held it to his face and broke the spikes off with his teeth.

Paul smiled, but was sympathetic to the fish. I noticed how he changed whenever violence of any order was being done. JJ killed the catfish with a blow to the head using the back of the machete. Then we started the motor and went cruising downstream, looking for the right place to use our new wealth of bait. We had to get a fish big enough to feed the three of us.

That's when we saw it.

THROUGHOUT THE DAY, TRAVELING the river in our little canoe with our 16 hp motor, we had seen riverbanks made of only one thing: walls of massive, unbroken jungle. The vegetation stood straight out of the water, ferns and palms and tropical hardwoods over 150 feet tall. That's how it was and always had been. But suddenly we were faced with something utterly incongruous with our perception of reality. Paul's face fell like he'd seen a demon. JJ's eyes went dark.

The forest was gone. The road was strikingly red. The earth freshly tilled and then flattened by heavy machinery. There was something surreal about it. Like one of those dreams where everything is just slightly off and there's something horrifying and it builds and builds until you wake up. But as we tied the boat and made our way up the bank onto the red earth, we didn't wake up. We were really there. The sky was black and growling thunder, the jungle tall and stark and still. We stepped barefoot onto the road.

I asked JJ what I was looking at, but his gaze was faraway

with guarded horror. "I dunno." It made no sense. Where did it come from? Who had built it? When the hell did this happen?

Looking back, there was no way for us to know. It was like the first time the Inca saw the white sails of the European conquistadors coming in from the ocean. I wonder if they had any suspicion that those sails were death incarnate approaching. The first time the Comanche saw wagon trains moving over the American West, they'd never heard the term "Manifest Destiny," and had no concept that the wagons were tied to a whole new country that was growing in the East—a paradigm shift, a war, blood, and ultimately the end. I wondered if the tribes in Amazonia glance warily at the horizon, where the sound of engines roar like a beast awakened from slumber.

There's an image in my mind of JJ, standing there barefoot, dwarfed by the towering trees on either side, the dark sky crashing down, the red road stretching dreamlike out into infinity. He just stood there for a long time, motionless, hands on his hips, one shoulder dropped, staring out into the future.

After we had investigated the road, the mood changed. We drove upriver in the direction of home. It felt safer.

It was afternoon now, almost four, and the world was already dimming. By five-thirty it would be getting dark, and none of us had headlamps.

We stopped between two waterfalls, and with the nose of the boat pointed into a stream, JJ threw a line in with a chunk of the bagre catfish. Within moments there was a tug. This one was big. JJ slid off his shorts and went over the side of the boat. He let the fish swim and take him. He guided it and nursed it, careful not to lose it. When the fish thrashed on the line, JJ pulled hard, sinking the hook home. Then he worked faster. He began taking in line until the fish launched out of the water for the first time. We all cheered.

Soon the two-foot-long, fat, juicy doncella (which means "river maiden" and is a kind of tiger catfish, officially a type of *Pseudoplatystoma*) was in the boat making loud grunting noises and flopping about. Tonight, for the first time in days, we'd have real food. On the way upriver Paul kept the fish in the back of the boat, with enough water so that it could breathe and not suffer. We had to keep it alive so it wouldn't spoil, and he did so with utmost respect for the animal's life.

We spent that night at Paul's camp, the homestead that had been made by his father, Satuko. We fried catfish and ate by candlelight while the chickens slept in the shadows. I was silent. I felt sick. JJ and Paul talked for hours about what we had seen. Even the fish, our great success, and watching JJ cut his foot to work his way up the ecosystem until we had dinner were not enough to dispel the portent of doom that we had all felt.

What we saw that day was the outermost filament of a monstrous beast, the toenail of the leviathan that was moving across the basin. A continent-sized demon that breathed smoke and flattened forests, killed entire tribes, and could wipe out species before they ever met a scientist's eye.

Behold the beast: the Trans-Amazonian Highway. Viewed from an altitude where the whole of South America is visible, it is a tiny line cutting across the great green jungle—a burning edge, or a little red tapeworm working its way deeper, a parasite with branching tentacles that spread in a protean kind of metastatic march that turns everything it touches to ashes.

We would learn that the clearing was part of a new road that had stemmed from possibly the most environmentally devastating single project in the history of the world. The highway was announced in 1972 by the Brazilian government as a strategy to access and utilize its country's full area. To do this they began cutting roads into unbroken forest that would provide access to the vast mineral, timber, and agricultural resources there. Funded by the World Bank, the project was part of Brazil's National Integration Plan. In the 1970s, Amazonian jungle dominated half of Brazil's territory and held only 4 percent of its population. The plan was to incentivize people to migrate west and settle it. A scary prospect when you consider that Brazil contains 60 percent of the Amazon in its territory.

This was decades ago, when Third World countries were expected to follow the Western model of development. Large swaths of jungle were considered economically impotent, undeveloped wasteland. In the 1970s, organizations such as the World Bank and the International Monetary Fund were more than willing to dole out the financial assistance that poor ex-colonies needed to pursue this model—they gave massive funding to the highway projects.

By 1975 the entire unpaved road had been bulldozed through, a laceration carving clean across the face of southern Amazonia. Behind the heavy machinery, farmers poured into the Amazon, striking out in right angles from the road and settling vast tracts of jungle by turning them to ash. From the air, the scars can be seen today.

The metastasizing offshoot roads blazed off the main highway and into the rainforest. This was Rainforests 101, something I'd learned in my Bronx Zoo days: Roads are kryptonite to rainforests. As soon as humans can get in, the ancient trees go down, the farmers drive in with machines and cows, the land burns.

At the time when the Trans-Amazonian was being cut, the world was also entering a period of significant discovery about the state of the environment, and a greening of international politics took place on a grand scale. When I was a child, "save the rainforest" was already a cliché, but it was one born decades earlier in a period of terrible loss. Part of this came from the Congo and other places, but largely it was the Amazon where

people saw destruction on a level that was historically unprecedented.

As the highway broke through Amazonia, construction crews
blasted through Indigenous territories. Naked Natives came
face-to-face with bulldozers and shotguns. Then, because these
isolated people often have few or no antibodies to outside patho-
gens, the mere contact they had with the invaders caused, in
some cases, entire tribes to be wiped out by diseases as simple as
our common cold. Knowing the rainforest like we did, knowing that an individual tree can house reptiles, amphibians, birds,
mammals, orchids, lichen, cacti, and hundreds of insect communities all within its branches and amongst its roots, we found
almost inconceivable damage the highway did as it slashed and
burned through the heart of the Amazon.

By the 1980s, under mounting pressure from an environmentally aware public, the U.S. government conducted a hearing on the environmental impacts of the World Bank's loans to
Third World countries—which an increasing number of people
believed to be more destructive than good. It was becoming
clear that giving vast sums of money to poor governments often
impoverished more than it empowered; millions of people were
displaced and catastrophic environmental damage was done by
highways and hydroelectric dams. The Trans-Amazonian Highway is debatably the single most lethal blow waged by man
against nature.

For the World Bank this pressure was real, and a sweeping
reorganization of the bank took place. It became more strict in
its lending and required more detailed environmental impact
statements before approving loans. The bank stopped its funding of the Brazilian highway system in 1985, effectively halting
all construction on the road, which would have linked Brazil to
the Peruvian border near Puerto Maldonado and eventually run
over the Andes to the Pacific Ocean, opening up the Amazon to

the Asian timber market by a direct land route to the sea for the
first time in history.

BUT ON THAT CLOUDY day at the edge of the world, more than
twenty years after the Trans-Amazonian Highway had first been
cut, JJ and Paul and I saw that the beast had been reawakened.

A year later there would be houses at the edge of the road,
crappy shacks with corrugated steel roofs built by people from
another part of Peru who had heard there was free land and no
rules over in Las Piedras. In the years after that, ten or twelve
more houses sprouted. With each new little hut came more people, and of course those people would cut a few acres to farm it,
which meant first leveling the trees and burning everything. If
you look at satellite imagery of the river from 2001 to the present, the cancer gets worse and worse every year; the forest looks
like it has mange, with vast areas of green turning black and
then red and then white as they burn. Suddenly it didn't take
two days to reach the research station. You could drive from
Puerto Maldonado to Lucerna, as the road's port came to be
known. Then it was just an hour by boat. Deep jungle no more.

By 2009 there were logging trucks where the road met the
river. Stores sprang up where there had once been just houses.
Soon they sold batteries and Coca-Cola and tuna cans. A few
lazy prostitutes began to hang around waiting while the loggers
transported wood. The logging trucks were tremendous machines with tall wheels that could handle the rough dirt road.
Timber companies sent them in to collect the wood that illegal
loggers had pillaged from our forests.

The stories of violent encounters between loggers and uncontacted tribes began to become all too common. Shotguns
against longbows. Men with motors were charging out into
jungle that was still the home of pre–Stone Age clans of hunter-
gatherers. The results were brutal. Slaughters would occur on

both sides. Men, women, and children would die, and as the death toll rose, resentment and pain grew. The killing would get worse, far worse.

Paul's father, Satuko, had no illusions. He said it was the beginning of the end. He would stand glaring at the edge of the river as the loggers went by. "Criminals! Criminals!" he would shout at them as they went. "I don't understand how it's allowed!" The world was changing before our eyes.

Our little research station and Satuko's house had always been a step past civilization. Somewhere you had to work to get to, somewhere special and deep in the jungle. That's why we came. It was the wild. But once word got out that there was a road that would take you into the jungle, past where the police would go, it attracted a certain kind of people. People who had nowhere else to go, who were desperate, who needed timber, gold, meat, and land.

"Isn't there anything we can do? Isn't there someone we can call?"

JJ was watching a logging boat go by. "We are the only ones here; no help is coming."

His words fell on me like a kapok tree. In the world I grew up in, there were rules. You couldn't just go burn things and cut down trees. If I ever saw anyone hunting a deer without a tag or chopping a tree without a permit, there were numbers I could call, police who would help. This was a crucial step in my education and understanding: the unlearning I needed to do to comprehend the world of Amazonia. I had pointed questions, like: Who owned that land? JJ said: Someone. Well, who? And where are they and why don't they fight back against the loggers? The answer was always a shrug. It was maddening. There was so much we didn't know.

Most of us live in places with rules to keep you driving straight and within the lines. Rules to keep you safe, rules to keep you from killing other people, even the ones who get under your skin, ruin your life, kill your dog. There's God's law. Society's law. Love thy neighbor. The Golden Rule. You can walk down the street and be reasonably certain no one is going to hurt you. But just behind the prop walls and stage lights, the illusion of society gives way to a breathtaking realization that it's all just an act. We are animals on this Earth.

Gradually the dark-laced jungle and the animals within it, the trees fighting for light—it all began to make sense.

Out here, the veneer of society had not yet been painted. The rules are as clear and ancient as the stars. Like that grim hunger in the eyes of a pacing jaguar. Every tree fighting for light. Every animal hunting, every cat crucifying a mouse, every fly waiting for a corpse. The jungle is where the ancient truths slither through the vines and there are glowing eyes watching from the shadows. It's a landscape of blood and muscle and scars and sky. Where God watches in grim fascination as the entropic symphony of creation struggles onward. It's run-for-your-life. It's the gasp of air. It's the fever dream and the mosquitoes and the mutiny. It's the wild rush. Your canines and the glint in your eye. It's the length of your teeth and the size of your muscles and the sharpness of your blades. Where you'll be safe as long as you can kill them first or run fast enough to hide where the hungry can't find you.

═══

Thank God for Paul. He was the antithesis of all the brutality we had to see. I spent a lot of days fishing with him, exploring little streams. He'd stop by the station sometimes to check on us, the only friendly face we'd see. He would smile with big eyes when I showed him snakes up close. His mouth opened with wonder the first time he held a rainbow boa. We could sit for hours and not say a word. His sensitivity and gentle nature set him apart. This was a landscape of hard men with big hands and chain saw wounds and adventure stories. Paul was quiet, watchful, and gentle. He spoke only when spoken to, was kind to animals, and made children smile.

A year later, I was trying to drive the boat one day when JJ wasn't around. The rusty old peke peke, a big, ugly, open kind of old-school boat motor, just wouldn't turn on, and I drifted downriver for over an hour trying to get it to start. When I arrived at Paul's, he laughed at me and knew I didn't want JJ to know. "He'll think you're a gringo or something," he said, leaning over to try to diagnose the problem. "Don't worry, your secret is safe with me." We worked on the motor for some time before he determined that a new spark plug was the only thing it could need. So we walked back to the house. In the dense bamboo forest a troop of tamarin monkeys were hopping and chirping, watching us. Paul became as excited as I'd ever seen him, a kind of wide-eyed wonder. "Look!" he whispered. "They are the mustached ones." Sure enough, the monkeys were emperor tamarins, a kind I had never seen before. Later on, the photo I got of emperor tamarins in that same bamboo forest would become the first record of the species on the Las Piedras River, a discovery I made with Paul.

That day, he got me a new spark plug and got the motor working so that I'd be able to get back home to the station. "Where's the family?" I asked.

He motioned somewhere far off.

"Estás solito?" You're alone?

He shrugged. "Como siempre." Like always.

I smiled. I told him he was a real hombre de la selva. He wouldn't go to town if he could help it. He always said it was too noisy there and too dangerous, too many people. His was a life lived so far from the madness of the world, all alone and quiet with the fish and the trees and the birds.

He was found face down. Whoever shot him did so from behind. During one of the times he was alone. Paul never saw it coming. Whoever did it stole his chain saw and went out through that horrible road, just like he'd come in. Whoever it was knew there'd be no consequences, not out here.

The jungle isn't a place, it's a state of mind.

THE SERPENTINE
SCRIPTURES

E XPEDITIONARY TRAVEL IN THE AMAZON ISN'T MEASURED IN miles or as the crow flies. Days pass while your tiny canoe motors up winding tributaries, the compass dial swinging in all directions as you follow the course of the water snaking across the landscape. We had been traveling from sunup to sundown, camping at night on beaches, penetrating places in the forest that had no name, just uncharted dream space, parts of the jungle where no one goes. It was just me, JJ, and two of his brothers, Pico and Chito, in an open-topped boat, being rained on and baked by the sun for days, at world's end. Up in one of these far-flung places was the first time it happened.

Hours of monotonous travel had lulled us into a dream state that was shattered when Pico began shouting and pointed to a tremendous pile of coils sleeping on a mountainous stack of driftwood on the river's edge. It was the first big anaconda we had seen.

Moments later, I made a mistake that almost killed me. I stalked up, summoned my courage, lunged, and was so focused on immobilizing the head that I just grabbed it with both hands and held on. It was the first time I'd felt the power of a fifteen-foot snake thicker than my thigh. I should have known they are all heavyweight black belts in grappling, with a specialty in choking and crushing their opponents into submission before swallowing them whole. The moment I "caught" it, the snake coiled around my wrists. I was handcuffed. Now I couldn't let go if I wanted to. I had started out trying to catch the snake, now it had me, and I wanted to run, but I couldn't.

I fell to the ground to work on the wrist problem, but as I did, an even larger coil came winding over my shoulders and neck, clenching around the front of me and flexing in a terrifying display of power that brought my shoulders dangerously close together. My ribs were constricted, my airway almost blocked, and my clavicle was a millimeter from popping. I tried to scream for JJ but a muted choke was the only sound I could make. The world flickered, and my collarbones were making sounds like a stick bent until it's just about to snap.

At that moment, JJ reached me at a full sprint, and fell to unwinding the snake's tail. Then came Chito, and they worked together. I remember drawing that first blessed breath of air after thinking I had taken my last. As I did, I never once released my grip on the snake's neck just behind the head, where the open mouth of the anaconda was flaunting six rows of recurved teeth. Pico pulled up in the boat: "Puta madre, Rosolie, mira este anacondazo!"

It was the first big anaconda we'd caught. Or so we thought.

≡

When Santiago, JJ's father, heard the story of how I'd almost died, he laughed heartily. "Esa es una anacondita," he said with his toothless, hollow-cheeked smile. He was well into his eighties and waved a gnarled hand, dismissing the whole thing. That's a tiny anaconda, he said, now truly laughing.

Meeting Don Santiago was like meeting a movie star in real life. He had palpable gravity. I was shaking hands with history. When Pico, Chito, JJ, and I had come back from weeks of expedition travel, we found Santiago living alone on the banks of the Tambopata.

Even at eighty-five he was a formidable human. One of those lean guys with a small head, but with sinewy muscles and broad feet. His hands were monstrous. He was barefoot around camp but wore old gum boots for work and a pair of shorts that looked like they'd been with him his whole life.

"If you want to bring me stories, you better get something worthwhile," he said.

Pico, who saw how close my bones had come to snapping, found his father's nonchalance hilarious. Pico slapped the table and laughed so hard that his cane fell to the ground and spooked the chickens.

Our bodies were aching from weeks of expedition: There are not a lot of comfortable ways to sit in a canoe for ten hours a day. This was our first night back at "home" in the jungle (though at Santiago's we still had to use our tents because all he had was an old palm-thatched shack in a small clearing). Despite our weariness, the boys were excited to share stories with their dad, and Santiago was happy to have the company and receive the gifts of peccary meat and a large chunk of ayahuasca vine that the boys had brought. I think he was also relieved to see that his boys had grown up to carry the torch of an adventurous, expeditionary life. "Tell me, tell me," he said as he kicked at a chicken and took a seat by the fire.

We told him of our adventures, the capture of the snake, how strong it was. How one night after JJ had caught a big catfish, a large black caiman had climbed into the boat and eaten the leftover fish stew, metal pots and all. We'd all come running out of our tents and just spotted the tail slipping into the water, leaving the boat rocking. "So you had no pots the rest of the trip?" Santiago's bony shoulders shook with laughter. Sitting next to JJ while the Durand men spoke, I had to rely on his translation sometimes, but over the next few hours I got to experience the brothers and father exchanging a century's worth of jungle lore.

Santiago was soon telling us what softies we were for using a motor. In his day, expeditions were done by pole. He asked me what I thought of Pico's boat driving, obviously proud that his son had become one of the most widely respected motorists of the region. In my limited Spanish I was able to tell him how none of what we had done would have been possible without him. Santiago liked that.

While JJ had never been a logger, Santiago and Pico had both spent years logging during the mahogany boom. It was a vile time of exploitation on the river, when the lawlessness was at its apex. Fights between loggers and tribes were common. The timber was free for the taking. There were so many loggers on the river at one point that the pimps from Puerto went mobile and brought boatloads of jungle prostitutes out into the wild. For a time these riverfaring brothels roamed the backcountry, and because no one carried cash, the girls accepted payment in timber—mahogany, shihuahuaco, quinilla, and cedro.

Of all the swashbuckling tales of the wild '90s, what stuck with me as Pico and Santiago spoke was that each trip had been not days but weeks up the Las Piedras, far past the station where JJ and I had spent most of our time. Far past where my wildest dreams lived.

Santiago described a world far beyond what we could imagine, places up small tributaries of the main channel and protected by quirks of geography where no one had ever been. He said there were ways to tell forest that no humans had visited before—the absence of trails, the abundance of fish, the kinds of trees and their size. He said there were good places and bad places in the jungle; some of them were haunted. Laughing a little, holding out a giant old finger, he warned us that if we were ever real far up the Las Piedras and heard the animals sounding "off," they weren't animals at all.

Sometimes the tribes would use the whistle of a tinamou, or the chatter calls of a monkey. Not only would they mimic the sounds to perfection, they had the intricacies down well enough that they could use it as a kind of secret language. It was chilling to hear and still haunts me to this day.

"One time I was out hunting up there, way up there, out past La Cachuela"—he nodded at Pico to see that he knew where—"and I had my gun. It was just about dark and I turned on my light and it was going to be a few hours back to the camp. I had hunted a spider monkey. I was following a stream back to the river when I heard the sound." He made the whistle of a tinamou with his mouth. His eyebrows rose. "I knew I wasn't alone."

"Puta madre, diablos!" Pico said in wonder.

"I knew they were tracking me. And you know them, they are tall. Not like local people. They're tall. And they're painted from head to foot in black and red. They are killers. Pure killers. So what did I do? I dropped the monkey for them and I shut my light. I got in the stream and I slithered like a snake down that stream. Over the caiman and the stingrays, I didn't care. I reached the river and was . . ." His hand slapped his chest like a heartbeat.

JJ told him what we'd seen on the Las Piedras—the road, the burned forest. Santiago nodded and shook his head in disgust. "They'll never stop. They think the jungle is something they can just take apart, like we can live without it. You see what's happening here, don't you? Look how many days you boys had to go until you saw good game. Pico, how many days was it until you saw peccaries?"

JJ nudged me; this was what he'd always told me. How when

he'd been a kid there had been animals and now there weren't. Santiago spat.

"If they come for Las Piedras, I hope those naked fuckers run them through with arrows. I hope they fight. They've kept it wild, you know?" He was looking at me now. "People don't go to certain places because they are scared of the tribes, because you never really know where they are. You could die at any moment. That keeps the forest safe, that fear. But it's changing now with these roads. They have the machinery to do terrible things."

"Like the forrestal," Pico said grimly. The excavator.

Santiago held up his hands like he didn't even want to hear it.

Pico was already lost in a flashback. "It's like a demon," he said, staring into the fire, "a demon that can just"—his hand cut through the air—"take away the forest like that."

"That's the thing," Santiago said. He was looking at me now. "If you want to keep this place wild, it has to be done now. Ahora. That's how we set up our village here, Infierno. You have to organize the people, you have to make it policy. Once the forest is gone, it's gone. Did you see the big trees I have on my land? You won't see those anywhere else. My father told me about the big trees, and Don Ignacio speaks about them when he journeys with ayahuasca. The big trees are our ancestors; they protect us. Cutting them is a sin. That's what I've come to believe. I know I used to be a logger, but now that I'm old, that's what I believe."

After a few hours of the firelight and Santiago's stories, I was motionless, suspended on a rare kind of raw wonder. There beneath the trees with these men, with these friends, was the shimmering threshold between real life and the mythical church of the Amazon.

Santiago's eyes were glowing in the darkness. He watched

the orange embers spark upward to join the celestial river of stars that arced across the night sky. As if the memories were written there, he squinted, his face as wrinkled and weathered as an old map of the world. Vast experience whispered in the firelight, as ephemeral as the breath that spoke the words, but powerful enough to latch on and sink down into some deep part of me.

"Papa, tell him about the anaconda on the blackwater stream," Pico said, yawning.

"Someone roll me a cigarette."

I did and handed it to him.

"Okay, let me see. First, there were other people there. So it's not a lie. Who was with me?" He was asking the boys now. "Ah, yes, Chikki and Elias were with me. And your mother. We had gone up some years ago. Maybe five days upstream. Camping, hunting. You know. It was good. But we turned around once we saw that thing. It was a dragon. Maybe thirty-six feet long. This big," he said, holding out his arms in a hoop. "And I'm telling you, it had horns."

That's when I stood up to go find a tree to pee on, shaking my head and making it clear that this kind of tall tale was beyond what I could tolerate.

"He doesn't believe it? Ha. He doesn't believe it!"

JJ tried to grab me. "You don't believe?"

"Hell no, I don't believe that! No snake has horns!"

Santiago dismantled my skepticism with an easy laugh as he drew on his cigarette. In that moment I lost the upper hand and went from shrewd rationalist to deluded inexperienced gringo. They all believed it. They had seen things I hadn't. In New York, skepticism is revered, but here I had just shown my hand, my experience level, and the fact that I was still new enough not to know that the jungle depths held secrets beyond the liminal boundary of modern imagination.

"Okay, Gringo Loco," Santiago said squinting at me across the fire. "If you want to play with something bigger than that worm you caught, then go to the Floating Forest. Go. If you want to find a true giant, a real one, and I don't know why you'd want to—that's where you go."

DAYS LATER WE SHARPENED our machetes and made the plunge.

As night gripped the world, down beneath the colossal canopy we made our way along a long-forgotten trail. Around us in the jungle, galaxies of wild animals stalked and slithered unseen. The Amazon at night is the greatest freak show on Earth, a teeming carnival of incomprehensible life, a festival of sex and death all around you. Beneath that canopy at night, every inch of the darkness is alive—hiking along a cave beneath leafy mountains is like traversing the bottom of a black hole.

We must have looked like insects with torchlights flickering between trees. Some of these trees were so large that as I looked upward they just faded into distant blackness. Nature's nocturnal cathedral. I kept tripping because I couldn't resist the wonder of staring up into the immensity.

Because his damaged leg made it impossible for him to hike, Pico had stayed with Santiago, and instead JJ's brother José came with us, shotgun in hand, ready for disaster.

We hiked through that dark jungle for so long that I remember gradually becoming worried that by the time we reached where we were going we'd have nothing left in the tank. It was exhausting, long, monotonous. It gave us time to think about all the things that could go wrong. There's something about walking through the jungle at night for hours on end that begins to play strangely on my mind. The fear slips in and begins to dance with the imagination.

When we reached the edge of the great swamp, the area that Santiago called the Floating Forest, JJ and I dropped our packs and José loaded his gun. We stood shoulder to shoulder, peering out over a landscape that was hard to comprehend. We had no idea what we were about to encounter. No clue that we were about to cross some kind of threshold.

Looking out over that midnight swamp, I was terrified. To be clear: I'm not asking you to believe what I'm about to describe. I myself am the world's biggest skeptic and it pains me to tell any story I can't prove. So I promise this will be the only one, for the whole book, and it's for a good reason because it sets up a lot of what came after. Because when you experience something so completely outside the boundaries of what you thought was reality, it's transformative.

This was the edge of the Floating Forest. A quirk of geography that caused an especially deep lake unlike anything we had seen. The tops of tall palms burst from the surface of the water, and an unnerving archipelago of floating vegetation stretched out before us.

With a cautious foot, JJ tested the buoyancy of the floating grass. It seemed to hold his weight. He took a step. Then another. I followed slowly, careful not to choose wrong and plunge into the black water. We made our way a few meters out onto the undulating alien landscape, then looked back at José, who shook his head. No way.

JJ smiled. There's an underlined note in my journal of that time that reads: "The hunt for giant snakes has led me to parts of the jungle most people wouldn't go with a gun."

We left José and continued out onto the floating island.

We spoke little as we went.

"How deep crees que lo es?" JJ asked, holding a small tree that grew from the grassy raft he was balanced on.

"I don't know." I was wholly focused on the step I was about to take from one good foothold, over a black span of water, to the next mass of vegetation.

Over the course of an hour we made our way across the surface. The Milky Way arched over the sky with all its purple-and-blue nebulous beauty. There were almost more stars than sky, and the reflection of the heavens rippled in the dark water, like an alternate universe, trembling. We had the sensation that we had left Earth entirely, and were hopscotching across dreams.

We were walking across the canopy of a subaquatic jungle.

Everything was unnerving. Caimans watched us from the shadows, their red eyes glowing in our headlamps. Owls hooted from unseen perches. As we groped our way across the terrain, rippling and bobbing with the water, there were sleepy wasp nests, waiting like land mines. JJ pointed at one with raised eyebrows until he was certain I had seen it. I nodded and adjusted course.

At one point I miscalculated and was instantly plunged into the water. Terror. Blinding terror. For a moment I lost my sight completely, over my head in pitch-black nightmare soup. My legs flailed as I scrambled back up onto the grass, trying desperately not to think of what giant, toothy things were looking up at me from the depths. I stood up, gasping for air, trembling.

"Look," JJ said. He was on a whole different wavelength. He'd found something.

He was staring transfixed at an area of bright green grass that had been flattened in a long pathway. Side by side we studied what we saw. I was thinking but didn't dare say what JJ voiced with a swing of his machete.

"Dis is anaconda."

"No, it's not!" I told him. It couldn't be. The drag mark was too wide, too thick. If that was the mark of a snake, it was a snake thicker than I was. It didn't seem possible, and I insisted it just couldn't be.

But JJ's eyes were dark with concentration. "There are no footprints, look."

I couldn't argue.

"Mira, Paul, lookadis." He shined his light out ahead of us, and suddenly it became clear that the wide trail moved in an *S* shape across the terrain. We walked on for a long time in silence, both too visually overwhelmed and at the edge of our nerves to communicate anything but the essential.

When it finally happened, it was well past midnight and we were lost, far out into the middle reaches of the vast swamp. When I first saw JJ go still, I could feel it in my blood. Looking down at what lay before us, my eyes saw, but my mind couldn't comprehend.

The larger of the two snakes—the female—was so big that from where we stood by her tail, her head was out of sight. Another anaconda, easily sixteen feet long, was draped over the larger one. They hadn't yet noticed we were there.

My brain fired a hundred thoughts all at once as her coils exploded into action. She was moving rapidly toward the water, where she'd be gone in moments if we didn't do something. I dove headlong onto her. But as I rode along, hugging the scaly trunk of her muscular body, my presence did nothing to impede her progress. My arms could not close around her, such was her circumference. I was carried more than seven feet on the anaconda, clinging to her, legs dragging on either side.

As she swept my body over the surface of the lake, I tried digging my heels into the grass but they never held. For the first time, it occurred to me that if she opted for fight over flight, that giant tooth-filled mouth would do irreparable damage to my face, not to mention she'd be able to collapse my rib cage in about half a second.

Instead, her head entered the water, followed by the first third of her body, and then the section of her body I was gripping. Digging both knees into the grass, I tried to brace. But her power was as unyielding as a horse—there was nothing I could do. She dragged me fully into the water, face-first, as JJ watched in frozen astonishment, his circuits too blown to move.

Cool black water swallowed my head and shoulders in a flash, and the rest of my body, clinging to the giant snake, followed into the dark abyss. I let go and paddled like a windmill for the surface.

With my head above the water, I held on to the nearest grass, where the last fifteen feet of the titanic snake sped over my shoulder and under my other arm into the water. I savored the last moments of her presence, hands recording the smooth, scaly immensity passing by. My heart jackhammered in my chest; it was a moment of unparalleled shock. I was at the mercy of perhaps the largest living snake on Earth. As her body narrowed to her tail, I released the grass and held the snake, my hands coming closer together and then finally touching as she departed. My last view of her was her tail disappearing into the black water below.

If you're rolling your eyes and just about to fling this book, I don't blame you. I wouldn't believe me either. But that's what happened.

We would only later see that I hadn't just jumped on a giant snake like an adventurous idiot—we had inadvertently conducted a valuable bit of field research. Discerning that female anacondas over twenty feet long cannot be caught on floating vegetation was a first step in developing a methodology for studying Amazonia's largest snakes—a field that at that time was lacking exactly because they are too cryptic to find and, as we discovered, too large to restrain. It would take some time and processing before we began to take the question seriously: How do we find a way to measure, sample, and study the upper limits of the most giant anacondas in Amazonia?

Some people might say, and many in the coming years would, that to launch into such an encounter voluntarily was somehow

grotesque. That it had the potential to stress the animal and en-
danger our lives and that the act itself was somehow a fundamental transgression against the devout naturalistic reverence
that one should have for one of the living gods of the jungle.
My only refutation is that, had you been standing there with us
in that alien swamp at the crossroads of fear and opportunity,
you would understand that it was something far too powerful
to turn away from. Like surfing a hundred-foot wave, reaching
the peak of an impossibly high mountain, or filming a deep-sea
giant squid, the chance to show the world the largest anaconda
anyone had ever seen was a type of treasure we had to chase.

It was not lost on us that we had penetrated layers of experience in the jungle that most people would find unbelievable. We
could hardly believe it ourselves. We had to tell and retell the
story, spend long hours awake at night. Something tremendous
had happened. You throw a stone and the universe ripples.

THE SHAMAN

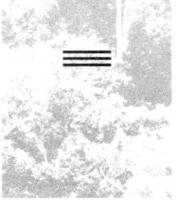

ONE OF THE INTENSE PLEASURES OF TRAVEL IS
THE OPPORTUNITY TO LIVE AMONGST PEOPLES
WHO HAVE NOT FORGOTTEN THE OLD WAYS,
WHO STILL FEEL THEIR PAST IN THE WIND,
TOUCH IT IN STONES POLISHED BY RAIN,
TASTE IT IN THE BITTER LEAVES OF PLANTS.

—WADE DAVIS, *THE WAYFINDERS*

WE COULDN'T GO HOME TO LAS PIEDRAS BIODIVERSITY STA-
tion because JJ and Emma had sold it. As far as we knew, it was
gone for good. It was heartbreaking to me not being able to go.
I thought we'd never see it again.

So instead, I found myself in JJ's home village—Infierno—
and the places and names he'd always told me about came to life.
Just like he said, it was different there. It didn't have the deep
jungle feeling of Las Piedras. It was a community. There were
sections of old primary forest interrupted by roads and farms.
The farmers shot anything that moved, of course, so around these
areas the game populations were way down. Predators like pumas
and jaguars and ocelots were kept at bay with shotguns to pro-

tect the cows and chickens and dogs the community members kept. There was some brilliant jungle around, but most of the old trees had been taken out. There were no more spider monkeys. No more peccaries. And the jaguars had long ago been hunted out, or they'd left for lands with better prey.

There were, however, other perks to being in Infierno. I got to be around a lot of local Ese Eja culture. I began learning to identify which vines could be pulled from trees and de-barked so they could be woven into baskets and brooms. We spent days at a time with Santiago, and we were always around Pico. José took us bow-and-arrow fishing in the Pitchyquoia stream, so we were constantly eating delicious fish. Chikki showed us how to find palm grubs thicker than your thumb, which we gathered and shish kebabed with salt and fried till crunchy—delectable. Elias explored colpas, natural salt deposits, deep in the forest. We went on several expeditions into areas of the forest only accessible to people with Indigenous status. I was learning a lot and was no longer a newcomer; I had cut my teeth in the jungle. We'd all survived rain for days on end. Cold nights on the brink of hypothermia, contrasted with inferno days being incinerated by the sun. On the rivers, in the jungle, I was one of the guys.

My dreams were mountains on the horizon that I had no clear path to reach, let alone climb. My heroes were the conservation biologists. When I was away from Infierno, back at college finishing another semester, I would go on Mongabay.com, the news hub mecca for conservation reporting, and read articles that would make my heart swell with wonder and envious longing.

Alan Rabinowitz was saving tigers in places like Bhutan. He'd written entire books on his work with jaguars in Latin America. He'd published scientific, peer-reviewed papers. There were pictures of him on elephant-back doing fieldwork. He'd met with the king of Bhutan and made an entire national park.

It was easier, he said, working with dictators, because they could just sign a decree into reality, no committees and no democratic voting, just a single person's decision. Protected! The man was a legend. And like me, he'd come from New York. He often told the story of how he grew up with a stutter so bad that he was barely able to speak, and how when he saw a habitat being destroyed, he felt especially connected to the animals because they too were voiceless. They were losing their home, with no power to protest or organize and explain to the humans the peril they faced. He was a fixture of the Bronx Zoo. His legacy and accomplishments were literally the scaffolding of my wildest dreams.

At that time, I was seeing so much destruction with no way to have any influence in stopping it. I tried contacting Dr. Rabinowitz; I sent him emails but never heard back.

Another conservationist I admired to no end was Mike Fay. He was a National Geographic Explorer, basically the coolest gig in the world. They pay you a couple hundred thousand dollars a year to just . . . keep being you. Essentially he was getting paid to be Indiana Jones, or the Most Interesting Man in the World. Mike Fay was known for being ornery and driven to extremism in his conservation views. But if you want to do things other people haven't done, then you have to be willing to do things other people won't do. You gotta burn to shine—and Fay blazed a trail so wild and long and dangerous it became known as the Africa Megatransect.

The Megatransect was his name for an expedition he undertook in Africa starting in 1999. It took him 465 days to hike 2,000 miles across the Congo Basin. Known for child soldiers and genocides and danger, the Congo is a place most biologists and scientists wouldn't go. Fay went in his Teva sandals with a few porters. He literally went where no one else from his tribe or country was willing to go, far beyond the line of safety and into a jungle where there was no guarantee of return. Along the way, he conducted a survey of the ecology and conservation status of wherever the path took him. There were photos of him and his team hiking in their sandals, up to their waists in water. Fay was unshaven and shirtless, with just a tiny backpack, his glasses, and a backward hat. It was about the most incredible thing I'd ever heard of. The things they must have seen. Elephants, gorillas, vast areas of the jungle that other people were too scared to explore.

What made the Megatransect the rocket fuel of my dreams is that after it was over, Fay managed to make a presentation to the president of Gabon to create thirteen new national parks. Then in 2002 his data, photos, and findings persuaded Colin Powell and members of the Bush administration to give $53 million to help preserve the Congo Basin.

Dr. Patricia Wright's work as a biologist and primatologist made her famous for discovering a new species of primate, the golden bamboo lemur, and establishing protected areas in Madagascar. She is the founder and executive director of the Institute for the Conservation of Tropical Environments at Stony Brook University, as well as the Centre ValBio, the world-class research campus near Ranomafana National Park in Madagascar. She has published over 150 articles and books. She has received numerous accolades and awards, including three medals of honor from the Malagasy government and the prestigious Indianapolis Prize for animal conservation. I could only shake my head in wonder. How did she do it?

I had grown up on stories of Jane Goodall and her time with the chimpanzees, her refusal to treat them like study subjects and her determination to name them. Some people accused her of anthropomorphizing the chimps, but Jane always saw how similar they were to us, and comparing them to us was not, in her opinion, contradictory to the veracity of her scientific work.

Goodall, of course, went on to be the first person to famously and publicly prove the use of tools in the animal kingdom, changing the long-standing axiom "Man the Toolmaker" forever. She literally upended and overturned our view of ourselves as a species. Even when I was a kid, Goodall was so legendary, it felt like she was on a historical list with luminaries like Lincoln or Einstein. I mean, there were black-and-white pictures of her from ages ago, but somehow she was still alive and working.

These people I read about were doing such important work. They were associated with universities. They had PhDs. They'd gone to grad school. Hell, they'd probably gotten good grades. Reading about their work made me feel sick with longing for something I was certain I would never have. I had had terrible grades. I was dyslexic. I had no affiliations or lofty degrees. None of those things shared by those on the cutting edge. And there I was, in my twenties, not in grad school, no plan, no national park. Just imagine how many trees these people were protecting. Entire species. Entire forests and ecosystems. There were herds of elephants that were safe because someone like Fay or Wright or Rabinowitz had championed saving their home. Tigers slept in the jungle with their cubs, in areas patrolled by anti-poaching units these people had deployed. The only reason the world wasn't completely devoid of authentic ecosystems and endangered species was the work of these incredible humans. I wanted to be one of them. I wanted it more than anything. It burned my heart, I wanted it so badly.

For years and years, I would read article after article on Mongabay. Every now and then, they'd profile an up-and-coming scientist. A prolific kid somewhere writing a book on tropical birds. A graduate student who discovered a new lizard on a remote island. One article I read was about a twentysomething researcher who had deployed camera traps in a forest and dis-

covered all kinds of animal activity that was previously unknown. I daydreamed about being like them.

AROUND THAT TIME, I began to focus on, and to see the value
in, being accepted by this wild gang of Nativos that was the
Durand family and Ese Eja culture. Santiago's acceptance alone
meant that what I lacked in academic prowess, I had at least
slightly offset with some irrefutably peer-reviewed jungle street
cred.

I had raised a giant anteater. I had gone out with poachers
and watched them work. I had launched my own solo expeditions, my version of a vision quest, alone in the Amazon, and
managed to live through the ordeal. I'd ridden trees down the
river with JJ. And I had become good friends with some excep-
tional Indigenous leaders who were very committed to the idea
of protecting the forest they had. We'd been places few people
ever went. I had gotten to do so many of the things I had once
only dreamed of.

Then of course there were our increasingly wild adventures
with giant snakes—so wild most people didn't believe them,
but I had a good idea how to fix that. We'd just have to catch
more, and actually begin to form our findings into a study. JJ
and I sat up many a night planning it, manifesting our future:
We were going to catch the world-record anaconda and launch
a study into their population dynamics.

On a whim, I reached out to the folks at Mongabay and
wrote a little intro about what I'd been doing, about the Floating Forest and how unique it was, and threw in some photos
and field notes and drawings. I'd hoped to plant a seed, make a
contact, and then continue working in the field with camera
traps and the preliminary anaconda research. To my utter amazement, a reporter named Jeremy Hance responded quickly, and

asked me to send him some more info. It was something. But I wasn't going to get my hopes up. I wanted it so badly that the thought of it was almost overwhelming. I knew that once they found out that I had no affiliations or advanced degrees, they'd change their minds.

I was shouldering the considerable weight of guilt and insecurity related to my jungle life. People back home didn't understand it. To them it seemed like I was just going on a lot of long trips. Self-indulgent vacations. I think they thought I was running away, enjoying myself, like a beach bum who happened to like trees better than sand. There was undeniably a delinquent kid in me who felt like at any moment someone was going to show up and drag me back to detention. I still had nightmares about sitting before a committee that had decided to sentence me to a life of school. Worse, I was keenly aware that when you chase your dreams, there has to be a direction, a goal, and I very much felt like I didn't have that. I knew who I wanted to be, I knew where I wanted to go, but it was so intangible that even I couldn't tell if I was on a path or just wandering. I didn't want to be just wandering.

When I'd left high school and gone to college, an irate relative had pulled me aside at a family barbecue. He gripped me by the arm with wide eyes and warned me, "You know this only ends one way: You drop out and you end up working at a gas station." Aside from the distasteful, misguided urgency and the grotesque facial expression, I resented the effect his words had on me. I was already scared, already making choices that challenged my courage. Once he said it, all I could think was *Damn, that's what everyone must be thinking and just not saying:* You're signing up to be a loser in life.

The thing is, I come from a good family. Italian immigrants who came to America and worked hard. New York City people. Brooklyn people. My grandfather was a cop, and my grandmother never needed to vocalize the pride she felt about his being a Marine in World War II or an officer in the NYPD. It just became her posture, her ocean liner confidence and rugged brand of New York tough love. Her children were teachers, hospital administrators, and a successful lawyer. They had married other successful people. These are people who go to church on Sundays. Who stay together for holidays. People with good hearts who believe you stay safe, protect your own, pray for the best, and trust in God. Naturally they were concerned when one of their own began making pilgrimages to places they could barely pronounce. I knew it was care, but still I felt it as a kind of pressure. An unspoken question: What the hell is he doing down there? This is often how it is when we discover a calling, or commit to our inner bearing. By following a "dream," you are determining to move toward something on the horizon, in the future, and it is often a treasure no one else can see. So you can't blame other people if they look at you funny, or straight-out call you crazy.

THERE MAY HAVE BEEN more going on than we thought. And the contrast I saw between the world I had come from and the one I had adopted was remarkable in its polarity. There were times I would be sitting on a boat with Santiago and Pico and JJ and marvel at the rawness of the experience. A single log dug out into a canoe, with extra wood added to the sides to give it some depth. Unpainted. The motor was uncovered, missing half its parts, but still working. We'd be smoking cigarettes and squinting through the rain as we puttered up some jungle stream. There was no way to convey to anyone back home the vastness of the wild, the size of the trees, the depth of the swamps, and the overwhelming diversity of what lurked in them. It was another world, and it was thrilling.

Culturally, the Durand family was its own entity, even in

Peru, even in the rugged Madre de Dios. Santiago had created an army of wild men—and the women were no exception.

The first time I had met Santiago, he was naked.

Pico had spat and smiled, squinting away the smoke with a cigarette in his mouth. "I hope you're ready, cachero, my dad is coming!"

JJ leaned over and explained "cachero" is a local swear word that basically means "fucker." "Don't use it around normal people," he warned, "it's a bad word."

I asked the room why I needed to be ready.

Another brother leaned over, beer in hand. "My dad, he has a big, big dick!"

They all burst out laughing.

JJ: "When you meet my dad, say: 'Hola, cachero.'"

The laughter grew in volume. I couldn't quite get the joke. "Hello, fucker" to someone I was meeting for the first time seemed a bit steep, but the hilarity that ensued in the room was electrifying. They started speaking and laughing in a speed setting of Spanish that was far above my ability to follow at the time. So I just smiled along.

When Santiago entered, I saw what they meant. The man was eightysomething, lean, muscular, and naked from head to foot. He had a smile on his face and a big old cannon swinging between his legs. The boys all cheered and laughed as we shook hands.

"Hola, cachero," I said warmly.

The room erupted in laughter. Pico came right out of his seat and onto the floor. Santiago's eyebrows went up and he chuckled as he passed, that toothless-old-man amusement on his face.

"Man, you weren't kidding!" I laughed to JJ.

"No, it's so big! He's the original cachero, he make all of us with dat!"

It was hilarious how unconcerned with nudity they were, and how proud of their dad's dick they all were. They hadn't been joking. They were genuinely excited for me to see it.

From then on, "cachero" became a term of endearment within our little tribe. Anyone else who heard it would have been mortified. If you translated the things we said, or showed anyone the way we ate (monkey, bugs, campfire), they would have been horrified.

It was like that here. "Infierno" literally means "Hell." It was named by the missionaries when they were trying to tame the tribes and were getting shot at by arrows and bitten by malarial mosquitoes. In 1919 a missionary was shot on the La Torre River and died trying to speak to these people. It was now only a little more than a Santiago lifetime later, so no wonder these were people who didn't care about manners and pretense. They were people who made their living from hunting things in the jungle, who fished to sustain life. They couldn't be bothered with etiquette, and were humble enough to find a good laugh when one came by. Out in the communities of Amazonia where even the most basic medical treatment is miles away, infant mortality, leishmaniasis, botflies, infections, and a whole host of other common medical complications all but erased by modern society still cause enough misery to make most people thankful for any day that passes without a tragedy.

"Vamos, cachero," JJ said one day as we were returning from the forest.

"Where we going?"

"I show you," he said, and started along a path that after some time became bare dirt, smooth, without leaves. No boot tracks, indicating it received regular barefoot traffic.

We had spent the afternoon setting up a research project in a patch of primary forest inside Santiago's land. At that time my main "research" was searching for huge anacondas. It also involved deploying the two trail cameras I had bought and brought down. These were rudimentary game cameras usually used by hunters to monitor where prized deer or hogs were moving. But around that time, the conservation community was becoming aware of the cameras' tremendous potential to illustrate the inner workings of any given forest. Insert your double-A batteries and a memory card, set it to photos or video, set the date and time, and then place it where you think animals will cross. A trail or stream are my favorites. But in Infierno the results were less than inspiring.

On Mongabay I had read about scientists who were gridding entire rainforests, running analysis on the population dynamics of Costa Rican and Panamanian jungles. Their work was groundbreaking. It also involved thousands of camera traps. I had two. But JJ and I took great care where we placed them. We got some sloths and tapirs, the odd ocelot, but little else.

We walked along the smooth earth path for some time. Eventually, by a certain tree, JJ stopped and we removed our shoes and put them in our packs. From here on we walked barefoot until we reached a clearing where there was a small thatched hut. This was the home of the village shaman, Don Ignacio.

Don Ignacio Duri had white hair that stood straight up off his head. He had narrow, serene-looking eyes and a friendly smile. He had known JJ since he was a child. For the last several decades, Don Ignacio had become the most famous of the region's shamans, known as the original article, the real deal. Word was he brewed ayahuasca that was strong and knew how to guide people through the experience in such a way that they were kept safe as they navigated the underworld of human consciousness.

Ayahuasca lies at the intersection of mystery and knowing:

Where some people pit science and spirituality against each other, ayahuasca twines them together like mating snakes.

The origin of ayahuasca is still debated. It is a brew that consists of combining two plants native to the Amazon: the vine *Banisteriopsis caapi* and the leaves of *Psychotria viridis*. What's fascinating is that the odds of discovering the combined effects of a particular vine and a particular leaf amidst the eighty thousand plant species that grow in Amazonia is almost incalculable. The caapi vine contains properties that allow the dimethyltryptamine (DMT) in the leaves of the psychotria plant to become active in the human body. If you consume the vine without the leaves, then the body's enzymes simply break down the DMT. But together, the effects are some of the most powerful shamanic magic we know of.

Trial and error makes for a weak theory. That early Amerindians were just brewing various leaves and vines and roots and fungi together in a place where many of these things can kill you is highly unlikely. By that method, the death rate would have been so steep, no one would have had the chance to stumble upon the discovery. Conversely, if you ask the Indigenous healers, any shaman will tell you that ayahuasca is regarded as a direct gift from the gods, a link between this world and the spirit world. A way for mortal humans to access the immensity of the universe through the Earth mother, Pachamama. A relic of the time of creation, when Yacumama, the great anaconda spirit, descended from the heavens to carve rivers into the Earth and shape the world.

There were a few times that JJ and I drank ayahuasca with Don Ignacio (who was, of course, close friends with Santiago). Each time was slightly surreal, colored by intricate geometric patterns and long periods of hallucinatory disassociation that ranged from the blissful to the deranged. I felt comfortable drinking in the company of Don Ignacio and JJ and his family because it was never too intense. I never saw the wild visions and life-altering messages that so many people report.

Until one night.

It started with the simple fact that on this night there was something we didn't know: Don Ignacio was getting old, had fallen asleep when he was cooking the ayahuasca, and in truth had no idea how long that batch had been bubbling. He knew he'd made a mistake, and later we knew it, because when it was all over, he told us—part of the aftermath when we were trying to figure out what the hell had happened.

The ceremony began like any normal ayahuasca journey. Ignacio donned his ceremonial garments. There were macaw feathers and a fan of leaves. He smoked hand-rolled tobacco cigarettes and with his smoky breath blessed the various items he would use for the imminent journey. He drew deeply on the ember, the candlelight reflecting in his squinted eyes as he whispered prayers in Ese Eja and blew smoke onto the cups and bottles, feathers, and his hands.

The jungle was loud. It began to rain lightly. The sound of raindrops falling on thatched palm leaves. There were monkey skulls. Just like human skulls. Hollow eyes watching us as we prepared to link between this world and the other. Ignacio made all those present sit in a circle in the dark. The jungle night seemed massive around us, throbbing with the song of frogs and insects. One by one he called us to kneel before him. He exhaled a jet of blue smoke onto the cup, singing softly until the sound became a whistle drifting out away from his lips in the curling smoke.

When he handed me the cup, I got a sudden sense of entropy.

I looked at him as the cherry of the cigarette kicked up a spark, igniting the earthen features of his ancient face. He nodded, and I drank, blanketed in a layer of protective smoke from his lungs. Soon after, JJ was drinking. The shaman drew the cigarette deeply into his lungs. The candlelight danced in his dark eyes.

I returned to my place in the circle, lit a cigarette, and breathed deeply, cross-legged on the floor. The forest sounds were growing in volume—from the normal chorus until it was almost a roar. I remember looking to see if anyone else had noticed, but the candle had gone out. Everything was dark. Don Ignacio was singing softly in the dark. It was the song of the Earth, in another language—a soft and beautiful melody from before memory or time.

One by one people seemed to be succumbing to a kind of gravity that pulled them to the floor. Some people lay flat, others curled up in the darkness. I closed my eyes, suddenly aware that I might be sliding sideways. The sound of cicadas and owls and night birds and frogs was now swirling around me. Throbbing up the sides of my neck and pulsing in my hands. I held on to the floor, trying to remain upright, but the world had tilted on its axis and suddenly I couldn't tell if my eyes were open or closed.

In the faintest light I stared panting at the floor. I could see a lone cluster of stars out between the leaves, and as the world turned I began falling toward them. I fell toward the stars, slowly at first and then rapidly. I was growing smaller. I felt myself shrinking, dematerializing to atomic scale and falling through my own body and into the Earth. Everything was rushing. Out the other side of the planet was a period of darkness and then blazing white light. Down down down. I tried to be okay. I tried to find the ballast of knowing that this was just . . . I was just on a trip.

Trying to remember I was okay was like attempting to hold a tall wedding cake while white water rafting: For a few moments I was able to maintain some balance, but eventually the turbulence sent everything overboard. Soon I had fallen off the Earth and was tumbling down a geometrically brilliant wormhole through the stars.

Then came eons in the blackness. I had died.

I am certain I died because when thought came back to me I was in the infinite blackness of space. I was suspended in the blank space between solar systems. The frigid unconstructed backdrop of reality. There was no light. There was no self. I could not remember my name, I had no form. There was just the cosmic press of darkness all around me. Nameless. Shapeless. Nothing. I was only dimly aware, like some Ordovician arthropod at the dark bottom of the ocean. But this was worse. There was no ocean. There was nothing.

There was a long time of worlds and visions but an overwhelming agony at no longer existing. Sorrow like I had never known was my sole identity. For a long time there was no world, no light, no water, no me. It was the worst pain I've ever felt.

Then, light-years in the distance, I saw a faint glowing. I began rocketing toward the glow. For a brief moment I saw the Earth, suspended out there, all alone, brilliantly blue and green. Colors so beautiful I could cry.

Then more darkness.

Moments or years passed. When vision returned it was of the forest. I was moving through mist and swamps, beneath the roots of trees. I could somehow comprehend the jungle in all its staggering complexity because I was slithering through it. By now I was flickering back online. It was exhilarating because for the first time I became aware that I was searching. I still had no form, no name that I could recall. But the worlds I saw had some familiarity. This was the jungle. Giant, dreamlike, and from the perspective of an ant or the smallest snake. Trees were titanic pillars rising hundreds of feet into the bright canopy above.

For the briefest of moments I came into a clearing where all the other animals were gathered around a great tree. There were jaguars and deer, anteaters and lizards, and birds on every branch. Butterflies filled the air. Everything was glowing and they all turned to look at me. It was a moment of fantastic and serene beauty, save for the fear in the eyes of every animal present.

Fire from the sky ripped everything apart. With nuclear force, the tree was lifted from the earth and incinerated as the animals all lost their flesh, becoming skeletons before vaporizing and swirling into the void.

When the storm ended I was lying in the rubble and embers before a beetle the size of a building. Its long antennae were hovering over me as its jaws widened. Its eyes were a bustling matrix of maggots made of geometric complexity. The ground was shaking now. In the cosmic wind and ash was the burned wreckage of all life on Earth. All the life there had ever been. In the howling gale I clutched the ground so I would not be swept away.

Its voice held tectonic depth that shook the world. "SPEAK."

I shouted back, "What?"

"SPEEAAAAAKKKKK." The world was collapsing. Imploding. The dream was falling apart and there were explosions in the sky.

"What do you want!?"

Then the beetle's mandibles opened. I felt it rise from deep within and rush upward. Light exploded out of me in a cosmic rainbow that shot from my mouth to the mouth of the beetle. The force of the blast ripped the world apart and catapulted me backward, upward, through the worlds and stars and a long wormhole at a velocity that felt like I would tear apart from the force.

I landed in the real world on the wooden planks of the deck
in the Amazon, beneath the palm-thatched roof. My eyes opened
and I projectile vomited everywhere in the darkness. I crawled
pathetically across the deck to the edge, where I vomited another glut of orange bile, which to my eyes still had hints of
rainbow and geometric embers. It went up and out my nose and
I coughed and gagged and drooled. All I can remember is smiling. My hand moved across my face to wipe the bile and slime.
I had a hand.

I felt my hair, my face, flexed my fingers. I was a person;
suddenly I was me again. I had a family. I had a life. I was alive.
I rolled onto my back and cried in quiet gratitude. After some
time I was "back," enough to not want to be crying openly and
worry the others, but not enough to realize that as I rejoiced
and felt my own features, I was smearing vomit and slime all
over myself. I cracked my neck, I burped, spit. I reached into my
pants just to make sure. I wanted to call everyone I loved and
tell them how much they meant to me. Defenseless, I realized
how badly I longed to be back on the Las Piedras, how terribly
I missed it. It felt like so much static had been erased from my
brain, like I had been reduced to my most basic form. Reset. I
wanted to journal. But all I could do was lie there moaning and
drooling.

When we all staggered to our feet in the morning, Don Ignacio was gone. JJ's brother Elias joined us in searching for him.
He was nowhere to be seen. We checked all the places he could
or should be. We even sent a runner to his house. He was finally
found lying naked in a stream, his tiny old body shivering in the
fetal position as the water flowed around him. He said that he
had badly overboiled the brew. The ayahuasca had punished us
all, especially him.

He announced that day that he would retire as shaman.

My journey with ayahuasca left me with more questions than answers. Had what I seen been real? Had I journeyed into some basement of the universe? Do our bodies retain some ancient internal record of the stardust in our bones, like an elemental memory of a time before the birth of the universe? Do the vines of ayahuasca truly, as the shamans say, have the power to open the portal so that we can peer through to see the truth of the universe? I felt like I had seen my own death and been scared out of my skin. And like anyone who has a near-death experience, I felt changed.

Real or not, I saw what I saw. It was a vision of a vast, frigid, uncaring universe, and within that endless cold: darkness. The only thing that stood out against the deathly dark was our warm little blue planet. I had seen it out there in the distance. I had wanted to go there more than anything I'd ever wanted. I wanted to go home. I wanted to be alive.

After my journey in the abyss, not only was I thrilled to have hands and a face and a family and so much more, I found myself wanting to ask people if they'd ever realized what a miracle this all is. Water—you can swim in it! Fire: Imagine explaining fire to someone who has never seen it? Have you seen these trees? How many leaves do you think a single tree has? I was brimming with wonder and love for the reality around me.

What the vines had not provided was any confirmation of directionality. Was I doing the right thing with my life? Was there any point to spending so much time in the jungle and away from home? Would I ever return to Las Piedras? I still had no idea. The ayahuasca had shown me a stark vision of the universe that took me months and months to work through and held no discernible trail markers. If anything, I felt more lost than I had been before.

It was later that year that the first trail marker would appear, the first sign that I was on a path of some kind. It came when the folks at Mongabay asked if they could interview me about my work with wildlife and the Indigenous people of Amazonia. They sent over some questions and asked for photos and info. I spent a week fastidiously preparing it all. The article came out on March 10, 2010, and was called "Secrets of the Amazon: Giant Anacondas and Floating Forests, an Interview with Paul Rosolie." I printed it out. At the top of the article, just below the title it read: "Paul Rosolie leads volunteer expeditions into the Peruvian rainforest with an aim towards education and grassroots conservation. Mongabay.com's eighth in its series of interviews with 'Young Scientists.'"

THE GOLDEN AGE
OF GUIDING

≡

FISH WERE FALLING FROM THE SKY ALL AROUND ME LIKE GLIT-
tering rain. It was late at night and I was rafting a stream that
snaked through a part of the forest that I had never explored
before. The small inflatable boat was yellow and glowed in the
light of my headlamp as I moved along the tiny waterway. As
with most streams, it flowed through a depression in the earth
and created a tunnel through the foliage. I was only vaguely
aware of how big the jungle must have stood above me. Far
beneath the lofty treetops, 150 feet below the black ocean of
foliage above, I was having the adventure of a lifetime.

The fish were making me laugh. I was using a kayak paddle
to navigate, and as I went, schools of several hundred small fish
would race to dodge the raft. Whenever they became cornered,
they would pivot 180 degrees and leap into the air. The confetti
of silver fish was catching the light of my headlamp and blinding me. They hit my face, fell on the raft, flopped around franti-
cally.

I tried to throw as many as I could back in, but the stream
was quick. I had to paddle. Sometimes the paddle stroked water,
other times I was pegging against rocks.

On this particular stream on this particular night, the jungle
was howling. In the beam of my headlamp, I saw a stingray of

sobering size drifting away ominously beneath the water. Sting-rays in Amazonia have a long, serrated venomous barb on their tail, and I've seen them sting a person several times in the flash of half a second. Paddling that night, I wondered occasionally if one might get trapped in the shallow water between the raft and the sand and sting upward—the anal implications of multiple venomous stab wounds were concerning.

But any worries I had were quickly whisked away by the wonder of swift movement. I had to duck to avoid hanging vines, logs, and palm fronds. I had to weave between rocks and navigate the channels. Everything in the jungle seemed to be out that night. I rounded one bend and came face-to-face with an ocelot, the closest I've come to one. The raft was silent on the water, and the chatter of the stream gave me further auditory cover—so the cat had had no idea I was coming. She turned and looked me straight in the eye, and for a moment I was confronted with just how fantastic they are. The stripes along the forehead, the spots, and the banded tail. The brilliant yellow coloration in the wild, arresting eyes. She watched me pass with a feline glare, and squinting back against my headlamp, her eyes shone a dancing electric green.

As the stream babbled its way through the bowels of the jungle, it carried me past curious owls and a family of huddled, worried-looking capybaras. I spotted some sort of snake on a high branch, but didn't have a chance to identify it before the stream turned and I lost sight of it.

I didn't bother counting the caimans that I passed; these crocodiles were all over the banks, on the left and the right. Some were facing the forest and some were hanging over the edges with their mouths open in the water, waiting for a fish. Head-lamps illuminate animal eyes at night, and caiman eyes glow orange (the cats' tend to be white or green, like the ocelot's). Some stretches of the stream looked like a vigil, with little orange candles all through the darkness. These were areas where a mother caiman had a dozen or so babies, all calmly waiting for fish by the water's edge. Most of these were smaller, prehistoric-looking smooth-fronted caimans. But at one bend I had a close encounter with a seven-foot-long spectacled caiman.

This trip lasted just an hour or so, but it was miraculous. One of the best moments I've ever spent in the forest.

Very few people know the surreal wonder of navigating the Amazon Rainforest at night. It is as overwhelming as it is awe-inspiring. The sheer tonnage of biomass, the stupendous amount of visual stuff around you, is enough to make you dizzy. The knowledge that you are surrounded by giant ancient trees and vines and leaves, combined with the spiders and snakes and strange eyes looking back at you from the inky-black shadows between the leaves—this is the Amazon at night.

═══

Not long after the article came out on Mongabay, several important things changed. For one, I felt as though I had received the Presidential Medal of Freedom. I might as well have been on the cover of *Time* magazine. It was a boost in my confidence and a recognition of my dream that meant so much to me, it's hard to describe. It was also a calling card that allowed me to say confidently that I had been working in the Amazon for years, had been interviewed, had a meaningful relationship with the local people and the forest, and that the work we were doing together was at least remarkable enough for someone to report on.

In New York, my close friend from growing up in Brooklyn, Lee Rando, was able to convince me to finally turn what JJ and I had started into a tourism company. At first, I didn't like the idea. JJ and I had never liked tourists. The people I wanted to emulate were explorers, biologists, conservationists. But by this point we knew one thing for certain: No one anywhere was taking people into the jungle the way we were. No one. The idea of doing it right made me wonder. What if we catered to the travelers, not to the tourists? What if we brought them out for adventures they could never have anywhere else, like rafting a stream at night or traveling to deep jungle, and made it safe? If we could bring people to the jungle, and show them the miracles of biological diversity we saw every day, they would be floored. I knew that if people were able to see what I saw, they would surely help us protect it.

During the months that I spent in the United States each year, it became easier to book venues for talks now that I had the interview under my belt. The article was something I could link in an email, and that made me seem legitimate. It was the only credential I had, and I squeezed every last drop out of it. In my mind, I was faking it until I could figure out a way of making it. Oh, also, by "venues," I mean libraries on a Tuesday night, outdoor stores on a Thursday. A room full of chairs and a projector screen, maybe five people watching as I enthusiastically told stories that sounded completely made-up and asked those present to travel halfway around the world.

Somehow, though, it worked. With the newly formed Tamandua Expeditions, Lee began taking bookings and dispatching trips to JJ and me. Usually we led one or two major trips a year, a group of five to seven people for a few weeks at a time.

For a while we continued to guide out of Infierno. It was brutal. We had no help whatsoever. Often JJ would get one of his sisters-in-law to cook rice and beans and eggs for the duration, but everything else was up to us. Pico would come as a boat driver, but his leg didn't allow him to do much walking or carrying. So JJ and I were the ones lugging the sacks of rice, hauling supplies, cleaning the station. We had to spend days or weeks swinging machetes until our hands had blisters from clearing trails. When that was done, we were arranging and

making beds and sheets and mosquito nets, and of course, leading day hikes, night hikes, swamp walks, and all the other elements of a great jungle experience. There's hard work and then
there's slave labor. What we were doing was no way to live, and
we knew it.

On top of the brutal amount of work required to run these
trips, the truth was that Infierno never really felt like home.
Home had always been the research station on the Las Piedras
River. And in the few years we worked out of Infierno I had
ample time to mourn the loss of my favorite place on Earth.
When JJ and Emma split up and Emma moved with their son,
Joseph, back to the UK, the research station had been sold to an
organization of gringo hippies who wanted to turn it into an
ayahuasca retreat. Only thing was, they never got around to it.
For well over a year we never went to Las Piedras. We assumed
the station was rotting. And so we continued to toil away in
Infierno, unsure of our future, of the mission, of everything.

Until something incredible happened while I was in New
York. Although in this book I focus on life in the jungle, in
those days, there was ample time when I would be back at home
in New York with my mom and dad, my sister Michelle, my
Michelle, my then-wife Gowri, and the dogs. (Gowri and I had
met when I did a semester in India during college, and we were
married soon after.) That was home life. Family life. I was now
in my midtwenties, an adult by all accounts, and fully invested
in the path I had chosen. But trying to make a living while living your dream is hard. For me, it meant traveling light, staying
with my parents, and working nonstop to organize trips and
figure out ways to get more people interested in coming on expeditionary vacations to the Amazon. Though I knew deep
down that nothing would ever be quite like when I had first
come to Las Piedras. Nothing rivaled the river's wild remote-
ness, its expansive forest and distance from everything. It was

simply the place I loved the most and dreamed of one day returning to.

So it seemed almost miraculous when one day JJ called me with the news: *We got the station back.*

I was flabbergasted, confused, suspicious I had misunderstood.

But I could hear the smile on JJ's face as he spoke and explained that the ayahuasca hippies hadn't been able to pay and they had just . . . given it back.

The first time we returned to Las Piedras Biodiversity Station, it was early 2012. We hadn't been there at all in over a year; we had no idea what state it was in. We came in on the Trans-Amazonian Highway and along the dirt road that led to that horrid town of Lucerna. It was the fastest way to get there—we could do it in a single day!

With us was a family from India. Two parents and their children, ages eleven and thirteen. Our first family trip.

The road was bad and we didn't arrive at the river until evening. We only reached the station late at night. What we found made us rub our foreheads and apologize profusely to our new guests.

The place was filthy and the roof was falling apart. The deck was beginning to wear. More than a year of disrepair meant that the pillars the station stood on were beginning to rot. The place was filled with bat shit and rat shit and moth wings and spiderwebs. It was disgusting. That poor family came in with us, and trusted us, and we had brought them to a dilapidated research station way out in the middle of the jungle. I had to do my best to smile and tell them it was all part of the authentic experience.

This is an important part of my training. In order to get people into the swamps with you, you have to be the kind of person who can sell sand in the Sahara or water to a drowning guy. If you can convince people to suffer with you in the wilderness and be happy about it, you can do just about anything. It was a skill I'd have to use often later on to convince large donors to give their money to save a vanishing Amazon Rainforest.

JJ and I were at the top of our game. And, thankfully, this was no ordinary family. They reveled in the realness of the expedition. The fact that we really were far beyond society—we had no power, no comms, no help, no light—was exciting to them. They seemed enchanted by the grandeur and magnitude of the forest. Their enthusiasm was infectious.

So on their second night in the jungle, JJ and I took them out into one of our favorite swamps. It was a place we knew well for its dozens of species of frogs and lizards and spiders and snakes. Soon we had these people from across the world neck-deep in a swamp with tarantulas and thousands of frogs. I was at the front as we moved through the dark water, pointing out various species. JJ was off at some distance. We had to go carefully, because the younger child, Isha, was almost up to her ears.

But then JJ called from somewhere in the darkness. "Paul! Big snake!"

I turned to the Indian family and said, "I'm so sorry, but I have to go help him. Stay here, don't try to move, I'll be right back!"

Their eyes were wide as I ran off, leaving them stranded in the jungle night.

When I reached JJ, I saw that it was a six- or seven-foot-long boa constrictor that I had to climb a tree to catch. It was a monster of an animal, as thick as a man's arm. Needless to say, it was a memorable first night walk in the jungle for that family.

There would be many more in the next two weeks.

Over the course of their stay, eleven-year-old Isha left a considerable impression on me. In the time she spent in the jungle with us, she was wide-eyed and thrilled at every moment. The boa constrictor delighted her. Monkeys in the trees held her attention. She acted a lot like my shadow and would go every-where I went. She climbed trees, handled snakes, and swam across the river.

Whenever a butterfly would get stuck in the netting by the kitchen windows, she would ask me to bring her a chair so that she would be tall enough to reach it, cup it in her hands, and then climb down and walk it outside, where she would open her hands and smile as the butterfly flitted off into the jungle. Her commitment to doing no harm, to saving every creature, even extended to mosquitoes. Every time I slapped one, she'd look at me aghast, as though I had failed at my job, let her down directly. I felt like I'd lied to my grandma.

How, she would ask, could I truly be the caretaker of the jungle if my love for it didn't include all of its creatures, even the mosquitoes? I found this train of logic maddening. It made no sense. JJ and I murdered ticks and mosquitoes with the local person's frustration at their constant attack. But Isha would never let that frustration grow. In the almost two weeks she spent in the jungle, camping and hiking and boating up the river, she never faltered once. Every animal was sacred. Even the hated mosquitoes were creatures in her eyes, and when she saw one perched on her skin, she would wave it away, allowing it to drone off in search of another meal. Often me.

If any mosquito landed on me, I smashed it.

But seeing Isha's genuine dismay gradually made me stop. Even JJ stopped killing mosquitoes around her.

JJ made eyes at me. "What is dis?" he said, laughing.

I shook my head. Her commitment was strange but also, on some indescribable level, heroic. You had to respect it.

On the last day that the family was with us, we brought them downriver and back to the road, where a car had come to pick us all up. The road that had once been so mysterious and sullen was now becoming an enemy we knew well. The shacks were becoming more complex and plentiful as people moved in and brought their families. While we carried our gear and loaded the car, JJ explained to our guests—Shonali, Anil, Anya, and Isha—that the people coming in were stealing the land. That they had come from another part of Peru; that this was a common practice. People came out into the remote areas, burned the jungle, and set up farms. They were hoping that because there were no police out here, they wouldn't be caught. They also knew that "squatter's rights" in Peru were tricky, and if they could build a little ramshackle house and a farm, eventually they could claim the land (stealing it from the government or whoever owned it). JJ explained that this was the cutting edge of the fight to save Amazonia.

As he told the Indian family all this, two men passed by carrying shotguns. They also had a large yellow-footed tortoise. When Isha saw it, her eyes went wide.

"What are they doing with that turtle?" she asked, standing, as she always did, just beside me.

"Well." I had to think. "They're going to eat it," I said gently. I knew how these guys cooked turtle. Sometimes they slit its throat. Other times they'd just lay the turtles on the fire and let them boil in their own shells. This large tortoise was hanging from a vine-strap over one man's shoulder, and they'd used balsa fiber to lash another stick across the front opening, essentially jamming the turtle into its own shell so it couldn't struggle or crawl away. It looked painful and cruel.

The tears in Isha's eyes and the visceral trembling distress she exuded was so upsetting that JJ and I looked at each other and knew we had to act. If killing a mosquito disqualified us from being junglekeepers in her eyes, what would allowing them to use an axe on this turtle mean?

"Paul Uncle, do something," Isha said.

"Isha, we can't . . ."

"If you don't do something they are going to kill that poor turtle. Think how old it must be. It's so big. Think how scared it must be. Please."

Now there were real tears in her eyes.

I cursed under my breath.

JJ shrugged.

"Go talk to them," I said to him quietly.

"No, no," he said, "they'll think there's something wrong with me. Betta you do."

Usually, the rule is that you never buy bushmeat from people; it only encourages them to get more. But in this case, there would be no consoling Isha if we just went on our way. Awkwardly I went to the two men, wincing as I spoke in a low voice. "Um, excuse me, gentlemen . . . can I, uh . . . buy that turtle?"

In the end the confused men sold us the turtle for fifty soles. Isha was thrilled and relieved.

The turtle would be transported somewhere safe and released into the jungle. JJ and I would look out the window for the next few hours, silent. Both of us thinking of the burned forest and all we had seen. Out here, watching the things we loved turned to ash had become a regular part of our lives. Little Isha with her childish certainty of right and wrong was an untarnished white flower on a landscape of mud and ashes and blood. If she only knew the things we had seen. For some reason it left us with pensive, distant eyes and a lump in our throats.

That's how it was bringing people to Las Piedras. Most of them, you met and guided and would never see again, but something about the jungle shows you what people are really made of right away. You live through experiences that just fundamentally fuse you together as friends.

One day a client showed up and told me his name was Mohsin Kazmi. I shook his hand and judged him for his flashy demeanor and expensive sunglasses. Although I didn't know it at the time,

Mohsin would play a leading role in the formation of Jungle-keepers, and on his first tourist trip, he spent five weeks with me and JJ on an expedition that was nothing short of hell on Earth. Many of the people were upset at the conditions and found the most basic things we did on a regular basis to be terrifying enough that they protested. JJ once listened politely as one guy, a grown man, shouted at us that he felt he'd been put into a very dangerous and distressing position when we crossed the swamp. Later we would laugh and remember little Isha, who had done all the same things with a smile on her face.

Five weeks is a long trip, and there was a lot of drama. The conditions were indeed rough. JJ and I were working so hard to bring these people into the forest and guiding all day long and doing everything else, and they weren't even happy. We were doing our best to sell the experience as the "real thing" and en-courage everyone to help, but the truth is, most people just aren't willing to help, and aren't capable of surviving discom-fort, much less smiling through it—as Mohsin did.

As the group devolved into chaos, it only made Mohsin shine more. He was having a great time.

Talking with him, I realized that he grew up not far from where I did. And though he was three years younger than me, we had spent our teenage years hiking in the same state parks, along the same exact trails and streams. Mohsin was fascinating because he was the son of Pakistani immigrants (dad from Paki-stan, mom Pakistani from England), and as you'd expect, they wanted him to go into the medical profession. But Mohsin had other ideas. He was still in college and had already worked with horses; he had been a veterinary technician; he somehow al-ready owned a movie theater; and he was very much still figur-ing it out. But despite being an above-average jack-of-all-trades, and in spite of his parents' hopes for his future, Mohsin knew exactly where his inner compass pointed: straight into the jungle, right through the lens of his camera. Mohsin was a photographer.

He asked me if we could go on walks together, just him and me. He had a lot of thoughts to share. "You're onto something here," he said. He felt qualified to tell me this because he had recently done a study abroad in Madagascar with Dr. Patricia Wright. You'll remember her as the woman who discovered the golden bamboo lemur. He had already seen a real conservation outfit. He had worked in the shadow of one of the greats. And so it meant something to me when he told me that whatever JJ and I were doing here was something special. That although it was still in its early stages (a complete shit show by any measure), something powerful was developing here.

In the five weeks Mohsin spent in the jungle, we quickly realized that we could burn hours talking about the way the light hit the forest. He, like me, had grown up completely obsessed with wildlife and rainforests. He, like me, loved the woods, hated authority, and wanted to blaze his own trail through life. He also was an expert communicator and an honest and reliable colleague, and he could stay cool under fire. We went through a lot in a short period and parted as friends.

Not long after his expedition ended, Mohsin began consistently calling me and emailing me, asking for a job. He was relentless and undaunted every time I told him I had no money and no position for him. I remember glaring at the phone after hanging up, confused by his persistence.

He called every few months. And every few months I rejected him. But his response was always the same: "You don't get it, man, I'm not taking no for an answer."

He sounded crazy to me. A job. That was a hilarious proposition considering I had about eight hundred dollars in my bank account and no concept of what it meant to employ anybody.

But before we knew it, Mohsin was back with us on another

trip. This time he had a case of lenses and a new camera. He had come fully loaded. He listened to my stories about my solo expeditions, saw how I interacted with the forest, and told me that we needed to document all of this. One day it would matter.

At that time, I had just come back from a devastatingly harrowing solo in deep jungle where I'd been turned around by the uncontacted tribes (you can read the whole story in my book *Mother of God*). It was a major life event, a monumental expedition through some of the deepest wild on Earth, and even though I knew no one would ever believe me, I had actually had an encounter with the Mashco Piro.

Mohsin found the story fascinating, and asked how I had documented it. I told him I hadn't. I had *lived* it. He laughed. "We need to fix this," he said, smiling. "You're gonna do a lot more interviews, and you're gonna need better photos." So we went out into the forest and I followed his instructions. I made camp in the jungle. I would cross log bridges, I'd navigate by compass, eat lunch, go fishing. Whatever. All the while, Mohsin took pictures. He took pictures of Pico weaving baskets and of community life in Infierno. He took pictures of JJ guiding and driving the boat. Most important, he took pictures whenever we saw people burning the forest.

I never would have admitted it then, but the encouragement from Mohsin went a long way. The fact that anyone saw anything in what we were doing was enough to hasten my heartbeat.

This new sense that what I was doing had value helped me think clearly. What if we really could create something meaningful? What if these really were just the garage days and we eventually would be known globally as the conservationists who saved the Amazon?

Sometimes I would make fun of myself for having such grandiose dreams. But then, someone had done it in Sequoia

National Park. John Muir and Teddy Roosevelt stood above the Yosemite Valley for a photo before the national park was created. Explorers and artists and visionary naturalists (not just conservation biologists!) had been protecting nature for centuries. Even in my home state of New York the legacy is long. The New York City water system comes from pristine reservoirs in the Catskill Mountains. The Hudson Riverkeeper organization works to restore the health of the Hudson River I grew up along, from source to sea, from the mountains and forests, from the eagles in the sycamores to the sturgeons that still swim in its depths. People can make a difference. And maybe we could too.

It was a time defined by launching my most extreme solo expeditions, dedicated wholly to experiencing the last wild places as intimately and authentically as was humanly possible. I spent weeks walking the forest alone. I heeded the myths and stories Santiago had told me before he died, and plunged into places so deep it took days just to get to the start of the expeditions. I relied on only what I had in my backpack for provisions and shelter. I had no way to call for help, no GPS or satphone. Only my trusty Alpacka Raft that could be carried in my pack and inflated in minutes. It was also at this time, as my connection to the forest began to mature, that I started to write the word in my journal. Say it when I was out in the forest. Try it on. Feel it move out of my mouth and into the real world: *Junglekeepers.*

It didn't take long for me to fall in love with the word, and to imagine bringing people from all over the world to see this very special place, and hope that one of those people would have the tools to stop the burning, save the forest, and protect the animals I loved.

We sprang into action. Mohsin helped design a pamphlet and I wrote the copy. He got it printed and sent copies to Lee, who took to the streets in NYC. He went all over, on foot, sidewalks and subways, out on the cobbles—uptown, midtown, downtown—and distributed physical pamphlets to every business he could. The pamphlets featured a picture of me driving the boat with some volunteers on the Tambopata River and said in big bold letters: BECOME A JUNGLEKEEPER.

===

In the last months of 2012, Mohsin returned to the jungle. We agreed to spend November, December, and January at the station. Our mission was to improve the place and bring it back to life as best we could. The station was in worse shape than ever. At the time, I was putting all the money I had into repairing it. But the roof was coming apart, the floors were warping from the rain. The posts that held the place up were almost nonexistent. It was beyond stressful. I remember thinking that if we didn't do something soon, the station would die, and that scared me; I thought about it constantly. It seemed like we were always fighting back the decay, but the jungle was determined to eat the place.

Meanwhile, JJ and I had developed our own culture of guiding. We had a brand of interacting with the jungle unlike anyone else's. It was wholly different from the sanitized, bugsprayed, binoculared, and clean-trailed kind of guiding he had learned on the Tambopata. No, we did the jungle like we were animals. We went into the rivers. We slogged through the swamps. We climbed the trees. We penetrated deeper and interacted with the landscape with an intimacy that most biologists would find completely irresponsible. We didn't wear boots, we wore shoes. JJ and I still often went barefoot. We did it for pure love.

For all my time in the Amazon I had been the student. Now suddenly I was becoming a teacher. Mohsin was unfamiliar with so much of this alien landscape that I had spent the last half a decade learning about. There are things in the Amazonian back-country that are simply incongruous to the modern mind. Mohsin was in disbelief when he saw what we had to endure with the peke peke motors of the region, and, like any rational person, horrified by how often they broke.

"There has to be a better way," he said one day, watching JJ and me struggle. We were stuck on the side of the river.

JJ stood and smiled, looked theatrically upriver and down-river. "You can see a better way?"

Mohsin rolled his eyes. "No."

"Okay, then hand me that mangera."

Mohsin handed over the hose. We worked for more than an hour, repeatedly pulling the cord to start the motor. We checked the spark plug, the carburetor—everything looked fine. We dis-assembled, reassembled, cleared the tubes between the tank and the motor. JJ said we just had to keep pulling. At some point the damned old thing would start. By my logic, it seemed that if it didn't start, it was broken. But JJ knew better. He knew the Secret, and he was artfully teaching it to both of us. There we were in the inferno of sand flies, working as fast as we could. We'd pull the cord. Then pull again. Every time we pulled, it took all our strength. Every time, the motor would splutter and die. But around pull thirty-seven, for some reason, it hit. The motor roared to life, and we were on our way.

This time of teaching gave me the perspective to realize that so much of what we did depended on not fighting the jungle. The motor was bound to break. The trails were always going to have fallen trees. The river would rise and ruin your plans. The way to survive the jungle was not to fight it. You can't hold back a river with your arms; you can't argue with the ocean. You simply have to float long enough to survive. In the jungle, you have to let go of the presuppositions of your programming and commit the sacrament of relinquishing control to the jungle gods.

On night walks we showed Mohsin our guiding highlights. We loved showing people how dark the night was: "Let's all turn off our lights for a minute." Not being able to see your own hand in front of your face is unnerving to anyone. A reminder of how crucial a torch is. And how helpless we are without it. We went camping and showed Mohsin the unique way of making a fire when every stick in the forest is wet.

Then came the species. Recognizing saki monkeys, howler monkeys, giant monkey frogs, whip snakes, whip scorpions, blue-and-yellow macaws, and red-and-green macaws. Learning the ironwoods, mahoganies, remo caspi, manchinga, lupunas, and some of the other fifteen hundred species of trees was daunting. But JJ took his time. He'd cut a piece with his machete, often he would lick it, smell it, then hand us the wood and tell us to do the same. We developed a multisensory library of jungle wisdom inherited directly from the original article himself.

When JJ was in town, Mohsin and I spent weeks together in the forest. We had to cook and find water for ourselves, and had only a limited supply of batteries and gasoline with which to charge our lights and cameras every now and then. We survived off beans and rice and eggs and cooked over an open fire. We became skinny. And then later we became gaunt. We didn't mind, though—we were living in the Amazon and going on adventures that would become the bedrock of our lives.

Crafting photos became our art. Mohsin was intensely focused on documenting my methods of traveling and surviving in the jungle. My packraft glowing in the dark, lit by my headlamp. The surreal up-close faces of the snakes and frogs of the jungle night. We would go out and hunt for the most beautiful creatures we could find and then spend hours photographing them in the most creative ways we could imagine. It was good to have Mohsin. He was a new friend, someone who saw the jungle the way I did.

We went out on night walks. So many nights we saw almost nothing. So many others were magical. So many days the boat motor would break and we'd have to wait hours to be rescued. We did a lot of failing, a lot of learning. Life in the jungle was hard but rewarding. We'd sit out by the side of the river at night, submerged up to our necks, watching the swifts and sparrows, the terns and the bats race over the water. We'd marvel at the mist coming off the canopy. We'd spend long nights around a single candle beneath the palm roof of the station that now had enough holes that rain or stars regularly peeked through, dreaming about the future and all that we could build.

What if we found a way to get more groups, improve the station, make people help us protect this river? What if we built the world's tallest treehouse in the canopy and everyone wanted to come—that would solve our problems! What if we could get legit and eventually get a study-abroad group and bring students? What if we could one day go on expeditions into the very deepest corners of the Amazon and take the photos that would show the world what we stood to lose? Our dreams were like the candle flame, a flickering little point of light in a thousand miles of rainy darkness.

=====

One day out in the jungle, I was six feet off-trail setting up a camera trap when I heard footsteps. They were loud. I had been out on my own for hours and so assumed I was alone. The only person it could have been was Mohsin. I turned from where I knelt with a hand in the air and was ready to say, "Could you walk any louder?" when suddenly I realized it was not Mohsin at all.

A tremendous male jaguar paced by. His mouth was open, canine teeth exposed. His tongue was hot and large in his mouth and his eyes were blank and disinterested. He nodded as he passed, as if to say, "'Sup," and then carried on down the trail without ever breaking stride.

I remained kneeling and frozen, hand in the air, awash with the brilliant adrenaline of the encounter. How massive and beautiful, how muscular and serene. Those enormous paws. He'd been no more than six feet from me. It was the closest I'd ever come to a jaguar like that. My heart didn't even have time to start pounding. I was becoming truly accustomed to life in the jungle.

One of the most incredible places in the Las Piedras forest was a spot that JJ simply called "the colpa." There are many colpas in the forests of western Amazonia, but this one where we lived was the most remarkable we knew of.

JJ explained that colpas are areas of exposed clay, usually along streams. Sometimes they are near a tree-fall, where the large buttressed roots have been pulled up to expose earth rich in mineral deposits. This colpa was far back in the forest. It could take us as long as two hours to reach it. Going away from the river and into the interior was always something to consider carefully, because if you got lost back there, it could be days, weeks, or forever before you were found. The trail was your only lifeline.

Reaching the colpa, however, was worth it. It was a place beside a stream where the ground was exposed. The earth was reddish and clear of vegetation. There were areas where you could see the tracks of deer, peccaries, and various other species. It was evident, at least to JJ's eyes, that this was a uniquely important part of the forest. He explained that a diet of leaves and plants often meant that the herbivorous animals of the Amazon were lacking in sodium, and they would go to great lengths to get it. The colpa was where they went. The salt in the clay was a vital resource for them. Peccaries would come and root in the mud and make depressions that rain turned into puddles. Deer would come and eat the mud, supplementing their sodium. In the night, tremendous tapirs would plod in with their strange, giant three-toed feet and feast on the salt-rich clay of the colpa. JJ said that because all the prey species were always close by, the jaguars loved to patrol the colpa, hoping for a meal.

Whenever we went, though, the colpa was silent. The animals of the jungle could smell and hear and see us coming long before we saw them, so all we ever saw was their tracks, the faintest glimpse into their world.

Sometime in December 2012, I placed two camera traps at the colpa. Just before Christmas—one of the only years I missed at Grandma's in Brooklyn with my family—I pulled the camera traps out of the jungle. When I checked the memory cards, I saw something incredible. The cameras had recorded over two thousand videos of dozens of species. There were razor-billed curassows, Spix's guans, brocket deer, tapirs, ocelots, monkeys, pumas, and even jaguars. Just like JJ predicted, the colpa was a hidden world of Amazonian activity.

As I reviewed the footage, my jaw fell open. It was more than I had ever imagined. The footage was mind-blowingly rich with new insights into the world of Amazonian wildlife. In one video, I was alone in the jungle, checking that the cameras were working. Crouched with my machete, I looked to see the infrared light, gave a thumbs-up, and walked out of the frame. Two minutes later, a jaguar stalked in and stopped to smell the exact spot where I had just stood.

The footage was wildly compelling. It felt like a revelation. I spent the next several weeks editing it into a video explaining the colpa and the various species that visited. It was a short piece, just five minutes long, but it was action-packed with animal life. I sent the video I had made of the camera traps around to everyone who might watch it. I sent it to Mongabay, I entered it in short film contests, I watched it again and again. I simply couldn't believe what I was seeing.

=

Months later, when I was back home in New York, I was in the living room with my dad and my sister one day when the phone rang. My dad was the first one there, and he laughed when he saw the caller ID. "It says 'United Nations.'" He shook his head, assuming it was junk, and sat back down. I raced to the receiver and lifted the phone to my ear. It was the United Nations. They had seen the colpa video, and they wanted to know if they could speak to the person who had made it.

THE UNIVERSE
CALLING

≡

MOHSIN AND I WERE STUCK ON THE SIDE OF THE RIVER. WE
had a small leaky canoe with a gnarly old peke peke motor,
which was refusing to turn on, as usual. The sun would be setting soon. We'd been out on adventures all day, but the afternoon rain had toasted the motor. Now we were faced with
either getting it to work or spending the night out on the river's
edge with absolutely no equipment. The bugs were brutal. Sand
flies in the millions swarmed us. It was also nearing mosquito
hour. We were being ripped apart. There was blood all over us.
We had to get the motor working.

With a normal motor, you switch it on, pull the cord, and it
starts. Peke pekes are not that. These are motors in their most
basic form. There's a fuel tank, a hose connecting the tank to the
motor block, spark plugs, a carburetor (also usually exposed
and unprotected). They're big, dangerous metal machines. And
they never work properly.

The way you start a peke peke is by wrapping a rope around
the crankshaft and pulling. When the engine doesn't want to
work, you have to wind the cord and set the motor before each
pull. After each try, the rope comes free, and if the engine fails
to start on the first pull, or the seventieth, then you have to

manually reset the crankshaft and wrap the cord again, and get ready to put all your strength into the next pull.

I wish JJ were here, I thought, feeling the pressure of having to do it on my own. He had a lifetime with these devils. He knew all the things that could be wrong. Most of the time when they didn't start, the culprit was debris in the hose that fed fuel from the gasoline tank to the engine. Other times it was water that had gotten into the gasoline. While running diagnostics, you could pop off the hose and blow out the chunks of sand and dirt and bits of water. Then you had to siphon the gas out of the larger tank into the motor's gas tank; for this you needed another hose to transport the fuel, and you had to suck gasoline through it. If you've never siphoned gasoline by sucking it through a hose, it's good fun—you should try it.

On the river with Mohsin, I was trying to embody the principles I had learned from JJ, but I was already losing faith. I pulled the cord and the motor turned. I pulled the cord again and got whipped in the back, no shirt. The pain was blinding. I looked at the sun slinking down toward the trees. Shit. I reset the motor and wound the cord. On the next pull I got whipped again and felt like I was at the edge of spontaneous combustion from pure rage. The task was Sisyphean. But here's the thing: If you give up, the sand flies will eat you. This is the Serengeti, this is the stock market, this is Jungle Law. Either you make it or you don't. So take off your shirt, rub gasoline all over your body— that repellent will give you ten minutes of diminished onslaught from the bugs. You're sweating and burning and high from the fumes. You're bleeding and seething and suddenly your whole life becomes that motor. If it doesn't work, you'll sleep out here on the watery hard bottom of that boat. If you don't get out of these bugs soon, you'll be sucked dry. It's life. It's all it is. Don't stop. You can't stop. You'll die.

I pulled the cord and the motor spluttered. Mohsin tried a few times. Then I tried a few times.

"How many times have we pulled this damn thing?" Mohsin said with wide eyes.

"I don't know," I said, panting, "but over thirty. We just have to keep going."

"Look, I know motors, if it hasn't worked by now, it's not going to."

I smiled. Because he was right. And he was wrong. This fucker was going to start. I could feel it. As he watched me work like a madman, Mohsin's expression told me I had gotten accustomed to a peculiar kind of suffering.

The sand flies were feasting as the pull count climbed into the sixties. Every time, the motor would spark and settle. Every time, I really thought it was the one. Every time, it wasn't. Sometimes we'd give up for a few moments and be left in the crushing silence with the high-pitched droning of the flies that were eating us. That was enough to chase us back into action: If you stop, you die.

Eightysomething pulls and I was on my last legs. *One more. One more.* I had Mohsin holding the motor still (the rebar was hardly fixed to the wood of the canoe). I told him to dribble some gasoline into the carb. "Douse that shit!" He put in way more than was safe. Enough to blow up the motor.

I wrapped the cord and threw my weight into the pull. The cylinder turned and the motor caught fire, flames shooting upward. In a moment, the fire burned off the last of the water in the system, and we knew we were close. I leapt up and wound the cord again. We readied all the things and threw more gas into the open carburetor and pulled the cord. The motor blasted into action, a swirling dangerous beast of metal and chemical activity. The propeller was turning and the boat lurched forward. We jumped in and shot upriver.

Just like that, we were racing through the cool, insect-free wind and howling with excitement. All the suffering ended and we were wild with our success. We slapped five and shouted and laughed as we went. Mohsin was shaking his head with a smile on his face. "Let me tell you something: You, my friend, are relentless!"

═══

Relentlessness can pay off. In 2012, not long after Lee had gone around New York City with BECOME A JUNGLEKEEPER flyers, we were contacted by a group of yoga studio owners who said they wanted to plan a trip with us.

It was an exciting new opportunity. JJ said that if we were going to bring such fancy people to the jungle, we'd need better food. That's how we met Roy Riquelme; he came in to cook for the original yoga trip. Roy was an expert chef who had grown up in the Madre de Dios and made his living working in lodges on the Tambopata. He had also done expeditionary cooking for organizations like the World Wildlife Fund, Conservation International, the Frankfurt Zoological Society, and more. He was the real deal, and his food was a testament to that.

JJ and Mohsin and I guided the yoga group, and having food that was better than rice and beans made a big difference. The guests were thrilled to be eating such delicious Peruvian cuisine. Roy ran the kitchen with a smile on his face, chopping and cutting, boiling and perfecting dishes that made us all moan with pleasure.

By now Mohsin was a trained guide. He and JJ and I had a flow. We knew exactly what we were doing. And in the week that the yoga crew from New York was in the jungle with us, we did it all. We climbed the trees, rafted the rivers, went on night walks, and showed them the imminent threat coming from the Lucerna road.

They left impressed.

So impressed that they said they'd take us up on our offer of becoming junglekeepers. They asked how they could help, and we told them that if we were going to have a conservation organization, the first step was formalizing it into a recognized Peruvian NGO.

They enthusiastically agreed to help us with the process.

Soon I was drawing the logo, sketching endlessly and arguing with designers. In Puerto Maldonado, JJ and Roy were working with lawyers to create bylaws and an organizational structure. If we wanted to be a real conservation initiative, we had to define our mission. That was easy: protecting the Las Piedras River. We formed a board of directors. We hammered out operating agreements. We hired rangers. We asked friends and family to donate, and our new friends from the yoga studios helped cover the cost of lawyers and official paperwork. It was all moving fast. Soon Junglekeepers would be a real thing.

Also, my camera trap video, called *An Unseen World,* had won an award for the best short film at the United Nations Forum on Forests in 2013. The person on the other end of the line asked if I would be open to receiving the award onstage in Istanbul, Turkey, and giving a speech on my work in the Amazon and what the future held for this forest.

Months later, I found myself on that stage, wearing a suit and trying to figure out what to do with my hair. This was the United Nations. Some of the other people present were Indigenous leaders from Brazil and filmmakers from around the world. I gave the best speech I could at the time. I don't remember it being anything special, but going with Lee to Istanbul and getting to see my film played on the big screen in front of a global audience was something else entirely. The forests of Las Piedras were of global significance. No one had ever seen so many animals! The film went small-scale viral, making the rounds on the internet. *Yale Environment 360* wrote a piece on it, and it was covered in another interview by Mongabay.

And yet what I took away from the whole thing was a simple and succinct little axiom I follow to such an extent that I need to remark on it here: Pick up the phone.

If I had laughed off that phone call from the UN as junk, then perhaps I never would have gotten the message that I was now an "award-winning documentary filmmaker." Just like that.

I'm telling you. Pick up the phone. It's worth all the spam and junk mail and wrong numbers for the chance that it could be something wonderful. Most often it is something mundane or annoying. But you never really know. When the phone rings, it could be the government trying to get you—or it could be the universe trying to reach you.

Another life-altering example of picking up unknown numbers came sometime after the day I went with my mom and my wife, Gowri, to see Jane Goodall give a talk in New York City. The legend herself. In person. She gave a rousing presentation, and afterward sat to greet and take photos with hundreds and hundreds of eager fans, folks frantic to get a coveted picture with a living historical figure.

I had been writing chapters for almost a year. My cousin Danielle, whom I looked up to immensely, had told me more than once that I should write a book. I wrote down the stories I loved the most and passed them around to family and friends. I got feedback. And before going to see Jane Goodall speak, I printed them neatly and constructed a cover letter explaining that I was working in the Amazon, hoped to write a book, and would treasure her words of endorsement beyond anything imaginable. It was a long shot.

Standing in a line of audience members, I waited for my moment with Jane. Watching her was slightly surreal. Even though she had just given a long presentation, and despite the thousands of people who were waiting to meet her, she greeted each person with surprising grace, creating a brief but meaningful moment that these people would carry with them the rest of their lives.

I thanked her for her work, and handed her a manila envelope with two chapters in it. I asked her to read it if she had time and told her how incredible the Amazon was. She thanked me and set the package aside on a table. We took a photo. And that was it.

At least I had given it a shot. At least I had tried. After seeing her, though, I knew there was little to no chance that someone so decorated and busy (and let's just say it: old!) would have the bandwidth or motivation to read every little thing some eager fan handed her.

I was wrong.

The next evening I received an email from her assistant. Jane herself had read the chapters on the train the following day and loved them. Her people said she would be happy to give her endorsement whenever I found a publisher.

Mom, Dad, Michelle, Gowri, and I all celebrated. It was hard to believe.

That catalyzed me into being an almost full-time writer. I constructed my chapters, laid out a story, went to Barnes & Noble to get books about the publishing world. I tried my best to construct the sixty-page marketing mammoth that is a book proposal. I sent it out to a list of agents in New York City and was quickly rejected by them all. Some didn't believe the stories I told. Others just passed completely. One high-profile agent took the time to go above and beyond a simple rejection. He told me I had nothing unique to add to the subject of the Amazon, that I was unqualified and little more than a lost man-child. He said we didn't need the voice of an enthusiast who was too young and full of self-important upstart ambition to know what was good for him. He said if I ever did publish anything, it would be years. He said I wasn't ready.

The brick walls are there to stop the people who don't want it badly enough.

I went back to the books. Most of them large enough to work out with. Hundreds of pages of publishing info. They also included professional editors who had once been agents or publishers who now consulted on proposals. I called several. Some said their rate was $10,000 to do a proposal. Others charged more. All were skeptical of my young age. It was around 2013, and I was still in my midtwenties, just a kid brimming with wild stories. One woman, Linda Carbone, called me back.

She talked to me for almost an hour about the Amazon and my writing, which she liked. She couldn't understand why my proposal was so bad. She explained that no publisher would accept a proposal unless it was professionally done. Mine was far from meeting the mark. I explained to her that I was severely dyslexic, and while I could write and form a story, I did not have the ability to follow the structure and detail needed for a sixty-plus-page marketing document.

She said her rate was usually $5,000. I told her I had $1,300 left in my bank account. She agreed to do it for $1,300, as a bit of charity, because she liked me, the work, and the jungle. Not long after I worked with Linda, she sent the proposal out to some of her contacts. More people passed. By now I had been rejected by almost everyone in NYC. I was starting to prepare myself for the reality that some kind words from a hero and your mom telling you that you are talented just might not be enough to constitute success.

Then came the email from Lindsay Edgecombe. Lindsay was a young and impressive agent with Levine Greenberg who read the chapters I sent her and responded with a glowing message that read, "Dear Paul, I took your material home with me last night and couldn't put it down. I think that this is fabulous and would LOVE to work with you. I feel a visceral need to represent you for this book! I think that the Amazon you describe is so magical and that your message is so important."

This was what I had been dreaming of! She loved the chapters describing the Floating Forest and my favorite anteater, Lulu. She offered to be my agent. And soon after, we met in Manhattan to work on our pitch. Months later we went together to meetings all over the city, with all the major publishers. It was New York. The monolithic landmarks of the metropolitan world I had come from suddenly cracked, and the doors opened. Lindsay and I sat side by side describing a book that would take people into the Amazon in a way no other had. Not long after those meetings, HarperCollins bought the rights to the book that would become *Mother of God: An Extraordinary Journey into the Uncharted Tributaries of the Western Amazon.*

I was going to be an author.

═══

I knew full well the good fortune I had received, and in the coming months, I worked on that book like my life depended on it. Sets of push-ups to the *8 Mile* soundtrack. Journaling for hours. Running for miles and miles. Suddenly everything changed. I was training for life. Most people don't get a shot like this. I stayed up all night. I leafed through all my jungle journals, and I sent the newborn chapters to my sister, the literary authority I trust the most, before sending them to Lindsay and then on to Harper. Once it was all accepted, it was time to get the endorsement from Jane.

And that's when, once again, the phone rang.

I was at home in upstate New York, hiking along the Hudson River with Gowri and friends, when my phone rang. It was Mom. She had gotten a call from a number she didn't recognize. It was Jane's assistant, who said Jane was in New York City to-night, and wanted to have dinner.

We changed plans, rushed home, showered, and sped into the city. Michelle and Gowri and I all went up to meet Jane in her hotel room. We ordered Indian food, vegetarian.

"What would you like to drink?" Jane asked.

I went with the safest thing I could think of. "I guess water?"

"Well, that's disappointing," she said with a very British pout. "I guess I'm drinking alone. I have this lovely whiskey that Dave Matthews sent over . . ."

"Okay, fine! That would be perfect!" I quickly pivoted; I'd be happy to have whiskey with her. I also learned that while she was almost eighty and represented peace and wholesome con-servation Mother-Earth-ness, she was by no means an old mare. She was a firebrand. A warrior who had been fighting the status quo and the fate of the natural world for longer than most of us have been alive.

We talked conservation the whole night. At one point, maps and laptops were spread out on the bed. She explained her strat-egy in places like Borneo and the Congo. She emphasized the importance of rainforests, which make up only 6 percent of the Earth's landmass but half the terrestrial biodiversity—they were top priority. Then came the ocean fisheries that were com-pletely collapsing. She asked me what my plan was. What was my strategy. She asked me clean and clear, and held my gaze, waiting for a response. Like a general asking for a report from the front lines. In her pragmatic, determined stare, I saw the antithesis of all the tragic environmentalism I had grown up with, and instead thought of the quote from the street artist Banksy: "From this moment despair ends and tactics begin."

I told her about Junglekeepers. I explained the Trans-Amazonian Highway as a threat and how we had to stop the deforestation before it reached the critical areas. I gave her an overview of how the Tambopata National Reserve, Alto Purús National Park, Manu National Park, and the Amarakaeri Communal Reserve were superlative protected areas and Las Piedras was at the heart of it all, completely unprotected. We both agreed that in Africa it was easy to rally people behind a single species, like elephants or rhinos, but in the Amazon it was the contiguous ecosystem itself that was the character in need of saving. "You must make people understand that the forest itself is something alive and almost conscious—that's your charismatic megafauna. It's a continent-sized jungle that's more beautiful than anyone can imagine. That's what you have to make the people understand: It's a treasure for our world."

"Can I show you something?"

"Of course," she said, smiling. She had a Gandalfian quality of wise amusement.

On her laptop, I played *An Unseen World*. "Oh, that's delightful!" she said, clasping her hands before her. "Just look how many animals, how full of life that forest is. It's so special. So special. And that's why I'm giving you these words, that's why I'm endorsing this book." She was looking at me disarmingly stern now. "This is something that you have to use to its full extent to protect all you can. We'll never have this chance again. Either we save it or we lose it forever. You understand this, I think. That's why I trust you."

I nodded, I told her I understood.

Afterward she showed me a video in return. It was a video of her releasing a chimpanzee in the forest to a place where it could be safe. A chimp she'd never met before, but before going off into the jungle, the chimp stopped, turned, and hugged her tightly for a long minute. "Can you believe it?" Jane's eyes were full of light. She was at the same time awestruck and proud. Her excitement was infectious. We were having fun. Drinking whiskey while strategizing how to save the world and sharing our favorite moments from the field.

"Let me ask you something," she said with a devilish grin. "Do you swim in the waters of the Amazon?"

"Every day!"

"Do you ever go naked?"

"Absolutely never."

"If I were a man, I wouldn't either. With all those fish and things swimming in there, dangling a big grub for them to bite off seems like a terrible idea, doesn't it?"

We all laughed and I told her that's exactly why JJ and I are never naked while swimming the Amazon. At the end we hugged and she reiterated: I must not forget the gravity of what she was giving me. It all felt like a dream.

When we got back down to the smoky streets and yellow cabs, I felt like something magical had happened. Nothing would ever be the same. We had to protect that river. We were going to protect that river. I was getting an endorsement from Jane Goodall. It was like someone had handed me Excalibur. I now had a kind of new hope, a weapon that would open doors and light the way and move the compass dial in the direction of true north. If saving the river was the quest of my life, now I had something that I could use to really fight. More important, I now believed completely that this was the journey I was meant to be on.

I needed to call JJ.

WHEN I FINISHED THE manuscript for *Mother of God,* I sent it over to Jane, and she sent back her words of endorsement. She wrote:

Mother of God is a narrative that is gripping, sometimes disturbing and always satisfying. There are parts that will haunt you, scenes you will never forget. Running throughout is his growing concern for the future of the forest and his desire to conserve this Garden of Eden in all its beauty and wildness.

—*Jane Goodall*
PhD and UN
Messenger of Peace

THE QUEEN OF
THE AMAZON

===

ANACONDAS ARE BORN LIVE, NOT FROM EGGS. THEY EMERGE from their mothers in a yolk sac, like a life starter pack, encased in a clear membrane.

They start life smaller than you think, just under two feet. Given this, it's incredible that they grow to the insane length and weight they are able to attain. Because of this drastic transformation in size, anacondas wind up straddling many different roles in the food chain in a single lifetime. They go from being little snakes in the pond, prey to herons and caimans and fish, to the apex predator of the Amazonian riparian world.

The technical term for the various tiers in the food web of a given ecosystem is "trophic levels." They represent the flow of energy and nutrients through that system. It starts with the primary producers, like plants and algae, that harvest sunlight into energy to form the base of the food chain. The trees and vines are all struggling upward in the jungle, everything in the forest surging, reaching for access to the sun. Many trees invest their captured energy capital into creating tremendous trunks with powerful branches to lift their leaves toward the light. Many plants expend great effort on chemical deterrents and thorns to defend themselves from the primary consumers of the ecosystem, the insects and herbivores. Leaf-cutter ants that march their leaf bits down into subterranean cities, where they farm them into edible fungus. Deer graze on young shoots. The secondary consumers are the snakes and birds and frogs that eat insects and small animals. Then at the top you have the tertiary consumers, or the apex predators: the jaguars, harpy eagles, black caimans, giant river otters, and the titan herself: the anaconda.

Energy is transferred inefficiently through the trophic levels, with some lost at each stage. This is one of the reasons a plant-based diet is broadly considered more sustainable for humans on a global scale. This is the reason there are many trees and few jaguars. The reason there are vast grasslands with millions of squirrels and birds and frogs, thousands of deer or elk, but only a few wolves. Ecosystems are energy economies. And interestingly, the same rules that govern balance and possibility within this framework of chemical-physical interchange translate into the global capitalist monetary economy quite directly. Deforestation and subsequent poor rains cause a drought that affects ten million farmers in India, and the drought spikes famine and the economy ripples.

As apex predators, anacondas are especially vulnerable to biomagnification of contaminants such as mercury, meaning they are probably absorbing the cumulative mercury from many lower levels of the food chain. This makes anacondas important indicators of the health of the rest of their community, and of course it puts the snakes at risk. Through predation and maternal transfer, these snakes could be accumulating levels of contaminants that may seriously compromise neuromuscular function. And for a snake that depends on coordination and power to make a living in the most competitive biotic economy on Earth, that's bad news.

In 2014, there was still no hard population information on anaconda numbers in the Peruvian Amazon, which made it impossible to establish a baseline for the species. There was no way to tell if they were thriving or in decline. If you look at macaws or jaguars or harpy eagles, there is data. Most species come with a CITES rating, indicating whether the animal is "of least concern," "endangered," "critically endangered," "extinct," etc. CITES stands for the Convention on International Trade in Endangered Species of Wild Fauna and Flora. It is a global agreement among governments to regulate or ban international trade in species under threat. But for anacondas in lowland tropical Amazonia, there was a simple line at the base of any scientific report on population dynamics or conservation status: data deficient. So perhaps it should not have been surprising that details of ecotoxicology for the large snakes were nonexistent.

Since the night that JJ and I had encountered the beast that I had tried to ride in the Floating Forest, we had dreamed of launching a study, and in 2014 we got our prayers answered. A television network offered to put a few million dollars toward the project. They'd help us handle logistics, funding, and permits, and make our study of anacondas and mercury contamination a reality. The plan came with a concerning caveat: At the end of the show, I'd have to don a special hard scuba suit to let the network execs see if the snake would try to eat me.

It was a dumb idea, but I figured it was worth the risk of the stunt if we got everything else we'd asked for. If we did this expedition, this study, and made a show that the world loved, we could protect so much forest, it was hard to even imagine. I signed on the dotted line.

Then we set about selecting a team.

JJ and Mohsin and I chose several of the people we trusted the most. Lee Rando, because he was my oldest friend, who had known me since we were practically babies. Patrick Champagne was a young Canadian biologist who had come out to guide with us before and shown an inordinate talent for herpetological science. Lucy Dablin, a British scientist. My wife, Gowri. Joonas Hesso had been Finnish Special Forces and was a good friend, also one of the toughest people I've ever met. He and I had tackled a seventeen-foot-plus anaconda a year earlier, and he knew well the difficulties of trying to wrestle a dragon.

WITH OUR DREAM TEAM assembled, JJ led the expedition and Pico handled the boats. Pico, who had always been economically challenged due to his damaged leg, was excited to get steady work. The expedition would last six weeks. For the production, we were dealing with a crew from Los Angeles, literally Hollywood. They'd been contracted by Discovery Channel to handle the shoot. I told them the day rate for boat drivers was $150, when the standard was about $30. When Pico learned he was going to be making that amount, he nearly fell over. He swore and spat and hugged me tightly. It was the most money he had seen in his entire life. By the end of the project, he was able to replace the mud floor in his house with a newly poured concrete base.

For the first few weeks of the expedition, we were based out of the Floating Forest. We found some anacondas but nothing big enough to be impressive on film. We pulled mostly babies, sampled them, and began adding data points to the study. We had some truly grueling times. Each day we had to hike to the swamp. Each day we were up to our necks. It was all day, all night, in the swamps. We were brutalized by the end of the first week. But we thought we were off to a good start.

The producers disagreed. Catching some baby snakes and sampling their DNA and mercury levels was in no way sexy enough for television. Science in the Amazon just wasn't good enough.

By the second week we got a call. It was some older studio exec in an air-conditioned office in L.A. who had no idea what the reality on the ground was. He only cared about his bottom line. "Listen to me very carefully," he said. "We need a danger beat. We need something to get the viewers pumped." I told him we didn't have time for that.

"You don't have time?" He explained in no uncertain terms how he would shut down the whole thing and hold me accountable for the three million dollars if I didn't comply.

The fact was, we weren't scared of the jungle. And we weren't actors. Making it sound dangerous for TV seemed disingenuous. So we all met and discussed. But the network sent over notes of the possible "danger beats" we could do:

1.   Paul gets into a fight with a bull shark.
2.   Someone gets bitten by a venomous snake.
3.   Piranhas and a bucket of blood!

For the first one, I had to explain that although search engines may have led them to believe there were bull sharks in the Amazon, this was a phenomenon that only happened up in Iquitos and was exceedingly rare. I had to remind them that the Amazon was the size of the continental United States—not everywhere was the same. Also, how exactly did they want me to fight a shark? They said they'd have one brought in, that the viewers would never know. I refused.

The venomous snake thing needed little explaining and instead I shouted back at them.

The bucket of blood and piranhas was the most hilarious. Their idea was that we'd manufacture a scene where we are going downriver, and "suddenly Paul stops the boat when he sees a school of dangerous black piranha. He heroically pours two buckets of blood into the river to create a diversion, and then safely leads the team around the school of murderous fish." *Heroically* pouring blood into the river. Sure. Now how in the hell would piranhas in the water pose any threat to us if we were in a boat? Did these people not grasp that we swam in these rivers every day? And where on Earth would we get not one but *two* buckets of blood? It was insanity. My fights with the network became worse and worse. It was stressful and scary dealing with these powerful men who were trying to get me to sell my soul to the demons of the entertainment world.

≡

News got around that we were on the hunt for the biggest snake there ever was, and a friend of a friend who worked at a research facility farther up the Madre de Dios River reached out to say he'd seen a snake of colossal proportions in a swamp near the site. We saw the pictures. He wasn't kidding. It was the biggest snake any of us had ever seen a photo of. And the best part: She seemed to bask there frequently. We changed course, packed the boats, and made our way upriver.

The facility we were going to was called Los Amigos Biological Station, derived from its location at the confluence of the Los Amigos and Madre de Dios rivers. We heard that back in the 1980s a biologist named Adrian Forsyth had gotten the area surveyed, secured funding from the founders of Intel (the Gordon and Betty Moore Foundation), and protected the whole mouth of the Los Amigos River. He'd gotten the gold miners out and established one of the highest-caliber, best-respected research facilities in the western Amazon. Forsyth was a legend.

But we were far from prepared for what we'd find when we arrived at Los Amigos. Until this point, everything I had done in the jungle had been with just me and JJ, sometimes Pico, and

later Mohsin. This place, however, was a social scene, a large
operation with various groups of scientists and researchers. We
walked into a whole new world. We were not the cool kids.
One of the head researchers at this place saw our rowdy gang
and the ten-person film crew and went to her directors to complain about her lack of a film crew. The perplexed directors
tried to explain that they had no answer for such a question.
The weather was terrible, cold and raining constantly. Our
team came in like a group of escaped zoo animals. We had
learned the jungle from the Indigenous ways. We were wild.
These researchers followed protocols. They wore gum boots—
the big rubbery heavy things that I had grown up calling rain
boots. The researchers walked on trails. The researchers followed rules. And above all, the researchers never swam in the
river.

We started exploring the swamps and mapping out which
places were most likely to have anacondas. A contact there
showed us a place called Pozo Don Pedro, where an "extremely
large anaconda" had been seen on numerous occasions. It was
strikingly similar to the Floating Forest. Just a deep pool in the
jungle at the center of a massive swamp system. Like the Floating
Forest, it had floating vegetation all over it. It was surrounded
by aguaje palms. And because it was part of the Los Amigos station complex, it had twenty-foot-long dugout wooden canoes
parked at the end of the trail. Perfect tools to paddle around
looking for signs of anacondas.

The first few days we spent up to our necks searching the
great swamp with no encouraging signs. If my expeditions with
JJ and Pico had taught me anything, the cold weather was prime
time for finding big anacondas basking and hoping for some
sunlight. That's why we always searched for anacondas in June,
when the cold spells blew into the Madre de Dios. But for the
first three days we came up empty.

Our bad luck didn't have to do with just the fact that we weren't finding anacondas. The administration at the research station absolutely hated us. There was a researcher whom I'll call Biggie. Biggie was a little Indian woman with a tyrant's eyes, whose research involved capturing monkeys, shaving bits off them, and gluing transmitters to their skin. She would also spray-paint their tails pink. All in the name of science, right? She found us utterly distasteful. And she must have worn the soles of her shoes thin racing back and forth to go complain about us at the head office. We smoked cigarettes. We didn't always wear shoes. And when we came back from long days searching the swamps, we weren't satisfied with a trickle from a little indoor shower. We wanted to go bathe in the river and swim and have fun. I found myself, as the team leader, frequently called into the administrative office—suffering flashbacks to high school in the principal's office. They would explain the rules, and I would explain why we couldn't follow them.

At least once, I theatrically marched over to the administrative office and explained that I found spray-painting monkeys and shaving their fur to be inhumane.

Biggie was livid.

She cornered me in front of the team and several local field helpers.

"What right do you have to open your mouth about me? Who even are you? Do you have a PhD? No. Have you published any scientific papers? No. You have no right being at a place like this and you are an embarrassment to actual researchers doing actual work. Did you even go to college?"

Feeling about five inches tall, I told her I had a bachelor's in Environmental Studies.

She laughed through pursed lips. Her beady eyes literally shook with hatred. "Stay out of my way," she warned me with a finger pointed right at my face.

She turned and left, and as she did, an old Peruvian man carrying crates of fruit got in the way of her storm-off. She held up her arms. "José, what did I tell you about carrying things this way? This trail is for the scientists."

Now, first of all, his name wasn't just José. It was Don José. The guy was old. Second of all, he had two crates of fruit in his arms. They were heavy. So heavy that as she began to scold him, the first thing he did was put them down. He couldn't not listen to her; she was one of the queen bees here. But he also couldn't stand there with that much weight in his arms. He held up a hand in defeat.

"Lo siento," he said submissively. "If you want, next time I can bring them around the other way. But today the truck put them so close, I thought I could just . . ."

She cut him off right there. "No," she said, finger out. "You'll do it now. Go around." Old Don José, his labor interrupted, his dignity destroyed, agreed and lifted the boxes with great effort. Then he turned and walked in the opposite direction.

Biggie stood there watching to make sure he followed through, and then gave a final look back at us to make sure we had seen the example she had made: a venomous thing checking to see if there was anyone else she needed to bite before leaving.

These kinds of research stations taught me something invaluable about my time in Amazonia. I had been fortunate to learn the forest from the Indigenous people. Here, I saw a bunch of PhD students who had come from various places around the globe and who were following a set of mandated protocols and the tenets of the teachers they had learned from. They walked on trails, wore boots—the forest was an alien environment. They didn't experience it the way JJ had taught me to. They were *observers,* one trophic degree removed from the source of whatever magic powered this place.

At the research station, dinner was served in a common cafeteria. The first few days it was our crew as well as the in-house researchers, and then a group of twelve or thirteen students on a study-abroad program, along with their professors. We were lepers. Sideways looks, whispered comments. They all judged us. The admin had complained that we were like animals, that we had no respect for the rules. That we were loud and gross and just some gaudy TV people. I was already known for being on social media with my shirt off. What a show-off. Not a biologist. Just a sensationalist.

We ate dinners with our heads down and got out quick. It was toxic and stressful being around people who hated us.

Then, some days in, the man himself arrived: Adrian Forsyth walked into the hall at dinner. He would sit in the corner and hold court. Whenever he paused his fork and opened his mouth to speak, everyone would lean in to listen. The river was protected because he had done it. The research station had been built because he had done it. The funding had been gained by him. As far as anyone could tell, he was the most experienced and knowledgeable scientist in the region any of us had ever met. He had the gravity of a small planet and his own weather system wherever he went. I'd never seen such a respected human. He was like a shark swimming with fish: His every movement created a reactionary ripple or response.

I used some spare time to look him up and learned that when he wasn't in the field wearing his gum boots and studying beetles, he ran something called the Andes Amazon Fund, an incredible organization aimed at finding innovative solutions to conservation issues. I heard him recount one story where an oil company wanted to go inside the Amarakaeri Communal Reserve. The traditional assumption would be that the oil company was bad and would do nothing but fight with the Native reserve. But Forsyth saw it differently.

The normal play would be for the oil company, Hunt Oil, to

cut a road and then go inside and drill and destroy everything. Forsyth went and met with them—he had a better idea. He told them that they could indeed scout for oil within the protected area, with a couple of conditions. First and foremost was that they did not create a road. Roads are how people begin pouring into rainforests and how rainforests begin to die. To solve the logistical problem that *not* cutting a road would present, he outlined a proposal in which they would fly all of their gear and operators in with helicopters, land at the drilling sites, and do their work. In this way, the heart of the reserve would remain protected. The second of the conditions involved support. That whether or not oil was found, the oil company would become allies in protecting the rest of the park and its Indigenous populations. By coming up with collaborative solutions, Forsyth was changing the narrative wherein environmentalists fight the energy companies. He was of the opinion that the energy companies were going to explore for resources no matter what, and so it was best to make friends. He was right.

Every single person at the station took full advantage of the opportunity to remind us that we were at the bottom. Even though we had our research permits. Even though we had our respected scientists with us. There was something about the film crew. I felt bad for my team. We weren't just misfits, we were outlaws. Not in a good way. We were the Dirty Dozen, visitors who couldn't follow the rules and didn't know any better. At that time, we didn't have the confidence required to stand our ground and explain that what we were doing was truly groundbreaking work in the study of the ecology of the lowland green anaconda.

But that all changed one night at dinner.

I had been called to the office for a good scolding; my team and I were all eating our dinners with our eyes downcast. It had been days with no anacondas. Hard days in the swamps up to our necks. The network was still harassing me daily, something I didn't share with the team. Mohsin had been stung by a bullet ant. JJ had an infected foot. We all had cuts and scrapes and gashes on us. Infections and fatigue were setting in.

We were minding our own business when Adrian Forsyth pointed a finger across the room.

"You," he said, looking squarely at me through his spectacles.

I stood and went to him and introduced myself. I said my name was Paul and I worked over on the Las Piedras . . .

"I know who you are and what you do. You're Junglekeepers. I saw that video you made with the camera traps. The United Nations one. Simply marvelous. I've never seen anything like it. I loved it. I show it to everyone I can!" Then he turned to his students and devotees, Biggie among them, and said, "That's how to use a traditional technology in innovative ways!"

"Thank you," I said. "What you've done here is incredible, truly."

He nodded and dismissed me. I went to get more rice and tried not to look like I was floating.

≡

It had been cold for days. But by six the next morning we knew the clouds would break. The air was warmer. Today there would be sun.

JJ came to me as we dressed. "Hoy día es," he said. *It's today.*

When the first sunbeams poked through the clouds and hit the forest, we began walking faster. I caught JJ's eye and he nodded. All those days on so many years of expeditions in the rainy cold of the jungle wild, we had learned things on an animal level. We knew. If it was ever going to happen, this was the day. The anacondas would have been cold for almost a week, and the first sign of sun meant they'd be out to bask in the warm rays. I felt my eyes brighten, a thrumming in my bones; I felt ready.

But within five minutes on the boats I felt the spark of excitement flicker. It was just like every other day. The film crew was asking us to cover some walkie-talkie beats. JJ was on the front scanning with his binoculars. People began to fidget and talk. Maybe we'd just gotten excited by the sunlight. Dammit. It had been three weeks of working the team every single day, and now today too would be a wash. I was doing my best not to look as shitty as I felt.

Then it happened.

JJ's eyes narrowed and the binoculars rose to his eyes. He whispered, "Paul, lookadis."

There's a rising teakettle sound adrenaline makes in my ears. It was low at first. The boats began positioning. We needed a better look.

JJ was laser focused with the binocs. "It's a *big* one."

I moved toward the front of my boat and triangulated based on where JJ was looking. Scales. Monster scales. "I need you out of here," I said to Dave, one of the camera guys. Standing on the front of the boat, I got my first true visual. My face fell. The snake was nearly black and of terrifying proportions. I waved for them to get me closer. There was no plan for something of this magnitude. I was terrified.

As the boat drifted closer, I cracked my knuckles and tried not to think of how deep that black water was. Tried not to think of being wrapped in coils as I sank to the bottom, thirty feet below. *This is what you always dreamed of. It's here now; forget the fear.* I breathed deeply, trying to ready my nerves. Each breath counts when you know it could be one of your last. The snake was so massive, awe filled my eyes, and suddenly I felt it happen: Thoughts melted away; the chatter cleared. It got quiet and peaceful and very bright. I exhaled and my eyes closed. When they opened, I was in the calm space of heightened awareness. No thoughts, only instinct.

The boat pushed into the island of vegetation and I leapt into the grassy water. The snake untangled and fled. Two big kicks and I made it to her and grabbed her by the tail.

The rest of the team leapt one by one off the boats, smashing and splashing their way toward me. The battle was on. What followed was a fight between ten people and a giant serpent, and I only have the clips of memory and the videographer's footage to recall the salient moments.

All I knew for sure was that I had the tail but it was getting away. The power of the snake was unbelievable, like a tractor or an excavator. She had gotten hold of something below and was using her fifteen thousand muscles and hundreds of pounds of weight to haul me down with her. It was happening again. If we lost this snake it would all be over. It was now or never. What came next were like moments from a Renaissance biblical painting: fighting, gasping, reaching, screaming. I knew I had one job: Don't let go. If I could hold her until she was tired, maybe we had a chance. We'd found the holy grail and it was getting away. Joonas's hand clutched my shoulder. He pushed past me and made meaningful eye contact before rising with a deep breath and diving under. His feet came above the surface as he climbed downward along the snake's body looking for the head. What the fuck!

Lee was beside me helping to make sure the last of the tail didn't slip through my hands. Mohsin came in on the other side. JJ came up out of the water, took a breath, and then went back down. He was also underwater looking for the head. Even in those moments I was shocked by his bravery. If the snake bit him down there, he'd never see daylight again. He was risking his life.

Looking over my shoulder, I could see only thrashing coils. Splashing water. The canoes were coming in closer but we were fighting a sea monster. Her thick body would surface and then thrash and vanish, only to emerge fifteen feet in the opposite direction, ripping us off our grassy moorings with each smash of her weight.

Joonas came up, and his eyes were wild and stone gray. He looked into my soul. He didn't have to say anything. I knew. He knew. He drew a lungful of air, and vanished into the dark water. The last thing I saw was his feet, as his hands clawed their way deeper, down the trunk of the great snake, into the abyss.

Then I lost the tail. It slipped right out of my hands. I cursed bitterly, "I lost her!"

JJ exploded upward beside me. "I have it!" Mohsin and Lee lunged in to help him. They were holding on to the last four feet of the snake as the noses of the boats came in. Lee climbed up onto the canoe and used its buoyancy as resistance, and with both hands he hauled upward. Mohsin was organizing the siege. "EVERYBODY, ON MY COUNT! ONE! TWO! THREE! Arrrrhhhhhhh!" Everyone pulled upward. The snake retaliated with a downward lurch of such power that the nose of the boat dipped and the back end rose out of the water, throwing Lucy and Gowri forward. Again Mohsin rallied the call. "One! Two! Three!" Everyone pulled at once. The snake was thrashing now.

Then, from the back of the boat, which was now a few feet in the air, Gowri saw it: "THERE'S THE HEAD!"

I followed where she pointed. The snake's head was surprisingly far from where we'd been fighting with its tail. The anaconda had exhausted her oxygen supply and come up for air. I scrambled over the grass and came to where her tremendous face floated on the water's surface. For a wild moment it was just me and the anaconda, my hands poised, every cell in my body begging me not to do it. Sign the cross. There was no time. Terrified, I grabbed her.

"I GOT THE HEAD! I GOT THE HEAD!"

You could hear the fear trembling in my voice. The coils of the colossus began winding, and if she succeeded in spiraling around me now, it would be moments before my ribs imploded and my eyes burst out of my skull. I was at the mercy of my team. And wrap me she did. But they pulled us in. I held on to her neck like my life depended on it, which it did. Soon there were hands on me. The others hauled me toward the boat. Coils as thick as my waist moved by my face. The boat tilted, took on water, as they tried to get me and the giant snake in. In an avalanche of unwinding coils, the great snake and I fell into the boat.

We all cheered and whooped and hugged.

The boats were paddled to solid ground. We made a line and held the snake gently in our arms; she was still winding and powerful but tired from the fight. We laid her down and measured her. From nose to tail she was about six meters, or eighteen feet six inches. JJ and I caught each other's eyes, mouthing, *Oh my god!* Then we weighed her: 220 pounds. We had a radio transmitter ready, which we fed her and massaged down her throat. Now, no matter what, we'd be able to track her until she passed the device.

The cameras were right in my face as I marveled at the animal. "Just look at her scars! Just look at how massive this animal is. She must have had so many babies over the years. This is one of the most incredible creatures on our planet. This! This is the queen of the Amazon!" I was in a state of suspended wonder. The scales, the size, the power. It was the most beautiful thing I'd ever seen, and I said as much to the cameras, trying to convey the wonder and awe and respect I had for this incredible dragon of a snake.

"That's all great," said the producer, "but what would happen if she bit you?"

"Well, she had the chance to and she didn't, she's a gentle giant," I said lovingly, and kissed her on the head.

"Yeah, but if she did bite you, how would that go?"

I gave him what he wanted. "Well, if the snake did bite me, with a mouth that size, her teeth would reach bone, I would almost certainly have my arteries severed, and then soon be crushed to death. If she got me, it would be the end for sure." I said something to that effect. Big mistake.

There had been no time for thinking.

Despite the distance, Pico came in on his crutches. When he saw the snake, his eyes were bulging. As he reached me, he dropped the crutches and fell onto me with a powerful bear hug, swearing like a sailor. His arms tight around me, his nose practically touching mine, he put a finger on my forehead: "You are one crazy cachero, Gringo Loco! LOCO!" He shook his head, smiling, and hobbled off to begin working with a team of locals to make a bag or cage big enough to restrain her on-site until we could film with her properly. But first, we all needed a break.

Back at the research station we came in filthy and bloody and wobbling on our feet. There was a lot to do. We had to plan how we would film with her. The cameramen were wide-eyed and silent. JJ had an easy smile and Joonas's blue eyes were blazing. Mohsin and I hugged tight and Gowri was grinning from ear to ear.

Before we could even settle in or shower, a cargero pulled up, the kind of ATV with three wheels and a bed in the back. Driving the cargero was Don José, whom Biggie had lambasted days earlier. He waved to me with a smile like Santa Claus.

Someone had told the park rangers at Los Amigos we were looking for anacondas and if they found any on their patrol to please let us know. We had absolutely not told them to catch the animals. But catch them they had. In the bed of the truck were several big sacks. One contained an anaconda that was three feet. Another with a six-footer. Larger sacks contained a twelve- and a fifteen-foot anaconda.

Barely able to believe our luck, we began to measure and weigh and process the snakes. The professor from the study-abroad program asked if his students could help. I knew this was a once-in-a-lifetime opportunity for them. We brought the students in, and let each of them hold the weighty coils of the largest anaconda. With a veterinarian we used a scalpel to take tissue samples and collect other data on the snakes like sex, length, weight, and where they were found.

As we fell asleep that night, we were poised between wondrous processing of all we had seen and done and drifting off into sleep after the wildest day any of us could have imagined. We had more anacondas than we'd ever dreamed. Our study was going to be a success. Our show was going to be a success. When I thought of my snake's scales and power, I felt a surreal sense of awe. When I thought of the selfless bravery and devotion of my team, my friends, there was a lump in my throat. It had all been so beautiful. I knew that few people ever lived through such a day, and I felt an immense sense of almost divine gratitude. We stayed up late that night having beers and smoking cigarettes and telling the stories again and again, because none of us could believe it; none of us wanted that perfect day to end.

The giant snake from the swamp, the kraken we had wrestled and caught, turned out to be the longest specimen of *Eunectes murinus* ever scientifically recorded. At eighteen feet six inches, she was a world record.

We named her Eleanor, after my grandmother.

THE END OF
THE GAME

≡

DESPITE CATCHING THE LARGEST ANACONDA ON RECORD AND all the other wild adventures we had, and in spite of my first book being in bookstores across the country, and in spite of Tamandua continuing to bring in clients, things were off. JJ was off. When Emma had left and taken their son, Joseph, with her to the UK, it had ripped away enough of his heart that you could see the pain in his eyes.

Late at night, I would see JJ lying in a hammock, zooming in on photos of his son. It wasn't just sometimes. It was all the time. Once, I saw him there, the light of the phone on his face in the darkness, scrolling through a photo album of Joseph. I went all the way down to the river and back. Almost an hour later, JJ was still there in the hammock, his heart a thousand miles away, just staring at the images of the person he loved most in the world. In the years to come it would be a routine of JJ's, a constant in his life. Time alone, to watch his son as a toddler, as a boy, a teenager, and a young man—longing into the starry distance.

While JJ was bleeding from the loss of his son, my own world was growing dim as the sun was setting on my marriage. Something had broken during the weeks of the anaconda filming expedition. Gowri and I hadn't been there for each other in the way we had once hoped we would be. The hull of the ship had been cracked and we were gradually taking on water. Soon it dawned on me that we might not make it—that maybe I didn't want us to. We both began to discuss that we might ultimately have no other choice but to abandon ship.

"What's the matta?" JJ asked one day when he caught me staring off into the distance. "They don' think you a biology?"

"It's not biology, JJ, it's biolo-gist."

"Ah," he said. "In Spanish it's biólo-*go*. I get confused."

I nodded.

"Hm. And qué pasa, cachero, with you and Gowri? You not okay?"

"No," I said. "I don't think so. We might start seeing other people."

This got JJ's attention. "Like other women, otro damas?"

"Sí."

He smiled knowingly. "Muchas chicas. Tu no eres biólogo, eres cachero-*logo*."

Half-hearted smiles.

We sat on the side of the river, each at our own crossroads, smoke coming up from the forest in the distance. The road we had found with Paul back in the day had now become a town. Every few months another house came, and with it another few acres burned. What had once been deep jungle, sacred wild, was now just charred wasteland.

"Ay, Paul, you think we can do something about dis?" He motioned to the destruction in the distance.

"I really don't know," I said honestly. I didn't see how we could.

"Sometimes I wonder if it is cursed." JJ threw a stick into the river.

"What is?"

"The jungle," JJ said. "Everyone is always cutting it, killing everything they see. And we have to just watch."

In the distance the sound of chain saws droned on. At times we'd hear great shihuahuaco trees falling. There were more and more loggers on the river. They were flooding in from the road. Flowing out were the logs, the ancient pillars of the forest, slaughtered and stacked, hauled away to go become someone's furniture on the other side of the world. Where we once had played in paradise, now increasingly we saw roads being cut, logging crews entering. People were coming from other parts of Peru because the shihuahuaco boom was getting underway. We could see the changes in the habits of the wildlife. There was a shadow looming on the horizon that we had no framework to accept.

≡

What can one do in the face of such reckless waste? I had grown up hearing rhinos were going extinct. Elephant populations were plummeting in Africa and Asia. In the year 1900 there were more than 100,000 tigers on Earth, and now there were fewer than 5,000. Salmon fisheries. Ocean fisheries. The pollution, the wanton destruction. The Living Planet Index report says we've lost 70 percent of the wildlife on our planet since 1970. The day I read that, I cried. I thought the newscasters would remove their earpieces, traffic would halt, and world leaders would rush to the United Nations to find a solution. But nothing happened. The great green forests, the bountiful blue oceans, they were all getting emptier, dirtier, quieter. And no one seemed to notice.

Part of this was generational amnesia. Each generation accepts their world the way it is, and then the grandparents tell their children how much greener and wilder it was when they were young. In New York I'd heard so many elders say, "Those developments used to be farms." In India, more than once estate owners had told me that just a generation ago there had been tigers in these hills. The silence. In the *NeverEnding Story* of Earth, we were the Nothing.

For years I had tried to subscribe to Jane Goodall's message of hope. Her whole mantra is that there's hope. It's not too late. But as I traveled the world and saw what was unfolding in Amazonia, it became harder and harder to rally that kind of optimism. It began to feel false. As what I saw in Amazonia went from concerning to all-out apocalyptic, my views began to change, and it was around this time that I truly sank into the work of the artist Peter Beard.

If Jane is the light in conservation, Peter Beard is the dark.

Peter Beard was born in the United States in 1938 and graduated from Yale in '57. He then traveled to Kenya with a camera to document the culling of over forty thousand elephants at Tsavo National Park. It was the "conservationists" who were doing the culling; Beard was there with an unflinching eye, documenting the pachyderm holocaust. He was there to see a lot of destruction. He documented the extermination of Nile crocodiles in Lake Tanganyika. He became close friends with Karen Blixen (*Out of Africa*). Beard was the kind of conservationist who redefined the word. He wasn't afraid to call it how it was, to show it how it was, and with no filter. He was an artist capable of capturing some wild essence of the magic and romance between Man and Nature. His photographs and scrapbooks are a treasure trove of stark beauty, a fever dream of mankind's fall from Eden, the unfiltered annihilation of nature.

His seminal book *The End of the Game* (1965) is the kind of tome that will bend the table it sits on. It's a dark account of

The snarling wild forests
of the Madre de Dios, Peru,
the headwaters of the
Amazon Basin

Don Santiago,
JJ's father, with
his son Elias

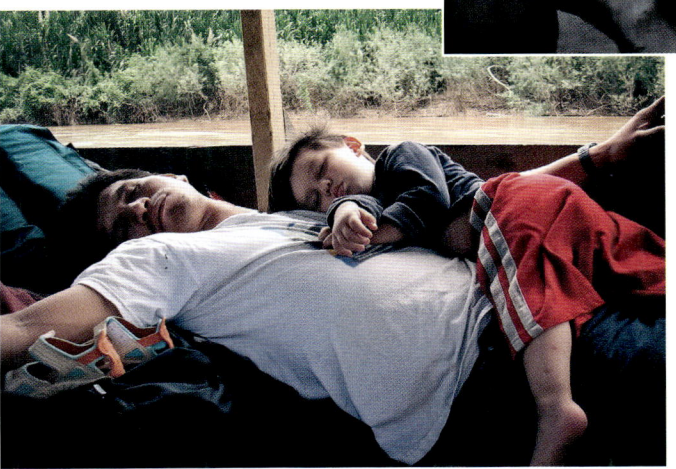

JJ and Joseph
passing the time
on the two-day
journey into the
jungle to reach
the station

Pico, the legendary motorista

Shaman Mario Durand preparing to lead an ayahuasca ceremony

JJ and me with our first "large" anaconda, which Santiago called an anacondita

At 18' 6", Eleanor was a world record when we caught her.

A close-up of
Eleanor's massive head
(PHOTO: MOHSIN KAZMI)

Time with
Dharma in India

Trying to write *The Girl
and the Tiger* with Dharma
vying for attention and
grabbing at my pen

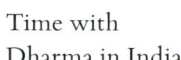

Walking through the
Indian forest with my
elephant friend

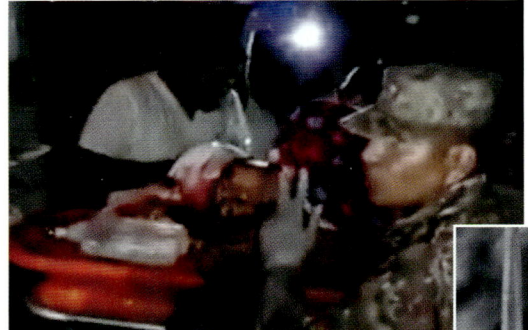

Ignacio en route to the hospital after being shot in the head by the Mashco Piro and airlifted by the helicopter in the background

Ignacio's scar from the six-foot arrow that nearly killed him

The ancient giants of the forest stacked at a logging mill along the Trans-Amazonian Highway

Primary forest being burned into ashes
(PHOTO: MOHSIN KAZMI)

Native girl on the Las Piedras having monkey for lunch

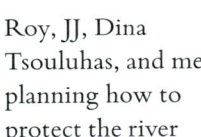

Roy, JJ, Dina Tsouluhas, and me planning how to protect the river

Flying low over the forest, scientifically surveying the immensity of the Las Piedras watershed

The little spider monkey who taught me how to speak their language

High in the branches of a kapok tree early in the morning, I feel like an insect in a giant world and am able to see the normally invisible mist river that flows over Amazonia.

The Mashco Piro warriors approaching on the other side of the river, bows and arrows ready (PHOTO: STEPHANE THOMAS)

Face-to-face with the Mashco Piro. This particular clan had never made deliberate peaceful contact before.

(PHOTO: MOHSIN KAZMI)

The moment that the boat full of plantains was pushed from our world to theirs and they rushed forward

A Mashco Piro man shouting in the rain, trying to communicate with us, the tribe across the river

A defiant man loosed an arrow in our direction and watched it sail to our side of the river. When it stuck in the ground he smiled and turned his back on us.

The most mysterious object on earth—a strange necklace that appears to be made of clay and decorated with animal teeth. Two of the Mashco Piro men had these around their necks.
(PHOTO: MOHSIN KAZMI)

JJ smiling on one of our many expeditions. This photo appears with his award as one of *TIME*'s 100 climate leaders of 2024. (PHOTO: MOHSIN KAZMI)

Piled into a tiny canoe, JJ, Roy, Stephane, Mohsin, and I explore tributaries and search for signs of invasion along the Las Piedras.

The Alta Sanctuary treehouse, the mist river flowing in the distance over the protected Junglekeepers reserve

The face of a Native girl, one of the many children who live a Native lifestyle far out in the jungle. They are the future of the river.

Devastation in its purest form: the annihilation caused by gold mining along the Trans-Amazonian Highway

The Junglekeepers' line: a drone shot showing the difference between ancient primary forest protected by Junglekeepers and the forest we were not able to save in time. With this image comes the understanding of the responsibility we face.

how Africa went from a wild place filled with wildlife and resources to a war-torn, desertified manifestation of an unfolding
apocalypse. He documented the end of an era, in terms of both
abundant biodiversity and colonialism.

One of his most famous images, the one I hung on my wall,
shows him lying on his stomach, his legs swallowed by a tremendous crocodile. His torso emerges from the mouth of the
dead crocodile, his face calm, his hands positioned writing in his
journal. Another is of an elephant walking along a shallow river,
with a quote in Beard's handwriting from F. Scott Fitzgerald's
The Great Gatsby: "For a transitory enchanted moment man must
have held his breath in the presence of this continent, compelled
into an aesthetic contemplation he neither understood nor de-
sired, face to face for the last time in history with something
commensurate to his capacity for wonder."

Beard's aesthetic was deeply hypnotic to me, and drew me in
like gravity. He was a free spirit who loved the wild. When he
obtained his own land, opposite Karen Blixen, he also made
some enemies. One of these was a warden of Kenya's national
parks, David Sheldrick, who banned Beard from Tsavo National
Park for his habit of hiking out alone, tracking animals on foot,
and getting lost. That made me smile, because that's what I did
wherever I went. Peter Beard seemed to look for the edges,
rules, boundaries, customs of society, and willingly cross them.

When he wasn't in Africa, Peter Beard lived at the east end
of Long Island, in Montauk. Famous in the Hamptons social
scene, he threw parties with guests like Jackie Onassis and Mick
Jagger. He had leading-man looks, an all-American dashing
quality, like Robert Redford but better. One friend described
him as being the smartest and best-looking man in whatever
room he was in.

One of Beard's images, taken from a plane, shows a herd of

756 elephants moving across the planes of East Africa. It is Africa at its wildest and finest. A glimpse back in time. He famously described it as an extinct image, something that can no longer be seen on Earth. As the decline of elephants continues toward extinction, herds of this size no longer exist. The photo is like a window into the Pleistocene. A vision of what—so recently—has been lost. In a single human lifetime, he managed to document a precipitous drop in the brilliance of nature. And a sobering magnitude in the visions of death.

I once saw a video of an older Peter Beard, sitting in a chair at his house on the cliffs high above the sea in Montauk. He describes a time when he was with the elephant hunters and a bull elephant came to look him squarely in the face. It was a time when the hunters were taking out entire family groups. You can't just kill the matriarchs, he explains. You have to kill them all. "You can blot out twenty-five elephants in about half a minute. Brain shots. 375's." Elephants are so emotional that if they see the death of their family, they become traumatized; they become killers themselves and hunt humans.

In 1996, Beard was out with some friends when an elephant charged. The elephant chased him and came down on him like a freight train. He ran until he fell over an anthill, and then the elephant proceeded to stomp and maul him. It crushed Beard's pelvis and ran him through with a tusk—entirely through his upper thigh. The elephant lifted him twelve feet into the air and spun him and then smashed him back down. The beating severed his optic nerve, rendering him temporarily blind. While he lay there, flickering in and out of consciousness, he was aware that the entire herd drew in, their trunks touching his skin and hair, exploring his nearly lifeless body.

Friends rushed him to the hospital (which was four hours away—apparently he bled out en route), and inside the hospital they were able to revive him. The severe physical trauma he suffered didn't stop Beard from showing up to his art exhibit in Paris in a wheelchair. The most interesting man in the world. An artist-explorer. An observer of the darkness. A libertine sensationalist and a man who saw the entropy and chaos of nature as something to be reveled in and celebrated.

He was cool and dark and edgy, and when I met him, he was very old.

It was a day in Manhattan when Lee and Gowri and I had nothing to do. I suggested that we go to see the Peter Beard studio on 57th Street.

But as we got close, Lee called me and said something that didn't make sense. He said he was sitting with Beard, and they were waiting for us. That couldn't be right.

I walked into the beautiful ornate lobby of an incredibly old building, and there, with wise eyes, abnormally large hands, and strikingly handsome looks even in his late seventies, was Peter Beard himself.

"Where have you been? We've been waiting for you!" he said with movie-star cool.

I almost fell over. Then he laughed easily and waved a hand. He said that Lee had arrived early and explained that I was a big fan and that we were inbound.

It wasn't long before we were engrossed in discussion about the state of the natural world. "You know," he said, "what you're seeing in the Amazon, the destruction, is very similar to what I saw in Africa. It really is the end of the game. Humans are a plague on this Earth. If there's any chance of saving anything, we're the last generation that's going to have that chance." He shook his head. "I don't know how it's going to play out."

I told him in detail what JJ and I were doing, and what we were seeing. I showed him pictures off my phone. I wanted him to see the tribes and the burned monkeys and the Trans-Amazonian Highway and the charred land. I wanted him to know I was in the thick of it. That I was really out there. We were talking up a storm. It was like meeting a great friend I'd just never spoken to in real life before. Then he paused.

"By the way," he said, vulnerable, "I'm sorry. I had a stroke not that long ago, so I apologize if my speech is slurred or if I'm not making sense at all." He laughed, the easy laugh of a person who has known the best in this life.

I reassured him that he was as smooth as ever, and there were no signs that he had had a stroke.

"Okay, good," he said. "Now show me more."

I showed him pictures of the devastation of logging. He shook his head and his eyes became dark. "You must continue," he said. "I don't think there's any stopping it, but you have to try what you can. I did what I could. And it was all for nothing. Africa used to be a paradise. Now it's ruined. Population is a disease. The only creature on this Earth capable of appreciating the miracle and beauty of all this is reproducing until we turn it all to shit—literally eat it, burn it, and turn it into our own shit. We are a plague on this planet. Now it is all stress and destiny."

About an hour and a half into our talking, Peter suggested we take it upstairs; he wanted to show us the studio. But around then a nurse showed up. She was frantic.

"Peter, you know you can't be welcoming guests! What did we say about stoop talk?"

Peter looked bewildered, with theatrical innocence. "Oh, but we were just speaking, my new friends are so nice, we . . . we . . ." Suddenly I could see the stroke showing.

The nurse signaled me with her eyes. It was time to go.

Peter and I said a hurried but heartfelt goodbye. It felt like there was so much more we could cover. But it was time for his treatment. "Don't ever stop," he said, looking right into my soul. I told him I wouldn't. I told him we'd meet again. We never did.

The anaconda capture and the television special that resulted were one of the worst things that ever happened to me. Or at least I thought so at the time. I lacked the experience and perspective to truly understand and internalize the importance of failure. If you listen to any entrepreneur or artist or actor or athlete, they'll tell you: Make failure your friend. Churchill said the key to success is going from failure to failure without loss of enthusiasm. But the magnitude and severity of the trainwreck that was the Discovery anaconda special smacked me right off my feet. I was devastated.

On the call sheet for the production the entire year that we worked on the show, the title had been "Expedition EA." They told me it stood for *Expedition Anaconda*.

When the show came out, they rebranded it *Eaten Alive,* and what they had done to the footage was even more devastating. They cut out every bit of the science, all of my appreciation for the animals and for the forest, and our conservation message. That moment that I had been holding Eleanor in the swamp and talking about her beauty and her importance: They used none of it. Instead, they used the part where I spoke about how dangerous she could be if she ever bit me. Fake and disingenuous, like just another TV personality trying to hype up how dangerous the animals are. It was the opposite of everything I had tried to do.

When I begged Discovery not to release this edit that they did, and told them I couldn't possibly endorse something so far removed from what I had intended, they had an unnamed lawyer call me late at night. He told me that they could sue me so badly that my grandchildren would be poor. I had signed a contract. They had made the film that they believed they had promised. Now my job was to go promote it. It was in the contract.

So I had to smile for the cameras and sell my soul. There I was on the couch with Matt Lauer on the *Today* show. The special itself became national joke fodder for everyone from Kimmel and Colbert to Conan O'Brien. They all had some disparaging remark. *What a letdown. What a pile of shit. Who is this guy? What a jackass.*

Around that time I began to be unfaithful in my marriage. Perhaps it was the depression of getting nationally humiliated. Perhaps it was a lot of things. As easy and good as it felt in the moment, I began to hate myself almost instantly. I tried to justify it, and came up with a whole ethos for it, that some people were just wild and needed to be free to express and explore. I came up with all kinds of bullshit euphemisms for the fact that I was a cheater. It happened again and again and got worse and worse. And as the secrets and the lies accumulated, my soul felt more and more like a rotting apple. I was moving further and further away from the values I had been raised on. As it turns out, we are born with a built-in compass for right and wrong—it's called a conscience—and in these times, mine was spinning. Everything was spinning.

There was also a feeling of deflated hopes because *Mother of God* didn't do as well as I'd hoped. It had been selected as a Barnes & Noble Discover Great New Writers pick, it had fantastic reviews from virtually all who read it, people loved it. I just didn't have the media reach at the time. Additionally, I had the sneaking suspicion that no one really believed a lot of the stories I told in it. I could feel it. The Floating Forest, the uncontacted tribes. It all sounded like madness to someone in a cozy apartment with a cup of tea and a book. Either way, I had put my heart and soul into that book, every last drop, and it did . . . just okay.

In the Amazon, the yoga people who had promised to help

us formalize Junglekeepers were working hard to get the process going in Lima. But I had been so busy with television and turning myself into a cheating piece of shit that I missed a lot of meetings that set up the bylaws and operating procedures that would become the organization. They capitalized on this, and stopped taking directives from me and JJ, and started constructing things in their favor. Slowly it was becoming their organization. I was losing hold of the dream. I wasn't right, and the sensation of it was all over me. My life began to seriously hurt.

Even worse, at this point, the destruction near the Trans-Amazonian Highway was at a horrific and historic high. Forest was burning. In the summer of 2015, I saw fires that sucked the hope right out of me. The ancient trees were going down, miles upon miles of ecosystem being leveled. I saw the scale of the fight and I remembered Peter Beard's wrinkled, handsome face. And his haunting words: *It really is the end of the game.*

Maybe he was right—it was all for nothing. Maybe my life's mission was not to protect the Amazon. Maybe I was just a delusional wannabe. Or maybe there was no fighting the entropic march of civilization. Perhaps my job was the same as Peter's: To witness and revel in the destruction. To simply watch and smile as the world ate itself. To see the elephants fall and the giant trees cut and just marvel at man's destruction. I lit cigarette after cigarette, crushed under the weight of so much guilt and pain, I could barely stand to be awake.

All I had set out to do was protect the forest, and it had become a trainwreck that refused to stop burning. A big, nasty public failure. I had shit the bed completely. Depression swept over me like the shadow of black clouds. I was lost and I knew it. All of the good and all of the positive direction that I had felt in the early days were gone. I felt like I had sold out, hit my

head against the ceiling, was hated by everyone on all sides—
and rightfully so, because I was just a piece of shit. I felt worth-
less and useless, and I wanted to be away from the world.

I wanted to get away from everything and everyone.

It was time for exile.

DHARMA

T HERE ARE CORNERS OF THIS WORLD THAT HAVE BEEN HIDDEN
from time.

I opened my eyes in the chill of morning. In the distance,
there was an elephant moving across the field beneath the great
jungle. The giant's tusks hung low, long and curved like a mammoth's. They swung side to side as he strode, like scythes cutting the spider-webbed, dew-laden grass. There were several
boys huddled on the elephant's back. I rose up onto one elbow,
squinting out into the distance. I rubbed my eyes at the edge of
dreams. It was barely dawn—blue mist still clung like a blanket
to the fields, dark jungle stood wild in the distance. The elephant strode like an ocean liner, ears like sails, a swirling of
white birds in his wake. The tribal boys on his back were
wrapped in blankets. They hugged each other tightly against
the morning chill, half sleeping on one another, rocking with
the giant's stride.

I had come to South India and traveled from Mangalore by
motorcycle, past goats and cows, village women carrying water
on their heads. At first I wore headphones in my ears, under my
helmet, and sometimes kept the helmet on the back of the bike.
The world gently melting into a montage of cinematic beauty.
The great waterfalls of the Western Ghats and the pungent, in-

toxicating smell of the coffee estates of Coorg. I rode for hours
and only stopped to drink from coconuts or take pictures. Way-
farer sunglasses and the wind in my hair, holding the handlebars
deeper into a dream.

I had come at the bidding of my friend Neeti. She was a
close friend of Gowri's and mine for many years. Since this
book is about the Amazon, there really hasn't been reason until
now to explain the dominating role India has played in my life.
In between stints in the Amazon, Gowri and I had spent months
of each year living in India. She has a wonderful family, and
there, we had a whole other life. I had originally gone to India
on a study-abroad program, but after we'd met and gotten married, India became a second home. Then, gradually, it became
home. I was no longer a foreigner in India. I felt South Indian;
I was South Indian, married in. I loved the food, knew some of
the local language, and felt more at home there than just about
anywhere else. On this trip, though, I had left Gowri in the
U.S., and come to India on my own. This was exile, and I
needed to be in the jungle, far from everything.

Neeti provided a pathway into a world so wondrous, I never
would have believed it existed had I not seen it with my own
eyes. So unbelievable, in the most literal sense of the word, that
I almost didn't go at all. The things she was telling me in the
weeks leading up to my time there sounded like complete fan-
tasy.

I launched myself without much thought, but in hindsight,
the experience would provide me with a powerful and motivat-
ing contrast to life in the Amazon. The Amazon, where I had
become used to vast forests and the fight to save an almost endless wild, couldn't be more different from India, where the animals and the forests are islands in a sea of swarming humanity.

The compound Neeti and I were staying at was technically

inside the forest reserve, where you needed permits to go. Neeti had been working with the Indian Forest Service and various conservation organizations there for years. She is one of the most dedicated and hardworking field conservationists I know. At that time she was focusing her efforts on the riparian conservation of the Cauvery River and specifically on its populations of mahseer (a large kind of endangered carp). It just so happened that at the exact time I was searching for an escape, Neeti was working in a hidden wonderland.

Here's the thing: Most people never get to see natural elephant behavior. Most humans interact with elephants on a safari. You drive up to elephants and you see them grazing. The elephants are confronted with cars and sounds and strange smells and a paparazzi-like atmosphere of gawking primates. Even the most accustomed elephants would simply rather not have to deal with that. An even less authentic possibility is to see an elephant incarcerated in a zoo.

What people rarely ever see, however, and what has always fascinated me the most, are elephants in the wild. I'm talking about when a herd is truly unaware and unconcerned that they are being watched. We all think we know how smart elephants are, and we are all wrong.

NEETI WAS THE ACTING caretaker of a site where a legend was born. Many years ago, a woman had saved two young female elephants from North India and brought them to the south. They had grown up and been allowed to walk wild into the forest. No fences, no chains. They had been rehabilitated naturally, and as they grew they had intermingled with the male elephants that existed in the jungle. The result was a family group of semi-wild elephants who were familiar enough with people to interact with them, but still wild enough to be dangerous.

The boys I had seen riding an elephant were part of the tribal community that lived in the surrounding area. The tribal reality in southern India is a harsh one. Many of them lived in mud huts with grass thatch roofs. Many of them still worked as mahouts, or elephant handlers.

In South India, the history of human-elephant interaction goes back thousands of years. And while Western sensibilities may be instantly outraged by the way elephants are ridden and trained, the fact is that in South India, humans and elephants have had to find a way to coexist. Most often this means that elephants are cut off from their old maps, their traditional migration routes, but here, in the protected forests along the river, in tribal villages, elephants and tigers and bears and ancient ruins all remain hidden in the tangled confines of the jungle.

And in the villages of the Jenu Kuruba tribal group, in collaboration with the official Indian Forest Service, there is still a need for elephants that can be worked with and ridden. When there is a man-eating tiger, the only way to track it through the jungle is on elephant-back. For this you need expert elephant handlers and elephants that know how to keep their cool and follow orders.

The semi-wild herd that Neeti was overseeing would sometimes come into camp. When they did, we would give them water. Just like humans, the elephants valued cold, clean water. Most of the surrounding area was arid at that time of year. The water in most ponds was stagnant and green. But at camp, there was a well. An idyllic little well with a stone wall and a roof, with a bucket and a pulley and a yellow rope. I had been there a few days, sitting on the front veranda, watching as the boys and their elephants crossed by. We made chai and coffee, and I was reading some of my favorite Fitzgerald at the time, *Tender Is the Night*. It was one of these sunny afternoons when the two matriarchs, Kunti and Kalpana, arrived with their families.

At that particular moment, Neeti was busy, on a call with some important director of her project. "Paul! Go! You know what to do! Don't let them break the well!" Then, with her head out the door, shouting after me: "And don't let them put their trunks in directly, they'll snot up all our water!"

I leapt up and ran out barefoot onto the grass. There were elephants emerging like parade floats from the edge of the forest. The size of Kunti and Kalpana was sobering. Flexing muscle and skin and the staggering size of their skeletal framework were enough to send an arcane panic up my spine. These were monsters. They were floating toward me in the way that elephants do: ears out, trunks up, excited for their fresh water.

If there wasn't a human to manage what happened next, they could collapse the stone wall around the well, or rip the bucket from its pulley. So I had to make it there first. I ran to the well, let the yellow rope glide the bucket down to the water, and pulled it up just in time for the matriarch to arrive and shove her trunk inside. She emptied the bucket.

Now there were trunks all around me. Pushing and grasping. One clutched my ear, and I had to jerk my head away; another grasped the rope, and I had to tap it. I spoke gently and calmly and reassuringly, but my heart was pounding. One of them stepped on my foot and I tried not to scream. I sent the bucket down and brought it back up and, again, one of the herd plunged in a trunk. While the matriarchs drained my bucket, I was being shoved and crushed by the others. I tried to keep the concrete well strategically beside me as I turned to refill. I threw the bucket into the well, the pulley whizzing. I was racing hand over hand to bring up another bucket as they surrounded me. I turned and produced the water: *Here here here!*

Those trunks weigh about as much as a grown human. So when they hit the bucket, it almost knocked me over every time. I did this again and again until I was exhausted.

My eyes almost came out of my head as another elephant foot stepped on mine. Somewhere in the confusion, a trunk wrapped around my waist and hurled me backward and out onto the grass. I sat there, panting, staring at a row of elephant asses as they all dipped their trunks down the well and drank indulgently. One of the herd turned to regard me with the elephant equivalent of an impish grin. He was thrilled with having thrown me so far. He kept his eyes on me as he drank deeply. Then he opened his mouth and belched out a long staccato roar, letting roughly a bathtub's worth of elephant snot fall into our drinking water.

Neeti finally arrived.

She smiled and shook her head as she vanished into the herd. There was nothing hurried in her manner. She walked barefoot between the mountains of wrinkled skin, swinging tails, greeting them each by name. Her gentle hand guided trunks out of the water one by one. Her hand was that of a painter or a violinist, the Shaolin monk practicing in the dawn. She moved with calm certainty. She spoke their language, addressing the matriarchs with a tone befitting their rank, and the young calves in the manner of a teacher admonishing an unruly kindergarten class.

"Come on, Kalpana, come on," she said, and laughed when the open trunk embraced her face. "Yes, yes, good morning to you too, Ma, now move back, Ma." Through a gap in the wall of elephants she caught my eye and nodded for me to come. We worked side by side—Neeti talking and calming and playing defense against the many thirsty trunks, while I hauled bucket after bucket up from the well. But for the duration of our work, one trunk remained affectionately poised by my ear.

"Oh shit." Neeti grinned. "I think you made a friend."

The elephant who had thrown me was named Dharma.

In the weeks to come, Dharma and I would indeed become fast friends. Whenever he was around, I would drop what I was doing and show him attention. Often, he would show up on his own; unlike the others, he liked to spend time with humans. Sometimes I would be reading, Dharma grazing beside me, and I would just pause. I would sit there scowling in disbelief, because no matter how many times I was in his presence, I simply couldn't fathom what I saw. Here was this mountain of gray flesh, muscle, and bone, with giant butterfly ears and an alien squid face. Yet the intellect he possessed, his manner, was so canny that sometimes it seemed like he was a human soul wearing an elephant's skin. Some days he was calm, other days stressed, and always brimming with messages he could not communicate. He would question us, with his trunk running through our hair or against our stomachs, learning things we could not know. It was surreal, it was beautiful, and I cannot describe how incredibly rare such a thing truly is.

Dharma was neither captive nor wild. As the son of Kunti, he had grown up between worlds as part of the semi-wild herd. The matriarchs wore radio collars so that they could be tracked. And nearly every day they would come to the station to drink from the well. So their level of human interaction was high. Dharma grew up familiar with tribal forest guards, biologists, children, and more. But when the herd would leave the vicinity of the research station, they were as wild as any other beast. Out there in the jungle, they foraged wherever the matriarchs led. They were careful not to step on king cobras, or get too close to a tiger. It was out there that they would socialize with the truly wild elephant herds. Massive males scarred from battle with farmers. Some who had killed humans.

Further solidifying Dharma as the sole citizen of the no-man's-land between humans and elephants was the fact that when he reached sexual maturity, it became clear that he was a makhna, a tuskless male. This meant that, like all males, he could be cast out of the female herd when he matured, but he couldn't hold his ground with the bigger, more masculinely equipped males. Their tusks were an advantage when fighting, and so an ordinary day of roughhousing with the bulls would mean a terrible thrashing for poor Dharma. The bulls' size was simply superior. So Dharma was, from the start, an elephant with no place.

It made life difficult for Dharma, and sometimes dangerous for humans. So much of Neeti's time was spent trying to keep Dharma safe from the trouble he would cause. One of his very favorite activities was to rob the local fruit truck drivers.

Coorg is a patchwork of protected forest, wild bush, farms, villages, and more. Many of the roads are long, winding through stunningly beautiful forest of one form or another. And this is where Dharma would wait.

There was hardly any traffic aside from the local workers transporting fruit to the market. Dharma knew their routes and schedule. Sometimes he would enlist the help of another male. They'd spend hours waiting. When the sound of a motor reached their ears, they would take their positions: one on the road, one hidden in the bush, waiting. For some reason I always imagine them jumping out with tommy guns and cigars: *This is a stickup, see? Hand over the bananas and nobody gets hurt!*

On a narrow road there's no way to drive around an elephant. So when the little truck came to a stop, Dharma would move in. Both elephants would spend some time harassing the driver. First by shouldering the truck and threatening to tip it. Sometimes one would wrap a trunk around a rearview mirror and snap it off. Ultimately they'd reach in and help themselves to all the bananas they pleased, as the poor fruit man prayed for his life.

Once news of the robbers got out in the region, a few of the drivers tried honking the horn and just speeding through. This made Dharma mad and scared, and the outcome was far worse. An angry elephant can easily topple a car. A single foot can crush a human body so badly that its guts explode out, leaving just an empty skin suit on the ground. Thankfully, Dharma had never actually killed anyone. Yet.

He'd been arrested several times. Tribal mahouts employed by the Forest Service would come on elephants of their own. They would corral Dharma, whack him with sticks, and use the larger elephants to force him to walk. They also tried shackling his feet, so he wouldn't be able to run fast enough to actually catch the cars. So we'd always be able to hear when he was coming. The *swish-swash* of the chains coming through the jungle.

On any given day he would often mope around the jungle alone. Spend some time kicking a stump, graze for a few hours, and then decide he was thirsty. *Maybe I'll go check out the well!*

Neeti's main objective was her fish study, but she was often sidetracked by elephant duty. Because she could see where they were on her GPS device, the Forest Service called her when the elephants were in trouble, which happened often.

One day a tribal Forest Service officer came speeding up in a Jeep. "Neeti amma!" he said with respect. "The herd . . ." They'd gotten into a farm. While Neeti raced off to the rescue, I was left in the hands of the Forest Service. On that day, Dharma came to camp. I was instructed to make him leave. If no one was around to control him, he would pull things over, destroy the well, or cause some other kind of creative chaos.

So I was told to take him at least one kilometer away from camp. I was shown a trail and given a staff and a backpack filled with bananas. "Let's go, Dharma."

The elephant and I walked off into the jungle. For almost an hour we walked side by side. Dharma would stop to inspect various plants. He would use his trunk to twist bits of foliage and rip them off and shove them into his mouth. Whenever he would stop to graze, I would remove a banana from my backpack and coax him onward. I didn't want to hurry. It's not every day you get to walk through the jungle with your very own elephant friend.

I was thinking about what that man had said to Neeti. He had called her Neeti amma. A term of hefty respect. This was contradictory to everything I had heard from Neeti in the months leading up to my visit. She had often lamented how ostracized she was as a woman. There were numerous instances of how horribly she had been treated. Outsider. City girl. Woman. They had made their position very clear. Once, I'd even heard a fat, curly-mustached Forest Service officer say the words "The jungle is simply no place for a woman." Often when Neeti spoke of the unfair treatment, I could hear the tears in her voice.

I wondered what had changed.

These and other things were being penned into my journal as I sat beneath the tree. Dharma stood like a big gray mountain beside me. There were bits of flowers in the hair on his head. He got scared when butterflies flew too close to his eyes. He was big and tough and strong, but also a total sweetheart. I was enchanted by what I saw, and took those observations from reality straight to the page through my pen.

After over an hour Dharma became bored with my writing and thinking. He had been twisting his trunk around grass clumps and kicking them free. He wanted attention and stimulation. So he started trying to grab my pen. I pushed his trunk away. But as soon as I did, it returned. He grasped the pen again, and again I pushed him away, this time more forcefully. When he tried a third time, I pointed a finger at him. "You stop it! Stop it right now!" Dharma flapped his ears and put his trunk in his mouth like a child biting his fist in frustration. He was sulking and moved off. I went to him. I kissed him on the forehead and rubbed him between the eyes. His long lashes shut in approval and enjoyment. He liked this.

Side by side, I walked with my giant elephant friend through the golden forest. Sunbeams lit particulate magic and set the foliage aglow. Dragonflies zoomed around us, and barbets and hornbills called in the branches above. When I thought we were far enough from the research station, I scattered the bananas from, around, so it would take him some time to get each one. Then I gave him a hug around the trunk and hustled back to camp just before dark.

Late one night I was awakened to the sound of a tiger calling. It wasn't long before Dharma came to camp. He was agitated. The sound of the tiger had frightened him. The fact that he could not go with the females or the males meant that he was alone in the jungle. I sat up that night, just him and me, talking to him for hours. It struck me that the tremendous heart he carried held a depth that I had no framework to understand.

I HAD JUSTIFIED MY exile to India for several weeks to work on my book *The Girl and the Tiger*. You remember the Indian family that had come on an expedition with JJ and me in the Amazon in 2012, the year we got the station back? Well, not long after that, Isha had sent me an email explaining that near her hometown, in the coffee estates, someone had found two tiger cubs, and she wanted to rescue them. Isha was an animal lover and had fallen madly in love with the Amazon, but I knew when she said she wanted to rescue the tiger cubs that there was no way for a teenage girl to do something like that. But Isha's dedication was the spark that lit an ember in my head that continued to glow. It became a reimagining of *The Jungle Book*. The main character's name would be Isha, and she would rescue a tiger cub from an Indian village, making the tiger the victim instead of the villain. The book would tell the story of wildlife in India, habitat, and fragmentation. It would be an old-school adventure and an action-packed insight into the realistic world of modern-day tigers and elephants.

The project was like a new drug. I dreamed about it, made drawings of its pivotal scenes, lived in that world. And now here, on the ground, in the world I was writing about, there was no more perfect consultant and proofreader than Neeti, in terms of both the natural history and the South India legitimacy of the book. Neeti was the archetypal conservationist, over-dedicated, underfunded, and wholly committed to protecting the natural world.

On a crisp morning, with piping-hot coffee and cigarettes, I asked Neeti about the Forest Service: Why the change in attitude? "When we talked months ago, you said they'd been terrible to you. All I've seen since I've been here is them practically kissing your feet."

Neeti nodded. "Ah yes, that."

"What happened?"

"The elephants did it. The whole herd was by the river, and we were all worried they'd cross from the reserve land into the farmer's fields. The herd was sleeping under a bamboo thicket. You can't rush elephants. Then this big tusker came, wild guy. He started displaying and acting defensive. All the Forest Service guys got together and started confronting him. Everything was getting more and more tense, like, that tusker could have killed everyone. The men shouted, screamed, tried to scare him away. But the tusker got madder, ears out, ready to charge. He was going to flatten them."

Then, just as the showdown between the giant bull elephant and the Forest Service men was about to explode, Neeti called out to Kalpana and Kunti. They came out of the bamboo and moved in between Neeti and the tusker. The herd began communicating with the tusker, calming him and blocking his charge path, and managed to deescalate the situation long enough for all the humans present to escape.

Neeti smiled. "Once they saw that, it changed everything."

I had heard of something like this before, elephants associating men with guns and fire and conflict, and having a completely different view of women. Almost like they are another species. Almost like they are gentler and more considerate and cerebral. But in this case, Neeti's presence had rallied the herd, averted disaster, maybe even saved lives.

It wasn't long until we again got news that our herd had broken into a farm and come into conflict with the farmer. The Forest Service called Neeti to help and allowed me to join them to mitigate the situation. Where no one else had been able to get the elephants away from the farm and defuse the mounting tensions with the irate farmers, Neeti was able to intervene. Once we had the herd located and docile, the Forest Service dispatched some of their tribal team to lead the elephants several kilometers back through the jungle to our camp. Neeti had to rush off to her laptop and a meeting for her research, but I asked the Forest Service men if I could join them on the march home with the elephants. They said yes.

And so we walked through villages and along forest roads. At one point as we came through a town, there were children on bicycles on their way home from school. Everyone stopped to watch the elephant parade. Women were carrying water on their heads. Motorcycles were puttering by. Then, the sound of commotion. My eyes went to where the largest matriarch had cornered a young woman against the wall. Oh no.

The elephant stood tremendous above the slender woman. Its trunk was moving over her mouth, scenting her breath. The trunk probed her neck and over her shoulders and around her face, then down to her stomach. Nobody moved. The woman was alarmed, but calm. Everyone was frozen, waiting to see what would happen next. Slowly the other female elephants drew in. More tremendous elephants standing over a frightened young woman. Trunks rising to touch her stomach.

A mustached man from the Forest Service came up beside me. He made a motion with his hand. Sign language told me: The woman was pregnant. The female elephants knew it, and were conversing avidly amongst themselves.

I spent that day and many others marching with the herd.

Toward the end of my stay in India came a day when the boys who rode on the elephant passed through camp. I followed them. Neeti was deep in work editing some paper, and there were no Forest Service men around. Dharma was off somewhere unknown in the jungle. I thought of how Peter Beard used to get into trouble for running wild through Africa. Although I knew I wasn't supposed to, I followed the boys on their elephant.

I simply grabbed my camera bag and jogged behind the elephant as the boys rode. They were riding a big old elephant that was blind in one eye. He had tremendous tusks. We walked through areas of luxurious forest. One of the boys pointed from atop the elephant to a spot on the ground where tiger tracks had crossed the road.

When we were deep inside the jungle, the boys left the elephant's back and began climbing a tall strangler fig. Tucked into their cloth belts were machetes with curved blades. I watched as three of the boys—all between nine and twelve years old—began to climb to the very tops of trees that were over a hundred feet tall. Soon they were in the canopy of the jungle, walking the branches, holding the blades in their teeth, balancing out to the very edges of the limbs. I was wincing, terrified they would fall, watching as they harvested ficus fruit.

With each cut, they dropped branches to the ground.

Beneath them, the elephant, which was of abnormal size even for his kind, was grazing placidly. Whenever a branch fell, the elephant would lift it up onto his back, where the youngest of the boys was waiting. The boy would receive the branch and place it neatly onto a protective blanket. As the hours passed, the older boys continued to weave through the canopy, even moving from tree to tree, harvesting fruit and dropping branches. The elephant calmly continued his work of lifting the branches up so that the child on his back could pack them tightly and tie them with rope.

At the end of the day, as we were walking home, I was following an elephant that was stacked high with fig branches. Atop the branches rode the four boys. Children. They spent the entire day out in the jungle working with a fully grown male elephant. It really was like something from Kipling. Something from a world lost to time. A vision no one back home in New York would ever believe. I felt a kind of warm wonder for which there is no analogy—in this magical place, the children rode elephants and tigers still stalked the jungle shadows.

Writing *The Girl and the Tiger* and living with Dharma and the elephant herd was an eye-opening look into the state of South Indian wildlife. National parks are packed to the brim with wildlife. In between them are roads and towns and villages and tens of millions of people. In India, humans and wildlife have been coexisting for thousands of years. But all the same, more than ever, the wildlife is losing ground.

The elephants know their old maps. The routes that ancient generations had trampled. Watering holes. But their old ways and customs and routes have been intercepted by highways and concrete and stores and shopping malls. Farmers have cleared the forest.

Elephants are hungry and large, and like humans, they exert a tremendous influence on their environment. They engineer it. Their dung carries seeds and produces mushrooms and nutrients. When the forest is cut, they go hungry. Farms filled with pineapples and tightly packed produce are too much to turn away from. They strike in the night and can level an entire person's livelihood in a matter of hours. I once met a man who lost $25,000 worth of bananas to a single male elephant plundering them in the night.

I've seen footage of villagers out with torches and pitchforks, throwing fireballs and fireworks and rocks at elephants. Farmers use poison. They electrify fences to levels capable of killing a pachyderm. In many ways, it is an all-out war between humans and elephants. And that is to say nothing of the millions of other animals that share the space that is the incredibly verdant and diverse tapestry of South India.

Elephants operate in sensory dimensions that we can't even imagine. Through their feet, they detect thunderstorms over a hundred kilometers away. They can communicate using seismic vocalizations from as far as twenty kilometers apart, and have a sense of smell five times more powerful than we have. Their brains are more than four times larger than humans', with unrivaled long-term spatial-temporal and social memory.

Elephants are self-aware. They can recognize themselves in a mirror, have complex social bonds, acknowledge death, experience grief, and even cry. Like us, their babies depend on their mothers for many years.

Most elephant communication happens using very low-frequency sound vibrations, from 1 to 20 Hz. Most of this is below our hearing range, but is often accompanied by rumbling sounds that we can hear. Their extraordinary ears can also hear birdsong as high-pitched as 10,500 Hz.

Oftentimes I spoke to Dharma. *What things do you know? What is held in that great heart of yours?* He bowed his head so that we were forehead to forehead. With flat palms I rubbed his eyes. I spoke to him for a long time, and for a long time he listened. The last time I saw him, I hugged him around the trunk, and he wrapped me around the waist. I kissed him on the nose, that great, wide soft part where the trunk affixes to the skull. *I love you. I love you. My big boy. Stay safe out there, okay?* Based on his reaction, there is no doubt in my mind that he knew it was the last time we would meet.

Dharma allowed me a window into the hearts of animals. Just like Lulu the anteater had. His incredible intellect. His sense of humor. The confounding ways he knew the things that I was thinking before I thought them. The way the matriarch knew that that woman was pregnant. He taught me things about the forest I would have never learned otherwise. He taught me things that would solidify and strengthen my relationship to the wild. He also taught me something that would directly save my life later. Things no human ever could have taught me. I thought I knew the souls of animals, but Dharma showed me I had not even scratched the surface.

That his name was Dharma is worth reflecting on. A person's dharma is their path. The path of righteousness and order in nature and in society—one's own highest, most ethical path. Dharma is the idea that there *is* a path, that nature is ordered for good and evil, right and wrong, and that there is such a thing as destiny. How could I not think of all the tens of thousands of acres that surrounded my river in Peru? The jaguars and the macaws and the spider monkeys. The anteaters and the anacondas. The leaf-cutter ants and the billions of other wild heartbeats that existed in the unbroken, untouched jungle. What an incredible and historic opportunity to save so much life. Like any good exile, I felt my perspective altered by my time with the elephants. It made me look back at the life I had left with longing and a renewed and curious focus. And pointed me back in the direction that I had come from with a new and clear vision.

I knew what I had to do.

A LIGHT IN
THE FOREST

PICO WAS DRIVING THE BOAT THROUGH THE MORNING MIST.
We both were wearing jackets and backward hats to protect our
hair from the cool morning wind.

I was about to do something crazy.

I had returned to the Amazon with new eyes. When I'd
reached the Las Piedras station I went to see all my favorite
trees—my old friends. I put palm to bark. I spoke to the spider
monkeys. I climbed and hiked the forest, swam in the river. I
longed to be gone from the world, deep in the forest, far from
anything human.

This place that I now knew and loved. This place that could
be gone within a dog's lifespan. I felt a love and urgency for the
jungle that made me want to wander its depths, see it as no one
else had. I wanted to be a part of it.

For this I would have to do a solo. Pack a bag. Sharpen a
machete. Take a headlamp and some batteries, a pot and whatever other basic supplies would fit in my pack. For a few days, I
was going into the wild.

Our tiny canoe under the big jungle. Pico would point out
caimans and teach me the river. Pico was a man who had taken
a life of not being able to walk well and turned himself into a
boat driver of artistic prowess. I kept alert and learned all I could

as the hours went by. When Pico's eyes began to tire, I'd put two cigarettes on my lips, light them inside my shirt, against the wind, and hand him one.

We drove two days upriver before we reached the point where he left me. Pico had told me that if I left the river and went straight west for two days, I would reach something magical. I believed him.

"Cuidado, cachero!"

I waved and then walked off into the jungle, alone.

I didn't care that I was risking my life. I hiked for hours into the trackless jungle. My cranium was still swirling with thoughts of Dharma and all the elephants packed in the little forest that was left. I kept thinking of the New York forests I had grown up exploring with my golden retriever—the majority of it thin stands of secondary growth. Not original. But out here was the real thing. The zenith of terrestrial biological complexity. The last endless forest. I hiked like I was a fugitive, and maybe I was. It had dawned on me that at some point I was going to have to make some decisions and realize who I was.

When I was a child, authority was the looming monster in my life. That one friend's mother had said that one way or the other, I would be stuck at a desk forever. That had haunted me ever since. It had chased me into the wild. Scared the shit out of me. I realized now that all of this, on some level, was the quest for ultimate freedom. That wilderness has always been ultimate freedom. The wild doesn't care who you are: To the jungle or the mountains or the sea, we are all equally anonymous.

In Amazonia, once you leave the river edge you are in places few people have gone. Once you go a dozen miles, you are far beyond where the trails drop off. It's raw wild. Unconstructed dream space. Forest from horizon to horizon. It towers above you. It engulfs you. The old hardwoods stand their lofty guard.

The shadows scurry with unseen life. There's a heavy silence, a presence, like in the greatest of churches.

I hiked for a day. Slept. And then I hiked more. Soon I was lost in the nameless places. I was searching for the edge of the world to find the spot where I could be alone with the jungle and the river and God.

Life is simple when you are out alone: Keep walking. Sharpen your machete. Make a fire. Boil water from the stream. After a few days, civilization was something as distant and blurry as last night's dreams. Reality became crystalline. If a tree falls in the forest and no one is there to hear it, does it make a sound? Does the universe exist if we are not there to observe it?

On day three of marching into limbo, I was walking along a stream when I heard splashing. I paused and waited—machete ready for whatever was coming.

A giant river otter with wide black eyes and bushy whiskers came loping and splashing around the bend. She was over five feet long from head to tail.

She looked at me without any hesitation or surprise.

"Hey," I said. It was the first sound I'd made that day.

She turned, took some encouraging steps, then looked back at me. I followed. It was clear that she wanted me to.

Soon we were running. I was slower than she was. At some bends she'd dive into the water and torpedo around the turn, but then she'd pop out and look back, waiting for me.

As we came around the last bend of the stream I realized we were approaching the edge of a lake. Something inordinately noisy was taking place in the direction we were going. The otter stopped, looked at me, then launched into the lake.

There, the rest of her family was rocketing and zipping through the water, vocalizing in the blaring alien dialect they speak. It is a sound that cannot be replicated by human vocal cords. I crouched in wonder. The otters were excited, agitated, and moving so fast and displaying such web-footed hydro-acrobatics, I could hardly believe what I saw.

Then suddenly, the surface of the lake erupted. A sixteen-foot black caiman lifted her tyrannosaur head out of the water and rolled her entire body with a wrath and power that shook the jungle.

The otters showed no fear or mercy. They cut through the water and took bites out of the caiman, taunting, harassing, slashing at her. The caiman lifted her great tail, an armored piece of reptilian engineering that was longer than I was tall, and thrashed and rolled and barreled off into the depths of the lake.

I stood holding the trees as the entire family of otters rejoiced and frolicked and spun. The one female, my friend, came straight up out of the lake as if to raise her eyebrows. *What did you think of that?*

I smiled.

I spent a week on this mini solo, camping in a new site each night. I made a long loop out into the jungle, where I met the headwater-trickle of a long stream. Just like Pico had said, it was magical. I hiked along that stream for days. I slept in my hammock, headlamp on, machete beside me, just in case I needed to get out fast in the night.

As the days passed, I didn't take pictures. I just lived, like an animal. I needed to let my thoughts play out. You can think out there. Without society deafening you and influencing your mind. I was the only person on Earth who knew where I was.

When I was a teenager in the forests of the Northeast, I had never used trails. JJ and Santiago had taught me the jungle without trails. Trails, like so many things, can either lead you home or whisk you swiftly in the wrong direction. At some point, perhaps from urgency for the forest or a vague longing for suc-

cess, I had stopped wandering and taken the wrong trail. I thought
I needed to go fast; I needed to learn what dangerous directions
they can lead you in. But now I felt like I had stepped back into
the truth of the forest, the untrailed calm space I had always
known and loved. I had found my way to my wandering home.
I had known this space as a teenager with my dog. I had known
it in the barefoot machete days with JJ. It is the peace of giving
yourself, completely and undistracted, to the wild. Any wild.

You can find it in the woods or the desert or a state park by
just letting the miles wash over you. Letting the rain come and
go. Spending long periods of time with only yourself as company. I still couldn't reconcile how I would live my life. On the
one hand was this love of the pure wild and the urgent need to
protect it. On the other hand, deep down, was the question of
whether I would ever live a normal life. If I should or even
could. It was a problem I had always carried with me like a
heavy rock. Just like the realization that no matter how hard we
try, sometimes we let people down. There were a lot of things I
was carrying that were tied to the world and to fear and to the
people I knew. But out here none of that mattered. Out here I
was just another one of the animals.

===

When I was a child, my dad would come home from work and
play with us. Underneath the oak tree, on the big rope swing.
At night at the dinner table he would quote Dostoyevsky.

"I'm a sick man . . . a mean man. There's nothing attractive
about me."

We'd all laugh.

Sometimes before bed I'd ask my father to tell me about the
kite creatures.

"The Tralfamadorians?"

"No, the kite-shaped creatures in the cave!"

"What were they called again?" he was testing me.

"Harmoniums."

"The harmoniums. Yes. You know this one, but I'll tell it again." My sister and I would snuggle into the covers and get ready to be transported as he retold the story from one of his favorite authors, Kurt Vonnegut.

"There were these two space explorers, Boaz and Unk, who got shipwrecked on some strange planet. They were in this massive cave. And the walls of the cave were completely covered in these calm, blue kite-shaped creatures called harmoniums. They didn't hunt or hurt one another; they didn't speak. They just moved around the walls of the cave, feeding off the vibrations of the planet. In the years that Unk and Boaz were trapped in the cave, Boaz sometimes played music. When he did, the harmoniums got excited and drew closer to feed off the vibration of the music. Boaz took great pleasure in giving concerts to the peaceful aquamarine creatures, while Unk spent his day restlessly searching for a way to repair the ship, escape from the cave, and return home. And in this way years passed.

"Finally, Unk did discover a way to fix their ship and escape. Spaceship ready, Unk urged his friend Boaz to board. They could finally go home! But Boaz was conflicted. He couldn't do it. As his friend begged and pleaded with him to be reasonable and return to the world, Boaz ultimately refused to leave. He chose to stay on the deserted planet, saying to his friend, 'I found me a place where I can do good without doing any harm, and I can see I'm doing good, and them I'm doing good for know I'm doing it, and they love me, Unk, as best they can. I found me a home.'"

My dad said the story reminded him of me. Me, who was always feeling the bubbling stream. Who would pick up a baby salamander out of the road and transport it to safety. From the time I could walk, I was drawn to the tiny things, the beautiful peaceful creatures, and would rescue them, whenever needed, in cupped hands.

In the summers we'd go on vacation to the beach. Out in the Hamptons, not far from Peter Beard's Montauk wild, the beaches were a quiet dreamlike wilderness. The grasses and the bay, full of endangered birds. The ocean large and infinite like the universe itself. Far-off water glittering with wondrous things like whales and pods of dolphins and horseshoe crabs.

One day when the wind was swift, we all headed to the beach. Mom, Dad, Michelle, me, and our golden retriever, Bugsy. We made sandcastles. It was glorious. This was that vague period when a young mind is still coming online. I remember that my mom was unwrapping a sandwich for my sister—a Lenore Special (pita bread, Swiss cheese, salad lettuce, and mayo: chef's kiss!)—when something down the beach grabbed my dad's attention in a deep and transfixing way.

When he started walking, my sister and I quickly followed. The wind manhandled us as we ran to keep up. Seagulls rose skyward as we went. The waves were crashing loud as we came up to an old man with wild curly hair and a thick, brushy mustache. He was looking upward, a spool of thread in one hand, the other poised on the string, the blue kite flying high above. For a time we all just stood there in the wind and the din of the waves, watching the kite fly.

"Are you Kurt Vonnegut?" my dad said.

The man turned.

"Yeah. Who are you?"

Here he was, the man my father had quoted, who'd written the stories he told us, of the peaceful kite-shaped harmoniums who fed off the vibrations. The men stood and talked. The kite rippling and diving in the wind high above like some agile, avian harmonium. Vonnegut's hand always on the string, feeling the vibrations.

≡

After days alone in a kind of wild that is difficult to describe, I came cut and bleeding to the edge of the river. I had sweat out a dozen pounds. I was starving. I made camp and fished. Boiled river water in a small pot. The next morning before light touched the world, I unfolded my raft. I set the paddles.

After days of hiking small streams, the Las Piedras River in all its wide grandeur seemed like a miracle. So much water from the sky, run from so many little streams in the forest—this was where it all went. This was the way. I climbed into the raft and placed my bag over my feet. I drifted off down the misty, lumbering current. Slowly, over the course of days, I was navigating earth and water in the direction I ultimately needed to go.

THE BLOOD
MERIDIAN

"I
F WE GO ANY FARTHER, THEY'LL SHOOT US," VICTOR SAID.
He was scowling as he worked, using balsa rope to secure the
body of a spider monkey to a wooden cross. I looked at Victor,
one of our crew members, but he wasn't joking.

We had been forced to stop on a lonely riverbend, high upriver.

The blast-furnace heat of the day had finally subsided, and
heavy iron-hulled clouds were scraping low over the canopy.
The boat was tied and dinner was being prepped. The undu-
lated tinamous sang their haunting song, the anthem of the
Amazon. The frogs and cicadas were tuning their instruments
in a chirpy prelude to what would soon crescendo into the night
chorus.

The clouds were a concerning color. The jungle here seemed
larger, more perilous. Perhaps it was the claustrophobia of knowing that for hundreds of miles in every direction there were
only ancient trees in their colossal, mirthless multitudes. They
crowded over the river, their branches spread powerfully, interlaced with vines freighted with orchids and mosses. To a thousand-
year-old tree, life beneath the shadow of their limbs is nothing
more than a moment of stasis against the entropic certitude of

death. There was going to be a violent thunderstorm this night—
you could feel it.

I sat making notes in my journal while the soggy little fire I
had made flickered and seemed to lose the will to live. We'd
need it bigger if we were going to cook this monkey. We hadn't
hunted the monkey, but that morning we ran into three hunters
who gifted it to us. The Nativos all ate monkeys. But way out
here, with no refrigeration, they'd shot more than they could
preserve. It would be wasted if it wasn't eaten.

Spider monkeys are larger up close than you think they are
when you see them in the trees. Victor wasted no time gutting
it. One slash down the stomach and he dumped the entrails at
the river's edge. Then he tied two sticks into a cross, while we
got the fire going brighter. He lashed the long black monkey to
the sticks by the wrists and ankles. The tail was wrapped round
the pole and tied off. Finally he laid the monkey, crucifixion-
style, on the flames.

The monkey hadn't been the only gift the returning Native
hunters had given us. They also had news: The tribes were on
the move. They had informed us with the stern warning not to
continue the expedition, but we had pushed on through the
day. But now as night fell, we found fear moving through us in
ways that were eroding our resolve.

The Las Piedras has several Indigenous communities along
its banks. These are people who are from the forest, and come
from Native heritage. The only two communities upriver from
the station are Monte Salvado and Puerto Nuevo. The tribes,
however, are a whole other kind of group—mysterious hunter-
gatherers who live in small clans, walk naked, and are completely nomadic. They are called the Mashco Piro. The infamous
"uncontacted" tribes. The communities and the tribes almost
never mix, except for chance encounters, careful bartering for
machetes and food, or rare cases of all-out violence.

Knowing that a clan of Mashco Piro was in the area meant all bets were off. Everyone was more quiet than usual. We all felt a certain sobering sense of humbling humanity before the vast elements around us—the mercy of laws more ancient than we knew.

"Qué pasa para mañana, Gringo Loco?" Victor said.

"If we continue from here and we run into them, could we make it past? What if we hug the other side of the river? How far do the arrows reach?"

"JJ, have you ever seen them?" Victor asked.

"The hermanos? No." JJ dragged a log up and joined the fire.

"Gringo Loco, this river isn't big enough."

I squinted: *What do you mean?*

"Es así," said Victor knowingly. "A shotgun has a range of, what, thirty meters? An arrow can fly a hundred or more easily."

JJ leaned in, speaking in English to make sure I understood. "The river isn't big enough, they can shoot you from across."

"When you saw them, they didn't shoot?" Victor asked me with a raised eyebrow.

"No," I said.

I was actively trying not to think about the time I'd seen the tribes.

Victor's encounter in 2004 had been far worse.

It was the dry season, when the river was slower and more tranquil. He and a team of loggers had been maneuvering a barge of fresh-cut mahogany timber downstream. On that particular morning, the cook and his wife had gone ahead in a smaller boat to find a beach to cook on.

Nearly an hour later, when Victor and the crew had rounded the bend, they saw a beach bathed in red.

The cook's body lay flayed on the sand, riddled with spear-sized arrows. He had been disemboweled, beheaded, and dissected. Victor and the other loggers had fired their shotguns into the air, drifting in horror and disbelief. They passed the beach without stopping.

Had the tribes taken the woman? Had they killed her? While they were still reeling from seeing their friend's ruined body on the beach, they had to contend with the reality that his wife may have been carried off for an even worse fate.

Not long after, one of the loggers spotted her. She was clinging to a log by the side of the river, delirious and weeping. They collected her and found that she had not been injured; she was exhausted and traumatized but physically unharmed. Gradually she told them the story of what had happened on the beach.

She said that when their boat had landed, she and her husband were preparing to cook on the beach when the tribes began their war cry. High-pitched screaming. Spider monkey alarm calls. Arrows began raining down as they ran. One of the arrows caught the cook through the thigh. He fell and she turned to help him, but by then the naked warriors were running from the tree line. He could no longer run, and there was no time. He told her to run, to run for her life.

She ran and hurled herself into the river, swam down as deep as she could for as long as her breath would allow, as arrows zipped through the water around her. She swam and never looked back, letting the current take her. She never saw her husband again.

The fire was popping now and flames lit the monkey's fur and began whisking it away from the body and into the air, bits of glowing matter dissipating to nothing in the dark sky. For a while after the story ended we all watched the flames, each imagining what it must have looked like. The cook was certainly alive when the warriors had reached him. Had he begged for his life? How did they end him? What did they look like? Sometimes they were dyed red head to toe. Other times black. Sometimes they used red and blue dye from huito fruit to stain their skin. The ability and volition to kill without hesitation or remorse. To be wounded and bleeding, surrounded by these painted killers . . . What that man must have seen in his final moments . . .

JJ shook his head and laughed, rubbing his face.

"Okay, today I smoke a cigarette, please."

"Smoke, cachero, smoke," Victor said. "Out here, other things kill you much quicker." Cigarettes were passed around the fire; we all smoked in silence with our thoughts.

"Ay, Paul," JJ said, the firelight mischievous in his eyes, "you remember what my dad said about the sounds?"

How could I forget? It haunts me to this day.

We retold the stories Santiago had told us so long ago. When he was out in the forest and the animals began to sound strange. The tinamous were slightly out of tune, and the capuchins seemed to be speaking a different dialect of their language than normal. After all, if anyone could understand the intricacies and variances in the tempo and pitch of the forest, it was Santiago. The chilling moment he realized he was being watched. He was surrounded. He had ditched his pack, hid, slithered like a crocodile down the stream and barely escaped with his life. Decades later he laughed about it as he warned us, poisoning our hearts with the terror of the tale. There was a time when we used to think these were just scary stories he'd tell. Even there, in the jungle, out so far beyond the last tentacles of society, it seemed so improbable that there could still be violent, naked Stone Age tribes hiding in the shadows of the forest.

IN ORDER TO UNDERSTAND the brutality of the nomadic, "uncontacted" tribes and their complex interplay with the remote communities of Amazonia, you have to look back about a hundred years.

From the 1870s through the early 1900s, the rubber boom consumed the Amazonian west. Several decades earlier, Charles Goodyear had made a monumental discovery: vulcanization. The process involved mixing the coarse sap of the rubber tree—natural latex—with sulfur, which transformed the sap into a durable substance. It changed the face of the industrialized world. The demand for rubber for tires, shoe soles, machinery, and thousands of other items during the Industrial Revolution in the United States and Europe caused a frenzy. In *Tree of Rivers,* John Hemming wrote of rubber, "It made the best gaskets for steam engines. It came to be used in pumps, machine belting, tubing, railway buffers, and later as coating for telegraph wires." At the turn of the century, bicycles were changing the world and the automobile was in its infancy; both needed tires.

All of this inevitably resulted in a mass migration to the only place in the Americas where the invaluable latex could be tapped: the Amazon.

In the fray, the Brazilian government designated the Amazon River an international waterway, opening it up to vessels from every industrial nation. For the first time in history, the Amazon became a busy highway filled with hundreds of ships from across the world, all seeking to exploit the region's rubber. The rubber trees, however, were scattered among billions of other trees within the untouched wilderness of the Amazon.

The only way to get at them was to walk from tree to tree, from dawn until dusk, collecting latex. Naturally, for the rubber bosses, Native labor was the most effective way of collecting the prized sap. The result was a period of genocide and atrocities so savage that the rubber boom ranks among the darkest chapters in human history.

Yet the rubber boom was, in truth, the second wave of devastation, an aftershock of the first period of mass destruction in Amazonia. Whether for spices, metals, slaves, timber, oil, or medicine, jungles have long cast their shadows over the most grisly acts in human history. It was the white men who brought the Heart of Darkness to Africa, and in the Amazon the Spanish and Portuguese swept across the basin in a slashing, burning, disease-spreading march of death. Paraphrasing the words of Winston Churchill, John Hemming wrote that "rarely in human history has so much damage been done to so many by so few. A thousand colonists gradually destroyed almost every human being along thousands of kilometers of the main river and its tributaries." One Father Daniel, horrified by what he saw, wrote of the Europeans, "They kill Indians as one kills mosquitoes. . . . And they use or abuse the feminine sex brutally and lascivi-ously, monstrously and indecently, without fear of God or shame before [their fellow] men."

Despite the basin-wide slaughter that began in the sixteenth century, there remained some tribes that refused to be made into slaves. As foreign enterprises forged into the Amazon dur-ing the rubber boom, many tribes moved deeper into the jun-gle. Already isolated tribes fractured and fled into the most remote and inaccessible reaches of rivers, where the white men couldn't come. When the rubber boom ended, these tribes re-mained isolated, out of sight and out of mind to the rest of the world. They became the legend of loggers, the only people who sometimes encountered them. Like JJ's dad.

When Santiago Durand came into this world in July 1922, Pancho Villa was still on horseback in the mountains of north-ern Mexico. The thylacine had yet to be hunted to extinction in Tasmania, and eastern mountain lions still roamed the Great Smoky Mountains of the U.S. Anne Frank was just a few years from being born. At a time like that, it is somehow easier to imagine that there were still numerous tribes isolated out in the Amazon. But by then, the tribes had already fully separated from any other remote communities they might have once bartered

or fought with. The stories of the elders radicalized their children, the conviction intensifying with each generation: The
outside world was dangerous and cruel, violent. Better to shoot
first.

For most of a century there was little report of tribes in the
Madre de Dios. By the 1990s many of Santiago's children, JJ's
brothers, joined the gold rush for mahogany timber on the Las
Piedras. They were learning from Santiago; JJ and his brothers
got their jungle training but also transitioned to part of capitalist society. They earned money, had motorcycles, watched the
news, had parties. They had boats, used motors, and worked
jobs, albeit mostly logging. It was during this time that the
folklore of the region was stoked by a sudden uptick in con-
frontations. More loggers meant more people pushing out into
previously inaccessible areas. It meant that logging mafias would
fund expeditions, finance the gasoline needed to reach farther
into the forest to get at the largest of the ancient hardwoods.

For the tribes it meant that once again, dangerous outsiders
were a threat. Throughout the '90s, arrows and shotgun shells
were exchanged, and many on both sides died. A history of violence passed down from the conquistadors to the rubber barons
to the loggers. It always made me wonder how we don't see it
more clearly, the human inheritance of trauma, from the moment Cain slew Abel. The terrors of the past have made it so
that somehow even in a world where we fly in planes and have
cellphones, can do heart transplants and reach the moon—they
are still out there in the last parts of the Amazon that are truly
wild.

And even then—even with Santiago's stories and Victor's
tragedy, even with the arrows the Native communities had found
on the beaches, even though I had seen the tribes myself—by
2019 they began to feel like a mirage, a figment of historical

imagination, a nightmare. Nothing that could reach out and actually touch us.

Until they attacked.

ONE DAY IN EARLY 2019 our boat pulled into a remote community far up on the Las Piedras. When you arrive in Monte Salvado, you have come to the last stop. There is nowhere farther than this. The river keeps going, winding on into the uncharted, unexplored depths of its own headwaters, but boats carrying people are prohibited from going farther up it because Monte Salvado marks the edge of the Madre de Dios Territorial Reserve. A sprawling two-million-acre reserve designated for the voluntarily isolated nomadic tribes.

Monte Salvado sits on a promontory with a great view of beyond. It is not a place that gets visitors often, so everyone comes to greet you. When we arrived, the children were lined up on the high sandy cliff. The houses were mostly thatched, though some had corrugated steel roofs that had been brought up from Puerto Maldonado by boat. Chickens and dogs were everywhere.

That day we met Ignacio Piño Diaz. He was twenty-two at the time and was noticeable not only because his hat said MINISTERIO DE CULTURA, but also because of the way he watched us. At some point Ignacio had made the weeklong boat ride to Puerto Maldonado, attended training, and been appointed by the community and the Peruvian government to be the one to monitor and manage the community's interaction with the uncontacted tribes, should they appear. But from the moment we landed in Monte, he followed us around like a Secret Service agent, watching every move we made. Even when we shook hands, he never smiled.

Ignacio's features are deeply Native, Amerindian handsome,

intense, and unflinching. He is the kind of guy photographers love because he is good-looking and does everything with a confidence that exudes experience and knowledge. Which makes sense, after all: He grew up hunting, fishing, and driving boats at the edge of the world. And as we talked to the village president, Ignacio stood by, regarding us with a gravity beyond his years.

When you are in Monte Salvado the conversation may drift over the weather, if the fish have been biting, the river level, but inevitably and always it must eventually flow in one direction: What is the news of the tribes?

The day we landed, all was quiet. JJ and Victor smiled and shook hands with men they knew. Everyone had known JJ's father. Santiago Durand had been dead for years but his name still brought a smile to many people's faces. Victor, on the other hand, was his own living legend. He would pick up children and bark like a dog to send them running off with their friends. He was a rough hugger, a well-known logger, and a charismatic flirt with the ladies. Like Pico, he had one bum leg, a big personality, and a reputation as a reliable boat driver. He limped through the community high-fiving, bowing, hugging, smiling.

Ignacio never smiled. Not once. What he did do, though, when we asked if we could go farther upriver, was sternly explain that there was no way. We would be killed. JJ tried sweet-talking him, but Ignacio was an immovable force. He would not allow it. To drive his point home he invited us to a community house at the edge of the cliff, where he showed us arrows from the tribes that various people in the community had found and brought back.

They were seven feet tall. The ones for monkey hunting were tipped with a two-foot bamboo arrowhead made of carefully crafted, viciously sharp cured bamboo. The fletching was thick black feathers from a vulture or a Spix's guan. The rope was thin twine made from plant material. The shaft was river cane. All of it weighed almost nothing. The arrows were delicate if you bent them, but fired from a longbow, they could fly vast distances, and the two-foot blade would mean devastating injury to their target. It would be like being hit by something between a steak knife and a sword at high speed.

Ignacio knew these things because he had been in the forest when the tinamous went weird. He had seen loggers shot by arrows. He knew the tribes would think nothing of killing you, right here, right now. "Most times, though," he said, "the brothers come out and ask for tools or food. If we can give them some help, usually they will go away peacefully. If we can communicate with them we can help them, make things better. They have a very hard life."

Victor listened to this, rolling his eyes. "Yes, sometimes they are peaceful and sometimes they aren't." He shrugged theatrically.

"Usually they are peaceful," Ignacio said implacably.

"Yes, and when they aren't, they come in and surround the village and try to steal the women and kill the animals and take all the pots and machetes. That's what happened in my community."

"I know," said Ignacio.

JJ was holding one of the great arrows, deaf to everything we were discussing. His eyes were moving over the bamboo, the cordage, the feathers. He was hefting the arrow and finding its balance. He was trying to imagine so many mysterious things. His mind was twisting and winding deeper and deeper, trying to understand the minds behind the hands who wrought the thing he now held. "How do they make fire?"

"They have their ways," Ignacio said.

JJ turned to look at him. "So you don't really know."

Ignacio shrugged and invited us to his house. His wife,

Carla, and their children greeted us there. Their house was really just a roof on pillars with a closed-in sleeping area. The living space was outdoors, a junkyard of pots, dogs, chickens, children, hammers, machetes, and various other bare necessities of jungle life. Two young women with dark eyes and black hair worked diligently slicing and salting fish and placing it in the smoke of a smoldering fire. A howler monkey swung down from the rafters and climbed onto my shoulder.

In Monte Salvado we drank masato (crushed manioc), and dinner was an assortment of creatures. One bowl that was handed to me contained a base of rice and was topped with a slab of tapir, a whole piranha, the hand of a howler monkey, and the scaly foot of a yellow-footed tortoise. This last item you can use as a spoon to scoop up the rest because it is wide and hard. Ignacio and the others watched us eat, and after we had, we all smoked, sat around the fire, and spoke long into the night. As the Milky Way drifted across the sky and we got drunker and the stories grew more brutal, Ignacio never let more than the trace of a smile cross his face. He was always watching, always ready. It was like on some instinctual level he was just waiting for something to happen.

As it turned out, he was right. On October 23 of that same year, only a few months after our visit, Ignacio woke to a commotion and ran barefoot out of his thatched house, his wife trailing behind him. The rest of his community was already standing on the edge of the promontory, and everyone was looking across the river. Ignacio ran to join them and then he saw: The beach opposite was thick with them. Uncontacted. Naked. Wild-haired and war-painted. Bows in hand. They were gesturing, calling, agitated.

Women lifted their children and went into houses. Men loaded rifles and prepared. The elders of the village used the few words anyone knew in the Mashco Piro dialect, particularly "nomolé," which means "brother" but is commonly used as a hopeful "Don't shoot!" It became clear that the tribe wanted something, but they were speaking in capuchin dialect. Chirping and whistling. People who had phones took videos. There's footage.

The standoff went on for some time before the decision was made to send them an offering. Ignacio and his brother-in-law began loading plantains onto a dugout canoe. The river was low, so they cautiously waded out into the water. There was no one else in the community willing to risk it.

They pushed the boat the rest of the way, and the tribesmen eagerly began unloading the bananas. They carried them off and handed the heavy plantains to unseen others in the cover of the forest, still only using monkey calls. Clearly they'd made enough code out of the calls that they could operate. It was a defensive tactic to make sure that their language was not stolen by outsiders.

Ignacio was in the middle of the river motioning for them to return the canoe. His gestures were gentle, his posture submissive but strong. He knew that by creating a bond, by showing them friendship and fraternity, he could undo centuries of pain. He knew that if they would just stop being so scared, they would stop being so violent, and if they would be less violent, his community would help them. They could share with them. Learn from them. Ignacio knew this was a pivotal moment for everyone present.

He used his arms to request the return of the canoe as best he could with patience and calm. But suddenly the tension was rising. *Give it back,* he motioned. *Push the boat back to me.* The tribesmen were talking more rapidly now. Walking back and forth, they were becoming more agitated. Ignacio stood his ground, but his brother-in-law began to back up slowly. Something was happening. The tribe seemed to be telling him to come closer.

Looking back over his shoulder with a scowl, Ignacio real-

ized he was now alone in the middle of the river. Standing
between his community and the uncontacted tribe, who were
growing more and more excited. They seemed to be having an
argument. Behind him, he could feel his wife and friends and
community watching, but he didn't take his eyes off the tribe
for an instant. *Push the boat back,* he motioned. But the painted
men on the sand seemed to want him to come to them. Ignacio
shook his head. It was clear that the men on the beach were arguing now, and it was also clear that there were more people
out of sight in the jungle. The air was loud with their voices.
One of the men knelt and gave the canoe a shove so that it left
the sand and began drifting downstream.

Now annoyed, Ignacio swam to it and climbed up into it. He
lifted the heavy wooden paddle and began guiding the canoe
back toward the other shore.

That's when they drew on him.

One of the Mashco called out to him; he turned to see the
arrow on the string, a man pointing his bow directly at his chest,
tracking his movement.

He watched the arrow leave the string, and was quick enough
to dump himself over the side as it zipped past him. Swimming
below the surface, he knew that with pants on he couldn't swim
his fastest and so dolphin-kicked and discarded them. Each time
he came up he had just enough time to gasp a breath of air and
see another arrow being loosed straight at him. He dodged it
and fell backward into the water, swimming as far as he could.

When he came up for air the final time, he turned to see how
far he'd gotten and was met with an arrow to the face. The arrow's course through the air would have led straight through
Ignacio's left eye and out the back of his skull. It was only thanks
to instinctual reaction that his face moved by millimeters—just
enough so that the high-speed bamboo blade entered above his

temple and impacted the side of his head, ripping the skin off his skull and knocking him backward.

When he crawled up on the sand, the blood was pouring out of him. His hand went to his head and felt bone where there should have been hair. That was the last he knew before he collapsed.

Emergency satphone calls were made to government officials, and just hours later the heavy staccato of army helicopters thundered over the jungle. The banana leaves and palm trees thrashed as the rotors came down. Men in fatigues jumped out, armed and ready. The people of Monte Salvado rushed toward the helicopters—women carried babies; men carried the elderly. Ignacio by this point was deeply unconscious. His head was wrapped thick with gauze, but they couldn't stop the hemorrhaging. They lashed him to a stretcher while medics rushed to get fluids into him, fingers on his neck—checking to see if he still had a pulse.

THE
TURNING POINT

"**L**OOK!" JJ POINTED TO THE WEST, WHERE BLACK SMOKE WAS rising a thousand feet off the jungle. I was driving and turned the wheel of the Hilux off the dirt road and began bashing through the grass. We were driving across farmland that had been cleared a year earlier. But the blaze in the distance was this year's burning. The pickup truck came skidding to a halt, and we burst out of the doors.

In my memory of crossing that field, I hear the soundtrack to *Interstellar*—music to accompany the sensation of running at full speed toward a life-and-death moment. The farmers were burning the fields, and it was dry enough that the fire had caught on to the edge of the jungle.

Towering trees and palms and vines were all thrashing in the updraft of the inferno. A troop of spider monkeys leaped through the branches as they fled. A kaleidoscopic explosion of macaws came screaming out of the branches. We ran until we hit the furnace heat of the blaze, which stopped us dead. The shock and awe of what we were seeing sucked the air right out of our lungs. Even at a hundred meters, the heat was so great that our clothing was melting to our skin. The ground was an obstacle course of fallen trees and branches. The great jungle lay dying on the ground.

The bodies of frogs and snakes and small mammals lay smoldering in the ashes. Many other animals would have gone into the trees for safety, into their holes and burrows, only to be cooked alive. The charred arm of a howler monkey reached for the sky out of one pile of debris. We penetrated as far as we could go. Trying to recover any survivors. But the flames had already razed it all. At the edge of the forest the blaze was seventy feet tall, ripping upward in a drastic crackle and roar of biblical proportions. It was like the firebombing of Dresden in World War II, when the firestorm created winds strong enough to uproot trees and suck people into the blaze. The wind was sucking us inward.

JJ's eyes were red and tearing, filled with smoke and desperation. "This can't keep happening! What are they doing!" He was shielding his face from the scorching air and wiping the tears from his eyes. He screamed in wild rage as an eruption of ashes and a rush of flames muted the sound. I cried openly as I watched him. The image of him there in the savage flames, his body twisted with grief and face streaked in ashes and tears, is something that will haunt me forever. I saw the pain of a lifetime, the depth of his frustration at watching what he loved burn, the brain-damaging reality that we as a species are sleepwalking right to the edge of extinction. If only others could see that we are a global society, that we are waging war against ourselves and our future. I saw JJ's open heart: the warrior, the protector, the human at a loss to stop the flames that scorched his soul.

Each tree could be home to thousands of species. We also knew that the drastic scale and gargantuan height of this single blaze were nothing compared to the fact that all across the Amazon at that very moment, fires like this were incinerating the jungle. It wasn't just our river, it was the entire Amazon basin. The Amazon was burning. It was happening before our eyes.

And no matter how much we cared, if we went any closer, we would be burned to death. The wind kicked the flames so they surrounded us, and for a moment we were running side by side. Running for our lives. Trees were exploding around us, cannon blasts that sent splinters into the swirl of ash and smoke. Both of us hit the deck, coughing and burned. We stood up and ran faster. There were holes in our pants, and the soles of our shoes were melting. We finally made it out into the grass.

JJ walked away, swearing in Spanish. I turned my camera on myself and began filming. My face was flushed and my eyes were full of tears. The ashes swirled through the air like snow. In the heartrending tragedy of the moment, I explained to the camera exactly what we were seeing: "We are losing the Amazon Rainforest, *every day*."

===

On a summer day just a few months before Ignacio would be shot in the head by the Mashco Piro, and about six weeks after JJ and I had witnessed the fire, I woke with a start earlier than usual. I was home in upstate New York, in a little apartment I was renting in Kingston. The sound of the phone buzzing was making it through even from the other room. I stumbled out of bed, staggered to the refrigerator, and put my hand on top of it. Every night I would put my phone on top of the fridge, but it wasn't there.

The buzzing was coming from the floor. I lifted the phone and saw a number I didn't recognize. I noticed that while the battery had been at 100 percent the night before, for some reason, it was only on 2 percent now. That was puzzling. Also puzzling was that I could swear I saw there were 30,000 notifications on the phone. That had to be wrong . . . but I didn't have time to think about it. The voice on the line was asking questions rapidly.

"Are you Paul Rosolie? Are you the one who posted the viral video about the fires in the Amazon rainforest?"

"Who is this?" I said, tripping over the couch.

It was somebody from MSNBC and they wanted to know if I could be in the studio within the next few hours. I was still completely confused. With one eye open, I did my best to keep up.

"Sorry, can you explain to me exactly what happened? And what exactly you want?"

"Absolutely: The video you posted last night from inside the Amazon fires has gone completely viral in a global way. It's horrifying! And by far the most personal footage from the emergency unfolding from within the Amazon Rainforest. If you're in New York State, we'd like to get you into the studio at 30 Rock as soon as possible to be on the morning shows. Are you in the state?"

I didn't have time to answer before another call came in. Hold. Hello? It was another news network, with the same question. With a lot of fumbling and still rubbing my eyes, I gradually put together what had happened.

The night before, friends all over the globe had been bombarding me with links to articles: Had I seen the news? The Amazon Rainforest was on fire.

Fire in the rainforest was not usually news—but this year, 2019, was different.

Some forest burning is part of their natural cycle. California forests, like where the redwoods and the sequoias are, experience regular intervals of natural forest fire that are part of the ecosystems' cycle. But in the Amazon Rainforest, fire is simply not part of the program. Fires in the Amazon occur because humans cut it down, let the trees bake in the tropical sun, and then set fire to it all. Fires in the Amazon are why we have lost almost 20 percent of the basin, why CO_2 is pouring into the atmosphere, why we are losing species faster than ever before.

But in 2019, something new happened. The government in Brazil at the time was encouraging people to go out and colonize Amazonia. Not just to inhabit it, but to expand and destroy and to carve further roads into some of the uncharted areas that make up so much of Brazil's territory. The burning and the cutting and the destruction increased with such rapaciousness that the fires were enormous.

The level of fire in the Amazon in 2019 surpassed anything recorded in the previous five years. But even then, human-caused fires in the Amazon are not usually newsworthy. They happen every year. Some years are worse than others. What really made the fires global news in 2019 was that people were able to see them.

Smoke from the biggest fire was blown eastward over São Paulo and Rio de Janeiro, and people began taking pictures of the sky. It looked like a postapocalyptic nightmare, purple and black. They posted photos explaining that the Amazon Rainforest was in a state of emergency. Those photos were picked up across social media and made their way to news platforms, environmental organizations reported on the rates of deforestation and the increase in fires over the course of a week, and outlet after outlet published articles. Suddenly it seemed like all anyone was talking about, across the globe, was "the Amazon fires."

And so, after reading all the articles my friends had sent, while sitting on my couch with Gowri in my little apartment in Kingston, New York, I had opened my phone and scrolled to a video that I had taken just a month and a half earlier. At the start of the fire season. There I was in the flames, with tears in my eyes, begging for help: "We are losing the Amazon Rainforest!" It ended with the now-infamous line: "Welcome to the fucking Anthropocene."

Now on the phone in my boxers at 7 A.M., I was recalling all this, and that I had actually posted the video. I had never posted anything that raw before; I had never said "fuck" on Instagram before. I had been unsure about whether to put it out there, but I had been so emotional, so fed up with seeing the windbag news articles from the night before, that in the end I had indeed set it free. It had gone out to the world just before I placed my phone on the fridge for the night and went to bed.

With my phone still on 2 percent battery, I was looking for a charger but bumping into things because I couldn't look away from the notifications that were flying in. The phone was buzzing and chirping and whizzing and moving in ways I had never seen before. For the first time ever, I had put rage and honesty and profanity in unedited form onto my feed, and apparently it had gone viral.

The rest of the morning was a blur. I called my parents and found out that I didn't really own a suit that fit. Brushing my teeth in the mirror, I had a hard time reconciling that I was going to go on TV with this unkempt disaster of a haircut. But there was no time to think. Within an hour, there was a big black Escalade outside of my apartment, and I ran down the stairs and climbed in.

When you get to the main lobby of 30 Rockefeller Plaza in Manhattan, it feels like the center of the world. Just in front of the skating rink with the world flags all around, you walk through the golden doors and into a cathedral of art deco magnificence. As I entered with my ill-fitting suit over my shoulder, I looked up at the grand imagery that adorns the interior of the lobby of 30 Rock.

The artwork is impressive and shocking, as is the building itself. When you look up, you see spiraling biplanes and great pieces of timber being hewn from the earth by muscular men. There are chains and locomotives, rocks and workers and slaves. It's all mystifying and tremendous, plastered over the vast ceilings and expensive walls of the building. It is the creation of

Spanish artist Josep Maria Sert: a sixteen-foot-high and forty-one-foot-long mural called *American Progress*. It is a masterful piece with powerful allegorical scenes, reminiscent of a da Vinci hybridized with a kind of Empire State Manifest Destiny. Man's struggle with nature, and with God and himself and the raw materials that life and society and our world are made of. Trees and animals, the human form, muscle and might, Abraham Lincoln, slaves and masters, and the magnitude of the powerful play.

But I was only able to appreciate the scene for moments before an intern met me, got me a key card, and escorted me past security and into an elevator. I was ushered into makeup, where two large Black women descended upon me to fluff and curate. I tried my very best to tell them I wanted to look natural. "Oh, honey, but you have such bags under your eyes." The other one laughed and tried to put blush on me. I let the one lady buff out the bags but told the blush lady I was going on raw.

"And you just gonna leave your hair like that?"

Pretty soon, I was sitting at a news desk. I was on a panel with Bill McKibben—somebody whose books I had read all through college. One of the environmental leaders of our generation. Someone with a clipboard and a headset began the countdown, and suddenly we were on. For the next three weeks, I would be in different rooms all around the country. Local news, various other outlets. I would hit CBS, ABC, NBC, CNN—pretty much all of the major networks.

For a few weeks, 30 Rock, that incredible building, would become a place I regularly visited. A place where I came to know the people at the doors. A place to which I had my own key card. I gradually learned how it all worked. It was exciting being there. It was exciting seeing how the news is made. How it's really just a black room with a lot of wires on the floor and a single, brightly lit stage and a desk and some people intensely focused on what's coming next. During the commercial breaks, they have time to touch up their makeup, make some quick remarks, and have a sip of coffee before patting their teeth to make sure it didn't leave a stain, and then they're reading the cards for the upcoming segment. It's no joke, and it moves fast and it reaches the whole country. This is where it all gets made. It felt like the central hub.

Sometimes it would be 1 A.M. when I finished work and hit the streets. Manhattan after dark. The street cleaners in the garbage trucks. The steamy breath of the night. The lights and the people. The city that I'm from. So different from the jungle. And so much a part of my bones and DNA.

The next morning I would wake up at five for a workout, to make sure I didn't look tired on the air. I would try to get control of my hair and fight off the makeup ladies, who by now had become good friends, and soon I got the hang of having my talking points ready. There's no reason to stress. When people ask you a question, you just tell them the answer. And for me, I found that that answer came with full enthusiasm and without any errors, so long as I just focused on that alone.

It was a new skill, and I was acquiring it fast. I learned how to avoid things that I didn't know. If a newscaster asked me what the Brazilian president's policies were on deforestation in the '90s, I would tell them that I worked in Peru, that my expertise was simple, but that the entire basin was important. It was like a boxing match. They tried to get you off topic. You had to back up and bring them in. Go back to what you know, to regain control. The other thing I learned was to stay in my lane. I'm not an expert on geopolitics. I don't know about the policies of various Latin American presidents. What I know is that I've worked with the Indigenous people for years, and they're losing territory and it's being burned and it's not sustainable, and that wildlife and forest are crucial for life on Earth.

I kept using the Carl Sagan quote: "Anything else you're interested in is not going to happen if you can't breathe the air and drink the water."

New York. Then out to L.A. Then some cities in between. Catch a nap in a greenroom. Jump up, put on the show, and then go back to sleep. Hotel rooms. Vending machine dinners. All this publicity was exhilarating, but it didn't pay a penny. In fact, it cost me quite a bit to keep up with it.

In Seattle, I had a long conversation with a woman at a hotel bar. The person next to us had a copy of *USA Today* in front of them, and on the front page was an article I had written, the title in bold: "I've seen the Amazon rainforest fires. They're a warning from the Ghost of Climate Future."

On the last afternoon that I would be in 30 Rock, one of the elevators was down, and so I took a service elevator. In spite of my pushing the lobby button, the elevator went up, high up. It let me out into a strange hallway. I walked out of the elevator and the doors closed behind me. I tried to use my key card to get them to open again so I could go down, but it said I didn't have access. I tried finding another set of elevators, but the floor seemed to be completely deserted. So I returned to the original elevators and swiped my key card again. This time red warning lights flashed. *You do not have access.*

I was so tired and so burned-out that I really couldn't think of what to do. And so I walked idly. In some large meeting hall, there was an old man with an old-school newsboy cap on, whistling across the great spaces. Bob Dylan's "The Times They Are A-Changin'."

I told him about the elevator and the key card and he never looked up from his mopping. "Just go find the corridor and keep going, you'll get there." I told him I had looked down the corridor and it seemed completely black, and I didn't want to get in trouble.

"You just do like I said, and keep walking. Don't worry about a thing and you'll get there eventually."

At the end of the long, dark corridor was a brilliant beam of light coming through the crack in the doorway. When I reached the door and opened it, I had to shield my eyes. It was a gigantic empty room that had floor-to-ceiling windows on one side. The view of Manhattan was simply breathtaking, the rays of afternoon sun flooding through. With my jacket over my arm, I walked slowly toward the glass. I knew I wasn't supposed to be where I was, but there didn't seem to be anyone around. For a moment, it didn't feel like there was anyone in the entire world. It seemed like I was above everything. Looking down on the city I had been born in. Everything was gold and light, the sun warm on my skin. I got this swelling feeling. Something was different. Something had changed. Without realizing it, without having time to analyze it, in the last few weeks, I had become the spokesperson for the Amazon Rainforest to America. An overwhelming and glowing sense of purpose came over me: Everything was going to be okay. Suddenly, and for the first time, I had found the path.

It felt like a hug from God.

≡

The media of those few weeks did a lot to rehabilitate the damage from my 2014 disaster. I felt like I was finally shedding my skin, ready to start over in mind and heart. It was time to get back on track. That clip went so viral, it was hard to believe. It was seen all over the world. Europe, South America, Asia, the whole planet. The number of people who shared the video was staggering, in the high millions, many of them names I knew— famous names. I was in the car when my cousin Michael called me with news that sounded impossible: Joe Rogan had even shared the video on his personal Instagram. I couldn't help but wonder: All the videos I'd made, all the words I'd written, and it had been a moment of filthy, desperate reality caught on a phone camera that had grabbed the attention of the world. In the days after Rogan shared it, the numbers on the video skyrocketed like they were never going to stop.

Jane Goodall and I had kept in contact over the years, and her words were ever helpful and encouraging. In the emails we exchanged I kept her abreast of things, the current fires and Junglekeepers. Of the controversy around the anaconda special from years earlier, she said, "I was not angry, but disappointed. I can see how it all happened—and maybe it was for the good. It did at least bring the issue to millions of people, even if the documentary was not what you wished. Anyway, when I warned you—even if I had been more forceful it wouldn't have made any difference. At the time you were sure everything would work out just as you wanted. And anyway, you had signed the contract! So now I guess I feel almost like a parent whose child has crept back to the fold!!!"

In the weeks that followed what had been a tornado of activity, many people reached out. Most of them had grand offers but really just wanted access. One guy offered to donate in the high five figures if I would connect him to JJ. Another one, a millionaire inventor and entrepreneur, offered to fund a pan-Amazonian sprinkler system to put out the fires. These people didn't understand. They were only interested in selfish gain. The guy who wanted JJ's contact wanted to go on adventures. The one who wanted to build sprinklers (moron) just wanted industrial contracts (and didn't seem to get that to install subterranean piping across the continent he'd have to rip apart the jungle!). Some people called offering to help with reforestation projects. Many offered firefighting gear and hoses. I had to explain again and again, as I had on the news, that the Amazon does not burn naturally. Discussing how to extinguish fires in Amazonia is like discussing how to cure lymphoma with a Band-Aid—the only way to cure the disease and solve the problem is to stop the forest from being cut in the first place.

At that time, I was fielding all my own correspondence. It was just me. I had my email and my phone. I didn't even have a working website. Being on the news for a few weeks meant that there was an incredible amount of attention coming my way. I was spending more energy than I had. I was traveling or on the phone all day. Mohsin and I tried to divide up the work of communicating, but we didn't have the systems; we simply didn't know how to deal with it all. We were fishermen in a dinghy out in the ocean with a hundred lines in the water, each one of them with a mysterious fish or a piece of garbage. But how to reel them all in? How not to tangle the lines? How on Earth not to capsize the boat? You pray for rain, you have to deal with the mud, and sometimes opportunity comes in such an avalanche, it can bury you.

But amidst the garbage that came in with the media blitz came a diamond in disguise in the form of a woman who reached out and did a very good interview for a small publication called *Never Apart*. A thoughtful, thorough piece. She said she worked with someone I absolutely had to talk to. She said her boss was a billionaire who was the CEO of a company called Lightspeed and was very interested in making real change and supporting environmental initiatives. I told her I'd be happy to talk to him. The man's name was Dax Dasilva, and one night he asked me to join him on a video call.

I happened to be at Mohsin's house at the time. While we had both continued spending weeks and months at a time in the Amazon, and launched all kinds of expeditions, Mohsin had also managed to meet and marry the girl of his dreams, a woman named Katlin. He had long ago shed his parents' hopes of his being a doctor. Mohsin had committed 100 percent to the plan we had hatched. He and Katlin got married in 2015, when he and I only had our dreams with JJ and a Junglekeepers-shaped framework, but no income whatsoever. That didn't deter Katlin. When we spoke of the future, she could see it too. And so she and Mohsin went all in and eloped. Soon after, their house in Virginia became a place where I spent extended time when I was in the U.S. And it was during one of these long stays that I set up in the fireplace room with my laptop and prepared to talk to Dax for the first time.

We all exchanged looks of anticipation. Katlin and Mohsin were watching from the doorway as I signed on. Dax was with his friend, the woman who had interviewed me, and suggested we all pour a drink. I remember catching Mohsin's eyes over the screen: This seemed like more bullshit. This guy just wanted to talk. He wanted to know all about Junglekeepers. But I kept talking, kept drinking, and played along, even if this would probably go nowhere. Katlin and Mohsin rolled their eyes as they tired of listening. I stayed in that room talking long into the night, certain I was wasting my time.

Dax said he'd be in touch soon.

THE BURDEN
OF DREAMS

"**L**ISTEN," MY DAD SAID ONE DAY WHEN HE WAS DROPPING me off, "whether things pick up or stay the same, or if you have to eventually jump ship and, you know, get a real job . . . we love you no matter what."

I closed my eyes tight against the nightmare of the moment. But it had been coming for some time. My parents had become delicate when they asked me how things were going. People were talking, I could feel it. At twenty-two, following your dreams is romantic, but at thirtysomething and broke, people start to worry. I had started to worry. What had once seemed brave now looked foolish.

Churchill called it the Black Dog. In *A Little Life,* by Hanya Yanagihara, they are the glowing-eyed hounds that are always chasing Jude. The pack of predatory thoughts that stalk you— following, hungry to drag you down to hell, through the Swamps of Sadness. They say that doubt has killed more dreams than failure ever has. For so many years I had rallied past the fear and surrounded myself with books and quotes and songs and a vision that all started to look rotted and old, like a bad joke. But by this point I felt I had some real evidence that I needed to reassess my life.

Earlier I mentioned that some folks had agreed to help us

form Junglekeepers. Well, they had followed through to an extent, despite the fact that they seemed to want all the credit. Regardless, with their help, for a few years Junglekeepers chugged along with a little funding and a few rangers. We bought our first parcels of land and were officially now protecting forest. But there was something wrong.

Somewhere along the way, the people who had promised to help us had woven themselves into the board of directors of Junglekeepers, which meant they could call the shots. They weren't kind people helping us get closer to our dream as much as they were grabbing power for themselves. They seemed more than happy to take the playbook from me and JJ. To listen to our hard-won wisdom and experience, and then go execute those plans and cut us out of the implementation. Outnumbered, we no longer had agency or control. JJ and Mohsin and I, as well as our chef-turned-paperwork-wrangler, Roy Riquelme—all of us who had started the dream—were slowly plunged into a purgatory of confusion as people from other countries vied to take credit for the work we had put our lives into making real.

The injustice was almost intolerable. JJ was furious with me. It wasn't supposed to be like this. I had done it all wrong. But there was no way out, there was nothing we could do. We just had to live with it. It nearly broke us as friends. Somehow I had assumed good people would come. That if you devoted yourself to saving the forest and the river and the animals, the universe would rally to help. But once again, things weren't turning out the way I had so badly hoped they would.

Our experience and years of toil were being robbed every day. The world seemed like a vicious and unfair place where everyone was just trying to eat one another.

Cigarettes became a crutch I leaned on. I could write poetry about those little sparks of warm comfort. As things grew darker and colder, I found myself drawing deeper and savoring each one, like a little act of suicide, like a gun to your temple, your eyes closed, and just a smoky sigh of relief, like it was all over.

But it wasn't over. I was still in the world and things were becoming more and more nightmarish for me every day. The depression I felt was like a tidal wave of darkness. Any resilience I had ever had was blasted away in the shock of the depths I sank to.

When Covid-19 hit the world, I was in India with Gowri and her family. I was emaciated physically and mentally. The pressure of continuing on with a relationship I knew was over was causing a dissonance that was tearing me apart. I wasn't just losing Gowri, I was losing all of our friends, her wonderful family, I was losing the India that had become my home. I walked around the places I loved, spent time with the people I loved, my family, feeling like a traitor and a failure and a liar. I was garbage. I was going to let them all down, lose everything. I knew it was going to happen. Gowri and I were in the cold ending stages, people whose relationship had ended long ago but were still together. We began finding subtle but penetrating ways of hurting each other.

When the news cycle first picked up the pandemic, I remember calling my dad and telling him I would ride it out in India. When they canceled the NBA season and bit by bit the world began accelerating toward an unknown tilt, he called me back. *Come home. Get home.* "You know how *Independence Day* and all those disaster movies start? This feels like that. This isn't going to pass quickly. Get home while you can."

I just made it.

At home, like everyone else, we were in limbo. From the perspective of a New Yorker, the view was grim. There were reports of bodies piling up outside the hospitals. Everyone was on lockdown. Soon the news of police brutality and the race war popped off. No one was going anywhere.

In Peru, JJ and everyone else were going through it. Roy's mom and daughter and wife all had Covid, and Puerto was in a state of emergency. Peru would quickly become the hardest-hit country of the whole pandemic. People were dying. For JJ and Roy, their loved ones were dropping all around them. Don Ignacio, the shaman, died. I called Lee and Mohsin and we emptied the Tamandua bank account to send money. Oxygen tanks were in short supply and vitally high demand, and our friends needed them for their families. At one point Roy's mother, wife, and daughter were all critical and needed oxygen. The local suppliers hiked the price by 1,000 percent, so that a single tank of oxygen could cost hundreds of dollars. Later, even thousands.

Mohsin and Lee and I agreed there was no point in holding back now, this was family. We sent them everything we had.

It was an afterthought that while people were dying in the city, loggers and invaders were charging out into the jungle to cut and burn as much as they could. On a good day the western Amazon is a lawless place, but in those early days of Covid, with the world distracted and society on its knees, the destroyers went flying out into the forest. Giant excavators called forrestales were used to bulldoze the jungle, slashing new roads across the face of Amazonia. I remembered Pico describing the first time he had seen one.

"Es un demonio," he said with the darkness of the memory in his eyes. "It's a like a demon. They can crush a forest, flatten the trees. They go right through and destroy everything."

Cut off from Peru, terrified of the precipice of divorce and losing half the people I loved, and being, like everyone else, captive to the rapidly diminishing orbit of the early days of the Covid-19 pandemic, I was back at my parents' house, thirty-three years old, with no job, no money, no plan, no hope.

I'm an Italian American Catholic kid: My people don't get

divorced. That's other people. We don't do that. I loved G and
her family so much, but knew it was long past due. I had failed.
Everyone had been right when we had started—we were too
young. I'd become the bad guy in her life, the deadbeat husband. Peter Pan of the Jungle. The boy who couldn't grow up.
No better than some forty-year-old idiot still trying to be Indiana Jones. I just couldn't give up the childhood dream. And because of that, I had not been able to give us a place to live, and
living with parents and always out of backpacks had taken its
toll. Months apart. The transgressions, the fights, the resentment. All because I couldn't do what everyone else did: buckle
down and just work, make a life, and do good.

Now, knowing that it was only a matter of time before I
worked up the courage or ran out of sanity and said the words,
I was going to ruin her life officially.

I hated myself.

For days on end I lay in bed in complete existential agony. I
was rolling back and forth in pain that I couldn't place or describe but filled my being through my bones and eyeballs and
very soul.

The day my marriage ended was sunny. I was sitting in the
car on the phone with G, who was in India. I just sat there crying. I said again and again that I just couldn't do it anymore. My
heart was broken for us, for our mothers, all our friends, the
smiles at our wedding. The pain was indescribable and all-
consuming. It's the worst I've ever felt.

In the weeks that followed, I had to come to terms with the
fact that if the jungle was no longer an option, I had to find a
way to live. I had no money. None. I looked on job websites.
What could I do? It was pathetic. I had reached rock bottom. It
was time to cash out. I had once thrived on people telling me
they were so proud that I was "living my dream." I had de-

ceived myself by pretending to be something I wasn't. If you try to fake it till you make it but don't ever get there, you're just a loser.

W. Somerset Maugham has a terrifying little subplot in his book *The Razor's Edge* where he describes a man who spent his life trying to make it as a writer. Only he never does. His family is poor and he dies a failure. "Many are called but few are chosen," quips one character. The words haunted me. I had been so stupid. It was so true. How many failed rock stars are there out there working at coffee shops at this very moment? Do we not take any warning from the fact that all the frozen dead bodies on Mount Everest were once highly driven, wealthy, and fully possessed with the vision of their own success? Now they're just corpses in expensive jackets. Not everything works out in life, and the longer you stay on the wrong train, the more expensive it is to get back home.

I drove to the dreary parking lot of a Dunkin' Donuts, in the car, the only privacy I had. I called Mohsin, feeling like Judas. How did I tell him that the things he had seen in me were just posturing? That I wasn't going anywhere. Or maybe at one time I had been. But now I'd arrived. The verdict was in: I couldn't save the Amazon, I couldn't be a good husband, I couldn't keep the team together. I wasn't a junglekeeper, I was just a guy who hadn't been smart enough to figure out what everyone else had.

I called Mohsin full of shame, and beat around the bush for some time. "Hey, have you heard from Pico? He's gone dark."

Mohsin said he hadn't heard anything.

"Shit," I said, "I'm worried about him."

"Me too," said Mohsin. We talked about JJ and Roy and what else we could send. We were out of money. The bank account was empty. Our "business" was travel, no one was going anywhere for the foreseeable future, and the people we loved needed cash more than we did. Peru was a disaster. Panic was in the air; the world was changing. It could be years before we went back, if we ever did.

"Listen," I said with my eyes closed. "I gotta talk to you about something." I don't even remember what I said. But I knew well that Mohsin had bet his life on our dream. He had committed himself to Tamandua and Junglekeepers. He'd proudly told friends and family that we were working to save a river. He'd even found Katlin, married her on nothing more than the promise of what we were building. I was about to let him down massively. I told him I wasn't who he thought I was, that I was terrified by having no plan or path, that the weight of the divorce was just too heavy. That it had all been for nothing.

Like a good friend he listened.

Every now and then he'd give me a "Yeah" or a stoic "Okay." And worst of all: "Sure."

I told him I was hanging it all up, changing course and going to get a job.

There was silence on the other side of the phone.

Then he began.

"Listen to me very carefully," he said. I grimaced. "Whatever you think you just said, wasn't it. I don't want to hear shit like that ever again in my life. I'm just going to do what you always ask me to do and tell you straight. Even if you are so fucked right now that you're ready to lie down, bleed out, and die, you have too many people who rely on you. You don't GET to die. Get up. You better get up. What happened to pulling the cord to start the boat? You better remember who you are and stop this shit. I'm serious. I reject whatever pathetic side narrative bullshit you are stuck in and delete this from the record. Access denied. I'm your best friend, man, so I'm gonna do you a solid and never tell anyone about this call, 'cause it's embarrassing. Don't you dare tell me shit like this ever again."

He hung up.

Something a lot of people underestimate is the seductive comfort of rock bottom. I was done fighting. I lay in bed for more days. I had reached the end. I remember sitting up all night, tears in my eyes, sitting in the dark by the fire in the woods, lighting cigarettes one after another.

Then the phone rang.

It was Dax Dasilva. "Hey, Paul!" He sounded excited.

He told me that he'd thought long and hard and read through everything I'd sent him, and he wanted to do it.

"Do what?" I said flatly.

"I want to make this happen. Let's save the river!"

Mayday! Mayday!

I had been so low that this conversation seemed surreal. Dax's energy was jarring, and the sudden rising sensation I was feeling was fast enough to give me the bends.

Dax and I talked for over an hour.

What I hadn't at first realized was that Dax's story, while so different from mine, had brought him to a place in life where he felt inspired, capable, and called to do something profound for the Earth.

He understood some fundamental truths. One was that the river was a race against time. If we didn't protect it now, we would lose it forever. There was no replacing those ancient trees and complex ecosystems. Two, JJ and Roy and Mohsin and I all had been doing this work for free for most of our lives. We were not just poor, we were poor squared, poor times the amount of years we'd put into this without having enough to even buy groceries. He constructed an operating plan for Junglekeepers—ranger pay, land purchase budgets, and even a salary for me and JJ. I was spinning. I had never had a salary. The life I chose had come with zero guarantees, no paychecks or medical insurance.

The thought of having enough to live on was almost beyond comprehension. It all was. On that miraculous phone call, Dax agreed to give us a ten-year commitment.

Dax said that he had grown up being a conservationist. He had seen brutal clear-cuts in Canada, and now that he'd amassed a fortune of his own, he wanted to use it to help conservationists around the world. He wanted Junglekeepers to be his first partner. He wanted to start a new organization, Age of Union, that would assemble a kind of superhero team of conservationists. He knew his funding could help struggling projects over the line to become effective. He could help them go from start-ups to real initiatives, from defense to offense, from dreams to reality. He said he was also looking at the Sea Shepherd Conservation Society, as well as inspiring projects protecting orangutans in Borneo and other places. He had plans of reaching out to Jane Goodall and supporting her crucial, global-scale environmental work. Basically, Dax was using the fact that he'd won capitalism to do what everyone always wished the billionaires would do: Use it to make the world a better place. He was assembling the conservation X-Men, and I was his first recruit. I hung up the phone and my whole world was spinning.

I rubbed my eyes. If I had heard correctly, Dax had just committed millions of dollars to Junglekeepers. I had a job. We had a future. Everything had just changed.

All I could think was *I gotta call JJ!*

I called JJ from New York and told him about my meeting with Dax, and he didn't believe a word of it. I think that after the last few years, he was loath to believe anything. Especially this. It just sounded too good to be true, so he dismissed it. Besides, there was something far more important unfolding.

No one had heard from Pico for weeks, and we had finally realized why. He had broken his right leg—the same one that had been crushed by a falling tree when he was sixteen—some months earlier, and in the open-air, developing world excuse for a hospital that they had in Puerto Maldonado, they had drilled his bones back together with a piece of steel and a bunch of screws that on the X-ray look like something from an Erector set. But since then his condition had worsened. An infection had set in, and gradually the leg had turned green. Pico had spent months in agony. He begged for someone to cut off the leg. He said it was going to kill him. He was certain of it. And when JJ sent the photo of the leg, I remember gasping and holding the wall.

Pico's right leg below the knee had become black with pus-filled lesions. The leg was no longer truly living. If there was any blood flowing, it was just barely.

If there was one advantage to doing all the media that I had done by this point, it was that I had a very large Instagram following. Mohsin and Lee and I arranged a fundraiser and promoted it on social media. We needed about $17,000 to send Pico to Lima for an emergency amputation. Incredibly, as soon as we began posting, people reached out from all over the world. Everyone knew Pico from my book *Mother of God*.

The notes were overwhelming. It was like something from *It's a Wonderful Life*. With each donation came personalized messages: "Let's get Pico better soon!"; "Viva the Mad Motorista!!"; "WE LOVE PICO!"; "You all are doing such inspiring work!"; "Thankful to be able to help!"

It took about a month of full-time work posting and responding to raise the money to cover Pico's expenses. During that time, I kept working with Dax to continue formalizing the budget and the plan and the vision of Junglekeepers. We set up a system that involved turning loggers and gold miners into rangers, and came up with a budget for that. The idea was not to take away their livelihoods, but instead provide them with a better, safer, more profitable and secure one. To help them build a future. We'd need to get those rangers proper pay, salaries, and health insurance, and make it all official. We'd also need to have a strategic framework to rescue areas of forest that were being burned. I explained to Dax that JJ, as the guy on the ground, would have the best and most comprehensive understanding of how to construct that part. Most important, though, Dax did the unimaginable and followed through on his promise to include salaries for me, JJ, and Roy. He also dispatched an initial emergency budget so that Mohsin and I could document the fresh wave of fires that were sweeping the Amazon that year, and agreed that Mohsin and I would be on the first plane to Peru.

The moment we reached our goal in fundraising for his leg, Pico was sent to Lima and the doctors amputated. The transformation was immediate. He instantly felt relief and became healthy. The doctor told us that a few more days and he certainly would have died.

I can only imagine the pain he must've been through. And I can only hold my heart in deep gratitude for all the people all over the world that had read my book, come to love Pico, and freely given money to support someone they had never met. They saved his life.

Dax wasn't kidding at all. He knew how to run major companies. There were pictures of him celebrating his company going public at the New York Stock Exchange. He wanted me and Mohsin on the ground photographing the fires that were undoubtedly taking place in November. But out of sight, out of mind—this was 2020, and the Amazonia news blitz of 2019 had been long forgotten. The jungle was once again burning, but the world wasn't talking about it this year. It was the height of Covid. That's how we knew Dax was on our level: He wanted to show the world what was happening to the jungle no matter what. So we masked up, faked some Covid tests (the real ones were impossible to schedule at this point), and were just about the only people on that plane. The Lima airport was empty. It felt like we were going to some bizarro version of the Peru we had once known.

But one thing was for sure: For the first time ever, it was game on!

THE
JAGUAR'S EYES

＝

MOHSIN AND I BURST OUT OF THE PLANE AND ONTO THE
street, shedding our multiple face coverings and gasping warm
jungle air. We met Roy and JJ in town, where we all hugged
tightly. Roy had lost a lot of weight. JJ had gone through an
even greater transformation. His jet-black hair had become
peppered with gray. The wrinkles around his eyes had deepened
and his cheeks were sunken. He wore glasses now.

We held a four-way hug, looking deep into one another's
eyes, smiling and touching the parts of one another that had
changed. I ran my hand through JJ's hair. Mohsin patted Roy's
shrunken belly. What we felt in that moment was an overwhelming sense of kinship and fraternity. Covid had brought
them right to the edge, but their families were alive, and we had
done everything we could to help.

We returned for the first time in almost a year to the research
station at Las Piedras. Even JJ had not been there. Everything
had been on lockdown, there was a police-enforced curfew, and
he didn't dare leave his family. We all were comically pale,
squinting in the sun, elated to be back out on our river.

At the station, I explained the funding that Dax had given
and how it would be spent. We talked nearly all night. We had
to build a ranger station, we had to hire more rangers, and we

had to come up with a comprehensive plan. For the first time, the dreaming was over and now the tactics had to begin.

At dawn we drove upriver. We all knew exactly where the ranger station should go.

We parked the boat at the mouth of the Loretillo stream. This was the first stream JJ and I had ever explored. This one was still untouched. When you think of green jungle, when you think of wild places, this is where you are thinking of. A crystal stream that winds through endless miles of trackless jungle. The vines and the treetops meet overhead to create a hallway of beautiful emerald brilliance. We knew this would be the crown jewel of what we were protecting, the home base for our entire operation.

That day we hiked into the forest, and with tape measures and bits of red flagging, marked out the location where the ranger station would go. There was an energy of excitement. JJ, with his gaunt salt-and-pepper look, was more handsome than ever. He had aged, but he had aged well. He was happy and dedicated, and I could see his heart was clear. A few years earlier, he had started a new family with a woman named Julie, and they had a son named Tristan. Lockdown had given them time to solidify and deepen their bond; they had survived as a family and come out stronger. JJ had a new life. The one thing he had been missing was the forest. For JJ, being kept out of the forest and stuck in the city had been torture. He was beaming the whole time we worked. Thrilled to be back with his boys. It made my heart swell to watch him.

Next, we headed out to assess the nearby deforestation we had been watching on satellite imagery for almost a year. If the imagery was any indicator, then what we were about to see was absolute devastation. We went along the main river then cut a few miles into the forest to the north.

What we found when we arrived ripped our hearts out. The

primary forest had been reduced to black ash. Great trees lay on the ground. Trees that we loved. Kapok trees. Mahogany trees, big old strangler figs, and Brazil nut trees. The invaders hadn't even used the expensive timber. They were interested in clearing land. To them, the jungle and all its biodiversity were nothing more than space. Space to be burned. And once it was burned, they could grow their crops. Their pathetic crops. Yuca. Papaya. The bottom of the market, things that sold for practically nothing. These people had come here and destroyed something priceless. We hiked through it all, Mohsin's camera shutter snapping. We had learned by now that showing people the reality of the threats we face is crucial, and so we continued documenting— even though it felt like there were knives in our hearts.

We walked through field after field of destroyed forest. When one ended, there would be a little section of jungle, and then there would be another one. For most of the day we surveyed the devastation, and by the time the sun was going down, we realized that we were lost. We tried to find our way back but kept getting turned around in the maze of destruction. The forest was unrecognizable.

JJ shook his head at one point, stopping to look at the earth that was still smoking. "They really burn the hell out of it? It's so sad. We couldn't do anything. We had to take care of our families."

Mohsin put an arm around JJ's shoulder. "It's okay," he said, "we're going to fix this. I always knew you were going to do something special, and this is it. It starts today. We are jungle-keepers now."

This made JJ smile.

Mohsin had brought a drone, and we tried to use it to see if there was any way to navigate out, but even the drone said it was too dark to fly. That's when JJ looked at me with a mischievous grin. He knew what he had to do. What he did best. He took his shirt off and tucked it into his shorts. "Okay," he said, "vamos, junglekeepers."

What followed was JJ navigating for three hours on dead reckoning. He managed to find the stream. So as darkness fell, we were hiking with only our cellphone lights. Mohsin's camera was his main rig, an expensive Canon DSLR that he'd have to hold above his head when the water got high. At times we were in the stream up to our necks. At others we were jumping off waterfalls. We were stepping over stingrays and slipping on rocks.

Over the course of the hike along that wild stream, despite all the destruction that surrounded it, we saw schools of fish, an aquatic opossum, snakes, an ocelot, about a thousand bats, a potoo, and several pacas. It was an adventurous night. But finally, JJ and his incredible jungle senses led us out to the mouth of the stream, where we were able to give a long hoot. Soon Roy came motoring up the river with the boat. "What the hell happened?"

As we explained our ordeal, JJ took over driving. He filled the tank and soon was steering the peke peke downstream. It was now fully nighttime and we were speeding through the jungle. Mohsin and I clapped hands on each other's shoulders and made eye contact—there was an understanding that required no words. This was the start of the reality we had always dreamed of—"one day" had just become day one. We were now actually doing the work that we had always wanted to do. We had investigated the destruction and had an action plan to stop it from progressing.

I looked to the back of the boat to where JJ was driving, standing tall in the moonlight. His eyes squinted, his jaw set. Watching him, I saw when something grabbed his attention. He crouched low and snapped his fingers at me. He was laser focused on something in the distance but moved his fingers across his face, indicating stripes or spots—I knew instantly what he saw.

He cut the motor and the boat drifted up the beach. We landed silently. JJ and I ran forward in bare feet, soundlessly over the sand. He grabbed my shoulder the way he used to when I was just a new kid and he wanted to physically show me where to look.

The jaguar was standing at the edge of the river cane. We approached so quickly and silently, obscured by the glare of our headlamps, that she didn't even have time to move. We were standing ten feet from a fully grown female jaguar. For a moment she looked ready to run. But then she sat. Her head bobbing from left to right, her eyes squinting, trying to see past our headlamps. We stood there silently. No breathing. For over a minute. The jaguar was assessing the situation. And what a glorious minute it was. Seeing this enchanting creature—the brilliant white-and-yellow coat, the blazing glow of her eyes, her massive paws. Her long whiskers. JJ was clutching my shoulder, wild with pure uncontrollable thrill.

Gradually the jag had enough of wondering what was going on and turned her back on us to slink off into the trees.

We motored the rest of the way downriver that night. I looked back and smiled at JJ in the moonlight. He smiled at me. I shook my head. I was so impressed with him. If it wasn't for him, we would've been sleeping in the jungle with no tents and no protection and no light. But instead, here we were blazing down the river together as a family. We had just seen the most incredible thing anyone could ever see. It was all because of him. This was all because of him.

═══

JJ and Mohsin and I spent a week on assignment for Dax and Age of Union. JJ casually told a logging company that Mohsin and I were American loggers and wanted to take a look at their operation. We got unprecedented access to see the horrifying piles of shihuahuaco trees inside the plant. The high walls of the factory kept the public view out. But now we saw it all. Mohsin's camera was firing like a conservation machine gun, while I was doing my usual thing, speaking to the camera, showing the size and scale of the trees we were losing.

Days later, JJ arranged another slam dunk. This one even more devastating. Our assignment was to film burning forest, and film we did. As usual, given that he knew everyone in the Madre de Dios, JJ had contacted a friend who was planning to clear an area of forest along the Las Piedras watershed. There was nothing we could do to protect it: The forest had already been cut, the trees had been baking in the sun for a month, everything was dry. We drove over in the afternoon just in time to watch the farmer hold a lighter to the ground. That's all it took. Mohsin and I exchanged a look of horror as we watched how rapidly the flames grew.

"Stay close!" I said.

"I will! Be careful!"

We split up and began filming everything. The flames were savage. We were walking through what used to be the Amazon Rainforest. Millennium-old trees lay dying in the dirty sunlight. As the towering flames ripped upward of seventy feet tall in places, the air became a swirling snow of ashes. Bamboo explosions fired off like cannon blasts. The air smelled like singed fur and agony. The last animals that had been hiding began to flee. The sky was filled with birds. The forest around the clearing was full of rushing, running animals moving through the leaves. What had for all of history been the loud, warm, dark green beauty was transformed to ashes before our eyes. The images we took were horrifying.

At one point while running from flames, I lost sight of Mohsin. I was running for my own life in the deafening roar of the flames. But something, some sound or call, or maybe just a gut connection, made me turn and call out, "Mohsin!" Nothing came back. I ran toward where I'd last seen him, but it was a hellscape of fire. When I found his camera on the ground in the ashes, my heart dropped. I lifted the camera and screamed for JJ. Now JJ was weaving and leaping across the charred earth to get to me. "HOO!" I responded in kind. We hooted loud and kept calling for Mohsin.

When we found him, he was face down on the jungle floor, just outside the burning area. He'd found some soggy ground and was barely conscious. JJ and I fell onto him. He was breathing but his eyes were floating—he was coughing violently. JJ took off his own shirt and pushed it into the swampy ground so it soaked with water. This he wrung out over Mohsin's head. Mohsin was moaning in relief as the water hit him. We kept telling him to breathe, keep his eyes shut, while we tried to get as much water on him as quickly as possible. He was a million degrees. We lifted and squeezed out multiple shirtfuls of water onto him and fanned him, and gradually he came back. It was a close call. If he'd gone down out there in the inferno, he would have asphyxiated before we ever got to him.

Sometime soon after we'd gotten back to Puerto and showered the soot from our bodies and spent a few days in bed, Pico was returning from several weeks of recuperation and therapy in Lima after his amputation. The Durand family held a welcome-home party at Pico's house. His wife and daughter and sons and grandchildren were there, as well as just about all of the nineteen brothers. People took turns speaking.

There was beer and chicken and duck and fish and rice. Pico and I hugged tightly. He pulled me down into the hammock with him and we rocked there. There were tears in his eyes. "Gracias, hermano, gracias, mi hermano."

Pico and JJ's brother Jesús gave a long speech and thanked me for being part of their family. He spoke about Santiago and the old days. And about how many years had passed. And about how real family are the people that you can depend on. When Pico relayed how the doctors told him that he would have died if it had been even just a few more days, his voice broke, and he had to pause. Everyone clapped and encouraged him, but he was overcome with emotion.

Pico was rocking in his hammock with eyes blazing. The pain was gone. He was happy. He had a new lease on life. I watched him there, laughing and wiping tears from his eyes and hugging everyone who came in. Disabled from such a young age, he'd had a hard life. The last year, that leg had gradually become worse and worse and finally so badly septic that he hadn't slept for months. He'd been sick and desperate and on the edge of death. But now? Now he was beaming. His wife, Melissa, came and gave him a kiss and he hugged her. His son Diego was helping carry sodas and beers. His daughter, Kiara, was serving food. Pico was a good one, a pure heart, with a good family, and now he was surrounded by the people who had rallied to save him.

The whole Durand tribe was present, most of the brothers and sisters and all their partners and children and grandchildren. We ate and drank and sang. Mohsin even sang a song a cappella while everyone listened. That night we made plans to launch a secondary fundraiser to get Pico a prosthetic leg. It would take some time, but we were certain that we could do it. I tried to explain, when it was my turn to speak, that people all over the world were invested in the story of Pico. He was famous. He had taken us on some of our wildest adventures, adventures that had changed my life, opened doors, and made me who I am. People in other countries who had never even been to Peru knew Pico's name, and the name Junglekeepers was becoming well known.

There was a lot of smiling and crying. When Pico's leg had become infected, we had nearly lost one of the best people any of us knew. I sat in the hammock, holding back tears, with Pico's arm tightly around my neck. He rubbed my hair and kissed my forehead in his affectionate, tactile, animal manner. "Mi hermano," he kept saying. When Jesús toasted and smiled wide, he said that Santiago had adopted Alex as the nineteenth brother in the clan of the Durands. Now, he said, pointing at me, Paul was hermano numero veinte—the twentieth brother.

===

Speaking of fraternity, the goodness of the world, and providence, it was around this time that fate decided to weave some of her most intricate and masterful work. It was a trajectory that began very far from the Amazon, and it had to do with seeds we had begun planting many years earlier. The hunch that JJ and I had originally had years ago was gradually turning out to be correct. All those years of guiding trips, honing our skills, punishing ourselves on long expeditions—all those years of working like Sisyphus, pushing the rock up the hill with no plan. That's how Mohsin had come in, and he in turn had brought in the study-abroad program and helped us build out Tamandua, keep the station alive, and keep launching ambitious expeditions. Then there was the book. When it came out, I felt like *Mother of God* had fallen flat, but the fact was that it was out there, and people still read it.

JJ had told me in year one: If we could bring people to see the forest, if we could tell the story and let people know we could save it, they would help us protect it. It's like walking for so many cloudy days and rainy miles, unable to imagine the future but sowing seeds wherever you go, and then one brilliant day finding yourself in the sunlight, the hillsides painted in the colors of a million wildflowers.

One of the first flowers we saw bloom was in 2018, in the form of Stephane Thomas. Stephane had grown up in France in a village so small it barely warranted a dot on the map—a cluster of sixty people tucked away in fields and forests. The kind of place where the cows outnumbered the humans. For young Stephane, life was quiet and often isolated. His parents worked tirelessly to keep their family afloat. His father was a carpenter, a one-man operation, working seven days a week, only sparing some time to be with his family on Sunday afternoons. His mother split her time between helping him and raising their three kids.

Stephane's younger brother was born with Duchenne muscular dystrophy, a cruel disease that would cast a shadow over their family's lives. For the first two years of his life, his legs were in a cast. Even after that, he required physiotherapy twice a week, a routine he kept up until he turned eighteen. Home life was hard, and Stephane's nearest friends were a six-mile bike ride away.

Stephane attended college, studying mathematics and computer science, tutoring on the side for extra cash. After college, he did what seemed like a great idea at the time and took a job in a bank in Luxembourg. It was a shiny, grown-up step into the real world, complete with a fancy title and a paycheck that made his friends back in France jealous.

Stephane found banking to be a lot of things, but "soul-stirring" wasn't one of them. His job was to analyze data, create reports, and make everything look tidy for the higher-ups. But here's the thing: He was faster at it than most of his colleagues. Soon he started automating parts of the process, turning hours of tedious work into minutes. While they were manually wrestling spreadsheets, he was finding ways to let the computer do the heavy lifting in a fraction of the time. Efficient, yes. Fulfilling? Not quite.

The trouble wasn't the work itself—he was good at it, and there was some satisfaction in finding ways to do it better. The real problem was what the work represented. Banking, as it turns out, is a master class in justifying the unjustifiable. It didn't sit right with him. His days were spent enabling a system of greed he didn't believe in, for people he couldn't relate to. But the paychecks kept coming, and he kept showing up, wondering how he'd ended up there.

As Stephane once wrote, "Those years were a lesson in the limits of pragmatism. Just because something is lucrative doesn't mean it's worth doing, and just because you're good at something doesn't mean you should keep doing it. A lesson that would help me much later. Banking taught me that sometimes, the fastest way to lose yourself is to succeed in something you don't believe in."

Stephane began to realize that he yearned for the work he had done in the years before banking, when he had been running summer camps for children. Planning daily activities, organizing logistics, and balancing budgets for the camp taught him how to anticipate challenges, allocate resources, and keep things running smoothly. From the tiniest challenges—a missing shoe or a homesick child—to the more significant ones, like navigating tight budgets, taking a five-year-old to the emergency room, or dealing with last-minute crises, he learned how to adapt and lead on the fly. Looking back, he realized it was this more meaningful work, and the problem-solving skills he learned with people, that were the building blocks of relentless optimism and pragmatic strategic power that would come to define some of his greatest talents.

What made this part of his life so extraordinary was the commitment it required. Stephane didn't take a standard holiday for an entire decade. Every break from work or school was poured into this world—creating something meaningful for children and supporting a tradition he had grown to cherish. The experiences he gained, the lives he touched, and the lessons he learned made it all worthwhile. In actuality, those summers weren't work—they were a calling, a period of profound personal and professional growth that shaped the person he would become.

But the banking world was his new reality, and by 2011, he had enough. He sold his apartment and his Porsche, and was left with $10,000, a compact video recorder, a backpack, and a one-way ticket to Nepal. He had no job waiting for him. No clear plan other than a longing to follow an imaginary line on a map stretching from Nepal through China, Southeast Asia, Australia, and the Americas. It was a vague idea at best—but promised the kind of freedom that's both terrifying and exhilarating in equal measure.

The first year was a series of events that you could easily imagine in a *Seven Years in Tibet* kind of film—Stephane in the blustery, oxygen-starved heights of Everest base camp. Hiking along and camping on remote sections of the Great Wall of China, mist swirling over the ancient stones. Swimming through kaleidoscopic schools of fish in the Great Barrier Reef. The year was a reminder that you don't need a high-paying job or a fancy car to feel alive. For Stephane, for the first time in years, every day was a new adventure, unpredictable and full of stories he never could have imagined or believed from the office.

But reality has a way of catching up. After months of exhilarating exploration, his savings were dwindling, and he had to face the fact that living out of a backpack wasn't sustainable. If he wanted to keep this adventure going, he needed to find a way to support himself—and put some of what he had rediscovered on the road to practical use. This was the first chapter in building a future that didn't involve a suit. It began with re-designing a website for a luxury resort in Thailand.

The owners were so impressed that they offered him three weeks of free stay. With a temporary home secured, he had a chance to reflect and plan his next move: If he kept using his coding skills, he could make a living. But for that, he'd have to make his way to the mecca of tech: the San Francisco Bay Area.

First, Stephane had to replenish his funds. Which he did in Australia, the next country on his adventure, where he had been invited by friends he had met months before in Nepal. So he dropped his bags for six months and clocked in at a cement factory. His task was updating spreadsheets to manage trucks heading up north with cargo. It was glorified data entry at best. But after two days of tinkering, he had automated the entire system. When he showed his boss, the man leaned back, nodded, and said, "Great, thanks." That was it. With his workload effectively reduced to "show up and exist," Stephane found himself with plenty of free time, time that he made the most of by exploring the west coast of Australia with new friends.

Once his finances were in order, he booked himself into coding boot camp in the Bay Area. The boot camp was only in its third iteration, but it promised to fast-track people into the tech world. He flew to San Francisco, ready to dive headfirst into three months of coding at one of the first boot camps of its kind. It was a whirlwind—a blur of long days, late nights, and a curriculum fueled by caffeine and sheer grit. By the end, he hadn't just survived; he had thrived. Demo day arrived, and he presented his final project to a room packed with tech recruiters and employers.

As a junior developer, Stephane worked tirelessly—logging eighty to ninety hours a week—and within six months, he became the client's primary point of contact at his first company. By his first anniversary, he had to hire a developer to help with the increasing workload. Over the next two and a half years, he kept climbing the ranks, from junior developer to leading a team of seventeen and becoming the company's second-in-command, generating half the revenue with a third of the staff. Do you see a theme emerging here?

The people at Apple sure did, and around that time they approached him with a very compelling offer.

Stephane would spend the next seven years at Apple in a period of steady growth. He started by managing a small team of six, which he expanded to thirty, reaching the upper limits of what was possible for a technical team within one of the company's big creative divisions. Looking for new challenges, he made the move to Apple's health software team, where he repeated the pattern: growing his team from four into a group of more than two dozen.

Working with Apple's health software felt purposeful: meaningful in a way Stephane hadn't experienced before. He knew that the tools they were building had the potential to improve people's lives. Even as a small—perhaps medium—cog in a massive machine, he had tangible impact. But over time, he began to feel the confines of his role. The further he climbed, the more he realized the limitations of his control over the broader vision. Decisions filtered down through layers of leadership in a massive company—while what he increasingly craved was something more direct, more personal. The gnawing desire for autonomy and impact began to weigh heavily on him.

Meanwhile, through all of this, he never lost his love for travel. Every opportunity outside of work became an excuse to explore. South America became his go-to escape. Chile, Argentina, Peru: He kept coloring the map. But something shifted the first time he visited the Peruvian Amazon in Iquitos (up north of the Madre de Dios). There was so much wilderness, so much untamed beauty—it was intoxicating. Every trip after that drew him deeper into the biome that spoke to him the most: the jungle. He explored Bolivia, Ecuador, Brazil, but always through some kind of lodge, all wonderful in their own way, but the jungle drumbeat of deep adventure had created a thirst he was unable to quench on the tourist trail.

Then, while planning a trip to Brazil, he bought a pile of books about the Amazon. One of them was *Mother of God,* by some numbskull named Paul Rosolie. When he arrived in Peru, Stephane told me that after reading the book he had figured there was a 50 percent chance whoever wrote it was dead. As we shook hands, he smiled and said he was glad to see I was still alive.

While I was still technically biologically alive, I was exhausted. That first trip he joined was well before the tides changed—before the press on the Amazon fires in 2019, and before Dax saved me from drowning in 2020. When I met Stephane, he was just another guy, a client, and I was bitter, tired, depressed, stressed—and scared of new people. So when he asked what help we needed, I brushed him off. But as you might have guessed by now, Stephane doesn't take no for an answer.

What I was too downtrodden to notice was the determination in Stephane's eyes—the moment he stepped off the edge of society and into the wild, towering jungle of Las Piedras, he recognized the elusive thing he had been searching for the world over. The mission, the place, the untouched wild—it all glowed with warm certainty. Just like it had for me so many years earlier.

When he showed up, I had no idea the epic journey he had been on, or the titanic caliber of skills contained in his slender frame.

Stephane's need to optimize seemed nitpicky to me at first. He asked why we used rotten old trail cams that gave us grainy wildlife imagery. I laughed and told him that if I had the fund-

ing, it was my dream to have some proper pro-level DSLR camera traps, but at this point, $150 Bushnells were going to have to
cut it. After all, they'd gotten me to the UN.

"Yeah," he said, blinking in frustration and repositioning his
glasses, "but don't you want to have better images?"

I looked him in the eyes. "More than anything. It's a dream.
But do you know how many things I'm dealing with here?"

"Tell me. I'm all ears," he said. Then Stephane did something amazing: He listened for hours. Maybe even days. He had
so many questions. The man who had automated his job at the
cement factory, who found ways to optimize and improve everything he touched, had a hard time concealing his surprise
when I told him some of the drudgery we had to endure to keep
the station running, how many times we had to pull the rope to
start the engines, to make this dream survive.

That first trip passed and by the end of it, Stephane offered
to be executive producer on the short film JJ and Roy and I
were working on, *Dark Green*. He also said he had an idea for
camera traps. When he came on his second trip, he brought a
homemade pro-grade DSLR camera trap.

When I opened the box I was amazed. "How did you do
this?"

"Well, I went to Home Depot and got a waterproof case,
then got a secondhand camera, linked the sensors and the flashes
and made separate casings for them and then . . ."

What he had done was tech wizardry on a level I had never
seen. And it wasn't long until we saw our first image from the
wild. A jaguar in all its stunning HD beauty walking the trails
at night. We knew immediately we had a winner. This new
window into the jungle world felt like a revelation. But what
was really going to change everything, and that I had no inkling
of at the time, was that Stephane had found his calling.

The only way I can do his entry any justice is to use the anal-

ogy that JJ and I starting Junglekeepers was like the impossible
task of pushing a huge boulder up a hill. Years of it. Just us
struggling and smashing ourselves against this huge problem.
Gaining inches, losing feet. But always recommitting. Through
the rain, slipping and falling in the mud. Just pushing, relentlessly pushing, for all those years. I'm talking about a ten-foot-
tall solid boulder. Early on, Mohsin had thrown his shoulder
into the effort and kept us going, just telling us he believed, and
helping to show the world. And then at our darkest hour, when
we'd been ready to quit, when I had finally given up, Dax had
come in like a titan and used his considerable muscle to give us
our first taste of momentum. Because of Dax things were rolling, we were making progress, but still with great effort, great
personal cost. And even with all of our strength, there was no
guarantee we'd ever reach the end.

Stephane came driving a tractor out of nowhere; his skill set
would be the heavy machinery that changed the game.

He was about to bring in the cavalry.

THE SECRET RIVER
(THE JUNGLEKEEPERS)

≡

N THE OLD BAREFOOT MACHETE DAYS, THERE HAD BEEN VIR-
tually no boats on the river. You could go weeks without seeing
another person. Now the logging boats were three a day or
more. We'd see them floating downriver. Men with poles guiding large beams of wood down the coffee-colored current.
They would motor up into the remote reaches of the river, cut
the trees, and then float the timber down for days or even weeks.

That road. That damn road had changed everything. And
Lucerna, that horrible little town that sprang up around the
road, had grown each year. In the old days it had just been a few
sad shacks. Now it was a place crammed with more than a dozen
boats. There were workers from all over Peru. Many of them
were loggers from other regions where the hardwoods were already gone and the day rate for timber workers had collapsed.
Many more of them were relatives or friends of the narcos.

The cocaine mafia in Peru had long ago learned that staying
out in the jungle was a good way to stay away from the cops.
During Covid the drug runners invested deliberate energy into
expanding their territory of safe areas. To do this, they gave the
poorest people enough money to buy some gasoline and chain
saws and sent them off with a mandate to go out and settle land
in remote areas. As a result, farms and little villages were pop-

ping up all over areas that had once been deep jungle. Places like Lucerna. They claimed to be innocent farmers, but it was a front, all a carefully crafted plan that tied straight back to the narcos.

There was still no law on the lonely Las Piedras River.

Between 2009, when the road first came, and 2023, JJ and I began seeing logging boats with a frequency that was nothing short of horrifying. There were traffic jams of logging trucks on the Lucerna road, all of them carrying ironwoods.

In the '90s it had been the mahoganies. Now it was the ironwoods. Ironwood is the English common name for what is locally called the shihuahuaco (*Dipteryx micrantha*), a tree that is one of the most crucial in the jungle ecosystem. They are revered by the local people and prized by loggers for their incredibly hard wood. They, with several other species, form the noble overstory of the rainforest. Shihuahuacos can reach heights of more than 60 meters and can grow for well over a thousand years.

JJ and I went with the Junglekeepers rangers and with expert dendrologists (scientists who study the natural history of trees) to the logging sites where shihuahuacos had been cut. We studied some of the trees, and what we found was that many of the largest shihuahuacos were older than we thought—over twelve hundred years old.

As threats to the river continued to grow before our eyes, the question of how to save it was more prominent than ever in our hearts. How could we truly stop the onslaught that we had been witnessing for over a decade? How could we stem the invasions, stop the loggers? How do you fight something as powerful and nebulous as a gold rush? It felt as hopeless and impossible as trying to hold back the ocean with nothing more than your arms.

Our little station didn't feel so far from everything anymore. We could just about always hear the motor of some boat taking timber downstream to Lucerna. We knew that the damage these loggers were causing would irrevocably change the forest. You can't regrow a thousand-year-old tree. No reforestation program is going to restore what these loggers were cutting— not in our lifetimes, and not in the lifetimes of our great-grandchildren. These trees were like the ancient sentinels, the structure and heart of the forest, the pillars of the cathedral.

By now you probably have a sense that every species in the rainforest is connected—that the jungle is a vast matrix of inter-connected life. A striking example of this can be found in the way that shihuahuacos provide nesting sites for the region's red-and-green macaws.

Macaws are a group of large parrots that are spread out across the Americas. But of the sixteen or so species of macaws, many are endangered or extinct. This is due to habitat destruction as well as direct hunting. Their feathers are beautiful. And every-one from tribes to tourist hotels want their feathers, making macaws prime targets for poachers. The illegal wildlife trade is right up there with guns, drugs, and human trafficking— some of the most powerful black markets on Earth. It's serious business. Rhino horn, elephant ivory, pangolins, feathers, and more—the demand for wildlife products can rapidly put iconic wildlife populations on the brink of extinction.

When I had first come to Las Piedras, back in 2006, it had been as a volunteer data collector on a macaw project. I spent hours and hours with the macaws, for weeks on end. The ma-caws gathered every day at a colpa that formed a riverside cliff. At our colpa there were mainly three kinds of macaws: red-and-green, scarlet, and chestnut-fronted. These were joined by a co-hort of smaller parrot species. On any given morning, I could observe between 60 and 150 macaws. The birds use colpas as meeting places; they all come from their various parts of the forest to congregate and socialize. The clay contains salt that helps them maintain healthy sodium levels, and it also works to neutralize some of the heavy chemical compounds contained in the fruits and nuts that macaws eat.

Watching a hundred macaws take wing all at once is among the most fantastically beautiful spectacles the natural world has to offer. It's a floral explosion of such vibrant scarlet, brilliant cerulean, and accents of fern green against the dark jungle that the rush of life and color is enough to leave you breathless.

The Las Piedras is one of the last places where macaws exist in such bountiful numbers. These are healthy populations that remain at prehuman numbers. But here's the thing. The red-and-green macaws only nest in shihuahuaco trees. They scour the jungle, searching for old shihuahuacos that have lost a branch and have a hole in the trunk. These holes, or hollows, high up off the jungle floor, strong, and insulated from weather and predators, are the perfect place for the monogamous birds to raise a chick.

But finding a large-enough tree with the perfect hole is difficult; studies have shown that suitable hollows are so rare that there is usually only one for every sixty-two acres of forest. This limited real estate means that the macaws in a given area of forest have to share, and as a population they compete and rotate who gets to breed each season. The result is that in any given year, only 10 to 20 percent of the macaw population is able to find a nesting site to reproduce. This limiting specificity results in a slow replacement rate once their populations are diminished. The macaws rely entirely on the most ancient trees in the forest—the exact same ones the loggers were now felling in ever greater numbers.

≡

In the area around the research station, the tallest tree in the forest—that we knew of—was a kapok that towered over the rest of the jungle. It was what the locals call an ancient lupuna, botanically a ceiba. At the base, its rocket-fin-shaped footprint was the size of a house. The tree itself rose in a titanic column up from the ground straight toward the sky. At over forty feet in circumference, it was a monster. The entire tree stood more than 160 feet tall.

The day I first climbed it, JJ and I were standing at the bottom in the predawn darkness with a seventy-meter rope, headlamps, and a set of rock-climbing gear. I'd seen this tree my whole Amazonian life. JJ and I had walked under it for so many years, we'd often dreamed of climbing it, but the thought of it had always terrified me. Until today.

I had had enough of wondering. Come what may, it was time. If you want to uncover the secrets of this world, you have to be willing to risk what others won't—do things that others aren't willing to do.

JJ had one harness and a belay device to feed me rope. I picked my way up the strangler fig vine that was the only purchase for my fingers. Barefoot, my toes found crevices or splayed flat against the bulk of the tree. "Good job," JJ said, "like a white spida monkey."

Pretty soon I was forty feet up. I used a piece of webbing to lash around the fig vine and attach a carabiner and feed the rope through. Now at least if I fell, JJ could slow me down. I was essentially trad climbing the tree up the single vine that clung to its trunk. It required a gorilla kind of brute muscle, and my arms were already burning. Every move was a power move that required almost all the strength I had. As I reached sixty feet, I realized that if I didn't put in another safety I was basically free climbing. But I kept going. At seventy feet another carabiner. Another rest. JJ said something from down below, but all I could see was his headlamp looking up at me from way, way down there. "What did you say?" I called down. "Holy shit!" he called up with a laugh.

"Holy shit is right," I hissed to myself, as I drew a breath and closed my eyes, blew out, found focus, and kept going.

Around a hundred feet I reached a part just below the crown. Huge branches, themselves the size of trees, spread out over me. But there was no way to climb straight up here. The tree bulged out, and so to continue climbing required me to lean out so that my back was facing the ground. There were no holds. I was scared and sweating. Deep breaths. Stay focused. Fuck fear. Another carabiner; at least I was safe here. Peering over to the right, I could see there was a set of vines lashed horizontally to the tree. If I made my way along those, I could theoretically reach another vine that was thin enough to grip. I just didn't know. I couldn't see where I was going—it was over the horizon of the tree's curvature. I had no line of sight. And at this height, JJ could hardly hear me.

With shuddering breath, I used my toes to move along the one-inch-thick vines that were lashed around the tree trunk. I was now super exposed. If I slipped and fell, even though I was on the rope, I would fall over thirty feet. I tried not to think of swinging. I'm not scared of heights, but up here was a different thing. That swing could still knock me out against the tree. A misplaced foot into a wasp nest could end my life. A blind hand reached into a crevice could get me snake-bit and envenomated. I just kept inching along the tremendous tree, like a window washer on a skyscraper, on holds so small my sweaty fingers were barely able to keep my grip. Then, with a trembling reach, safety. I had made my way farther around the circumference of the tree, and now could see a way up. I had to shout down to JJ. "I need slack!" He didn't know what that meant. I smiled. I hauled it out of him myself.

From here it was twelve blind, heart-pounding vertical feet until my left hand found something good to hold. Then a muscle-up finally brought me into the branches and over into the tree's crown, safe, and I lay panting in the bowl from where all the gargantuan branches stemmed. I shouted down to JJ that I had made it. I MADE IT! I was safe. I made an anchor and established a safety and stood. My mouth opened with wonder. This was my first time in the canopy not on a tower, not in a platform, but in the wild of the jungle canopy.

"I'm up!"

"Todo bien?"

"Sí! Estoy seguro!"

"Muy bien, cachero!" JJ shouted so it echoed up to the branches.

I smiled as I worked the ropes. My lungs were heaving. I had to concentrate on what I did—there was no room for error. JJ knew how to belay, but up here I was on my own, and had to haul up the ropes and set my own anchor. If I got hung up, tangled, or worse, it could be days until I got help. When I had made a double redundant safety and checked it five times, I finally allowed myself to look around, to draw a breath of misty wonder at the savage gigantism of the jungle canopy I stood in. How could something so tremendous even exist?

My headlamp illuminated the particulate interior of the cloud scraping over the jungle. This stood above them all. At such a size, it seemed safe to assume this tree was at least a thousand years old. Which means it would have been pushing up out of the earth when the Vikings were pillaging, Genghis Khan was growing his empire, Pope Urban II was calling for the Crusades. It would have already been a few centuries old by the time Europe was dealing with the Black Death and the Renaissance was getting under way. This tree, viewed in time-lapse through the centuries—its branches thick with birds and covered in monkeys and reptiles and amphibians, armies of ants and termites, and just incalculable iterations of life, generations and generations racing over it. Thousands of species. All the storms it must have weathered. Through the centuries, as empires fell, inventions were made, wars were won and lost, this tree was out there, silently reaching for the sky in the depths of the Amazon jungle.

In the childhood stories that my parents read us at bedtime, the princess could only be saved by fighting the dragon. In *The Hobbit,* Smaug guarded the gold. In those old stories, the really daunting dragons always had lairs littered with the bodies of knights who had tried and failed, charred skeletons of men cooked inside their armor. Indeed, many are called, but few are chosen. The brick walls are there to keep out the people who don't want it bad enough. And whether it's the princess or a pile of gold or whatever your most enticing metaphor is, if it's a dream that is truly worth it, truly full of value and brilliance of the highest order, there's going to be a hell of a fire-breathing monster between you and the goal. It seems to be the way life works, the secret to the game—you have to find a way past the flames.

The climb had been terrifying. But now, in the crown of the millennium tree, I walked freely on branches that were thicker than the largest oak trunks I had grown up with back home. I was a tiny human in a giant world of vines and branches, and bromeliads the size of cars. There were cacti and orchids and various creepers and large-leafed monsteras with glorious fenestrations. The veil of mist still clutched the canopy of the forest, although the world was growing lighter by the moment. I was navigating with a headlamp, and the particulate rush moving past my eyes was magical: The air was full of moisture, particles of water visible in the headlamp's light. I watched as below me, howler monkeys paused to look up, across from their tree to mine, with perplexed expressions on their faces. The canopy, the rarely seen world, the last frontier, where over 50 percent of the life in a rainforest lives without ever touching the ground. No wonder all the new species are discovered here: It's impossible to reach. My eyes were wide with wonder as I caught sight of a lizard resting on an epiphytic plant that I had never seen in my life. *My God,* I thought, *this is another world.* I ran off forty feet of slack, anchored myself, and then stood and walked out along the branch. After twenty feet the incline made it dangerous to walk upright, so I went on hands and feet, out and upward. Finally I was forty feet out from the trunk, another two stories higher than the crown, straddling the branch, high in the blue jungle morning.

And then I saw it.

At that moment the sun broke over the horizon and cast its warm beams across the world. Orange light burned out of the east, and the jungle responded with a crescendo of birdsong and a rush and thrum of life that sent ripples across the green ranges. Kaleidoscopic clusters of macaws took flight, screaming into the air, red-and-green and blue-and-yellow feathers racing across the sky. Everything was rising toward the warm embrace of the day, the first light, as if the world had begun again. And in this sudden rebirth, the warm rays heated the leaves and air, sending the vapor into mass exodus. For the first time, I was seeing something I had only ever read about: the mist river.

How long ago had I read that each of the great trees of the Amazon can pump a thousand liters of water into the air per day? That the rainforest exhales twenty trillion liters of water into the air daily? I had read and always remembered the words of Antonio Nobre, who had described an invisible mist river that is larger than the Amazon River itself. I had dismissed it as a scientific technicality, something filed away with other unseen fantastical facts about the cosmos—the number of galaxies or the unseen molten core of the Earth.

Now, in the branches of the greatest tree in the jungle, I watched as the mist river caught the morning rays illuminating golden currents, swirling as it rushed over the canopy like a stream from heaven. In the troughs and basins and lower areas, the river was deep blue, but then as it flowed up and over the taller trees, slow rapids washing over the canopy, the mist river became ignited, electrified in the gold magnificence of the sunlight. Scores of birds flew in and out of the churning currents. The life and breath of the Amazon was flowing from north to south, along the basin of the Las Piedras, over the jungle. My God. My God. I thought of everyone I loved, of every creature contained in the leafy distance. The jungle itself was like a great being, a monstrous leviathan of warm green might. I wanted to call down to JJ and tell him to find a way up. I wanted my mother to see it, I wanted the world to see it. The light filled my eyes, and I found myself wiping away tears.

Carefully, ever so carefully, I stood, my bare feet for the first time in a place where I was certain no human could have ever stood before. As I did, a pair of red-and-green macaws, side by side, came rocketing past me. They were so close that I could hear the air rushing through their feathers. Their colors were so brilliant and their beauty so great, I had to kneel to steady myself on the branch and keep from falling. I was gasping. I felt like I had seen something so beautiful that it was almost beyond what my senses were able to accept.

That moment changed me forever. It was beauty on a scale that could break you, but not for its absolute kindness and warmth, its biblical magnitude. As I stood on those branches with tears in my eyes, I heard the words of Fitzgerald, "for a transitory enchanted moment"; Gandalf's gravelly voice, de-

scribing "a far green country under a swift sunrise"; and the
McCarthian description of a place beyond any common merid-
ian with "burned worlds past all reckoning." Confronted for
the first time with an observable magnitude of symphonic out-
put, the heartbeat of the forest—sunrise igniting the world and
casting the miraculous spell of the divine, peeling back the quotidian curtain of the observable world to render the unseen
fleetingly visible.

I had read but never understood. I had known but never believed. Now I stood there barefoot and wide-eyed in the swirling illuminated world of gigantic biological magnitude and I
felt transformed. For a moment I was still and quiet, thinking of
my younger self, with a cedar sword, exploring the forest—and
how far beyond his wildest dreams this truly was.

Back down at the crown of the tree, I did a final check of the
anchors and ropes. No knots, all smooth, all good. Here we go.
When my feet left the branches, and I swung into the air, I left
the golden world, and rappelled back down into the shadowy
depths of the forest, where JJ was yawning. It would be another
hour before the light hit the forest floor—we'd woken up early.
And while I was bleeding and panting and full of exuberant life-
changed wonder, he had seen none of it; he was getting sleepy
from waiting around. "Good climb, cachero, good climb!"

That night in the candlelight at the station, I sat up late writing. Thunder was shaking the heavens as a steady nocturnal rain
fell. I remembered the day so many years ago when JJ and I had
been exploring the streams and he had drunk from the water
and shown me the vapor rising off his skin. We knew well that
the jungle creates its own moisture, but today, at long last, I had
seen with my own eyes the previously invisible link in the cycle.

Dip your hand and drink from the river. Watch the mist
snarl off the canopy in the first blue light of dawn. When the

sunbeams stroke the golden river, wisps of vapor play on the current of new light. Beads of sweat form on our foreheads as the tropical sun draws the river from our skin and back into the rising air. Birds float in and out of the gathering clouds, the breath of the forest, until the heavy sky falls to the land. The clouds scrape their black bellies across the treetops. Then comes the rain. We huddle in the downpour, cowering in the swirling genesis of the river creating itself. We are reminded in shocking clarity that the universe is not a place, but an event unfolding around us. That the river and the sky are flowing through us. We reach out to run our fingers along the surface of those truths. And, gasping, allow the breath we borrowed to rejoin the wind.

===

There are drawings in my journal from as early as 2015 that show an imaginary treehouse in the tallest branches of the canopy. They're all rough sketches. Nothing more than pencil musings. And now that I had walked on the tallest branches, I found myself dreaming of making it possible to stay up there. I imagined what it would be like to sleep up there. More important, I wanted to share the beauty I had seen with others.

Do you remember when I told you Stephane was going to bring in the cavalry? Well, the way he reacted to my vision of a canopy-level treehouse was perhaps his first and most defining example of it.

When I told Stephane my dreams of a world-class treehouse and showed him my drawings, he listened with undivided attention. It reminded me of the way he had listened back in 2018 when I told him I wished I had camera traps that could take professional-grade images—and not long after, he had constructed and returned with exactly that. When Stephane hears an idea that piques his inspiration, he listens with the concentration of one used to turning dreams into reality—it's like he's collecting schematics, blueprints, nuts and bolts, every detail captured from the raw material of imagination to be forged into reality.

It didn't take him long to begin making calculations. Soon he and I met with the rest of the team. I told them of my experiences in the canopy and showed them my drawings. I shared my conviction that if people were able to see the magic I had seen, surely they would help us protect it. To build a treehouse so tall would be a first, perhaps even a world record. It would allow students and scientists and tourists unprecedented access to the canopy of the Amazon.

If you build it, they will come.

If they came, surely they would join us in saving it.

By the start of 2023 we began. Stephane offered not only to fund the construction of the treehouse, but to use his experience as a project manager to oversee the build and manage the project's execution. It was a tremendous undertaking. If we were going to construct the tallest treehouse in the world, we would need to find expert treehouse builders, hire a small army of local workers, and begin constructing a vision for something that had never been done. It was a mammoth project.

To begin in earnest, the first thing we had to do was find the tree. To do this, JJ, Mohsin, Stephane, and I brought an expert treehouse builder to the jungle, and we all made the hike to the giant lupuna, the same tree from which I had first seen the magical mist river. From the high branches, with a walkie-talkie and binoculars, we were able to find a tree on the horizon that fit the bill—tremendous overstory height positioned at the edge of a ridgeline, so it stood far above the valley below.

Soon after, we were rappelling down from the lupuna. Then we were hiking up from the floodplain to the high ridge. When we arrived, we identified a massive ficus, and we knew we'd found our giant. This was the tree that would make history.

Months later, construction began.

≡

The year 2023 was when Junglekeepers found its footing and when we began to push back against oncoming threats that faced the forest. What allowed us to do this was a huge surge in support. Much like in 2019, it came in the form of a media hit that would take us to new heights. And although I still always pick up the phone, this particular story started with a simple message from someone I greatly admired.

I had been a fan and a listener of the *Lex Fridman Podcast* for years. Lex was well known across the globe for his outstanding podcast, on which he interviewed scientists, actors, inventors, CEOs, and interesting innovators and thinkers from all walks of life. Lex's style is a no-bullshit, straightforward conversation that often lasts three hours. He wears a suit and tie to the conversation. He does his research. He asks deep questions and isn't one bit scared to disagree or touch on uncomfortable truths. For a long time, I listened to him because I felt he was the most intelligent, intellectual, educational thing I could put in my ears. I listened because each episode was an exploration into a new topic or field or country or story.

And as you do when you watch an actor or listen to a person talk for hours and hours, you begin to feel like you know them. You don't. But you feel like you do. I liked Lex, and I respected him greatly. So when he messaged me one day in January 2023, I sat up straight, mouth open.

The message was simple: "Would you be interested in coming on this podcast I do?"

I almost responded, "The Lex Fucking Fridman Podcast?"

His humility made me smile.

A few months later I traveled to Austin, Texas, where we spoke together for hours. The episode we recorded went viral, breaking the top ten most-watched episodes of the *Lex Fridman Podcast*. Our episode, number 369, rose to beat out conversations with Elon Musk, Jeff Bezos, Kanye West, Matthew McConaughey, and many other luminaries that I would have thought would have far outweighed mine. Within a few months of it being up, our episode became one of Lex's top five podcast episodes ever. Ever. That said a lot about how people felt about the jungle, what the reminder of deep wilderness could do for the human heart.

The result was a tidal wave of interest. From the moment the episode dropped, we saw our emails, DMs, and website contact form submissions skyrocket. People wanted to know how they could help.

Remember what happened in 2019, when my video of the fires had gone viral? Suddenly, the whole world was reaching out to me once again. I had felt like I was a fisherman with a thousand fish on a thousand hooks and no way to reel them in. That was then, when it was just me in the boat. This time, I had an expert team to field the surge.

When the episode dropped, the numbers were daunting. Thousands of people from all over the world wanted to support Junglekeepers. Once again, Stephane proved himself invaluable, this time with Mohsin by his side. They went for days on end, emergency updating the website and establishing a donor platform with various levels of support. We constructed a system where people could sign up to donate on a monthly basis at various tiers: $5, $10, $100, $1,000, or custom amounts. This required Stephane to build systems and web pages from the ground up. Projects that should have taken weeks or months were completed in hours.

The surge of interest and the sheer amount of opportunity

were the necessity that forced us to invent the system that would make Junglekeepers unique. For the first time, people around the globe had a way to directly support the Indigenous leaders who were fighting to save the Amazon Rainforest. There was no red tape, no advertising, no complicated admin—nothing but our ragtag team. So when people asked where their donation would be sent, we could proudly and truthfully tell them that 100 percent of their money was going to protect the forest. No bullshit. Thankfully by this point, we had 501(c)(3) charity status, so donations were tax-deductible. We also had several years of wildlife surveys and ranger reports, thousands of acres protected, and a large body of work that proved we were capable of doing what we said we would.

It was during this time that JJ, Mohsin, Roy, Stephane, and I were able to get together and make a plan to take back control from the people who had tried to take Junglekeepers from us. I won't muddy these pages with the whole story; it's too ugly. But the creeps who had infiltrated us and tried to rob us of our life's work had brought us down for years. You'll remember I told you that they had control, and over time they'd locked us out of the bank accounts and social media, and given themselves a majority on the board of directors. It had gotten so bad that a lawyer told me we'd be better off starting over.

But with the new wave of support, we found a renewed store of resolve. We spent months planning and laying blast cable, preparing for our coup. Then, with Stephane's tech wizardry, some taped phone calls, and a final push, we were able to deliver a roundhouse punch to the parasites, which allowed us to take back the board, reopen the accounts, and finally be in control of Junglekeepers. At long last, we had won. After so many years, it was all happening at once.

The Lex episode was a rocket booster that launched us into a new echelon. Suddenly we had thousands of donors, people from all over the world who had heard our story, seen the images, and wanted to help.

With this overwhelming wave of support, we had the funds to begin purchasing parcels of land from the loggers and saving forest that would otherwise surely be cut. With the ongoing annual funding for the ranger program from Dax through Age of Union, we could patrol and safeguard those parcels once we had them. Suddenly we were climbing upward, gaining elevation rapidly. The area we were protecting began to grow, then it began to soar. Soon we were protecting over fifty thousand acres.

═══

In all the years that JJ and I had been alone, hardly anyone had paid any attention to what we were striving toward. But now that we had begun notching wins, as humble as they might have been, there began to be a steady trickle of attention. You might find this in your own life. That in the times when you need encouragement most, your efforts go unnoticed. It's the all-nighters spent writing, the lonely miles running. It's the unseen practice and the years of patient study. And that's why you'd better truly love the thing you are chasing and be doing it for reasons with roots that lace deep into the bedrock of your heart. Because people only start cheering for you when they see you winning.

One of the most authentic and important collaborations that emerged as we began taking steps forward came from an incredible crew of friends from ABC News, led by Matt Gutman. Gutman is ABC's chief national correspondent, and when he came we showed them everything. The deep forest, the raging fires, the ranger team. We even gained access to the infamous and brutal mining area to the west of Puerto Maldonado where a hundred-mile scar of deforestation is ripping the western Amazon. Matt and I stood there, drone in the air and mics on our collars, reporting from the wasteland where the Amazon Rainforest had once been. A sandstorm blowing in the distance. It was shocking footage, horrific to behold. The footage and stories that we told from the front lines of the fight to save the Amazon went on to win an Emmy Award for on-the-ground climate coverage.

Not long after, we were in Montreal for COP15, the United Nations Biodiversity Conference. Stephane gave me a warm smile and a thumbs-up as I went onstage. I sat beside Dax, who outlined his vision for Age of Union. He wanted to unite conservation efforts across the globe. He shared my long-held belief that this is the most crucial moment in history, and that the loss of biodiversity is the defining issue of our time. He said that we as a people need to think as a global society to repair the relationship between humans and nature. That we are not apart from nature, but inextricably tied to it, part of it, a manifestation of it.

I watched Dax as he spoke, the blue United Nations flag behind him, and felt a hurtling kind of gratitude. I found myself in awe of the true magnitude of what Dax had done in his life, the fortune he had amassed, the company he had built, and the heart required to decide to use all of it to create light in the world. One night in the jungle together, Dax had lit a candle. He'd used that candle to light another. He said it was the perfect illustration of how he felt about life. That one flame can light another, and that we each have a responsibility to fight back against the darkness.

Not only had he agreed to fund Junglekeepers, but he had stuck with us through hard times. He had the wisdom to know that any new company or organization was going to struggle in the early stages. He had believed in me and trusted me to figure it out.

That day onstage, Dax made public his donation to Junglekeepers: $3.5 million over multiple years. Camera flashes went off as we shook hands, me in my yellow jungle jacket with its Junglekeepers logo, Dax with short hair and a black beard, muscles filling out his suit. It was official—together, we were going to try to save the world.

≡

Back in the jungle, we sprang into action on a complete overhaul of the old station. It had been crumbling since the barefoot machete days, tilting, rotting, slowly being consumed by nature. But now the pillars were straightened, the wood was sanded, the roofs replaced. We added staff quarters, a kitchen upgrade, and about a million other things. We had solar panels and internet (which is also how we were now able to dispatch rangers in an emergency). Our goal was to keep the authenticity but upgrade the comfort, so people from all over the world could visit the wildest place on Earth. The station and the treehouse were a pinprick, a blade of grass on an endless field of wild jungle—upgrading them to the level that people felt safe and comfortable to visit would allow us to appeal to a much wider range of clients that could include potential donors for Junglekeepers.

When we began the treehouse build, JJ had had to stay in town hiring laborers and ordering materials, coordinating all the logistics to make the work possible.

When I finally led him to the jungle to see it, I knew it was going to shock him.

There was no denying that there was something surreal about seeing it—the herculean strength needed to move the great beams of wood, the Egyptian-style, leaf-cutter-ant ferrying of nuts and bolts and climbing gear and saws and tools. It was a project of epic proportions. The staircase spiraled up out of the jungle like a double helix of glowing red wood.

The first time he saw it, JJ looked upward with dizzy amazement. He had to sit down. His hand went slowly to his head as he removed his glasses. He ran a palm over his face as if in a dream.

I sat beside him, howler monkey on my shoulder.

"What do you think?" I asked gently.

"Paul, I mean . . . dis is . . ."

"I know," I said, grinning. JJ was speechless.

He looked upward, whispering to himself, "Su madre." I watched him quietly, just taking it in. The boy who had grown up in an Indigenous community with no shoes until he was thirteen years old, the young man with the dream of saving the forest—the man who had had so many losses and dark days and yet never stopped—was now watching the lights come on. He was watching his life transformed before his eyes. Soon he would be on the phone, being interviewed by *The New Yorker;* soon we would be standing up there, looking out over the jungle while his picture was taken. Soon people all over the world would read that an Indigenous conservationist had erected the tallest luxury treehouse in the world down in the Amazon.

Twenty-five years after he started, JJ's dream of creating a world-class way for people to experience the jungle was becoming real. He just sat there staring upward, the light from the canopy—and a new brilliant world of possibility—dancing in his eyes.

In the months that followed, we began fighting back against the loggers that were dismantling the land along the river. We held our meetings at the station. JJ sat at the head of the table, Mohsin and Roy and Stephane and I with notebooks and laptops. This was our war room. The table was a skyline of coffee cups, camera traps, candles, and maps. There were monkey skulls, open books, and a variety of insects chasing the candlelight.

We had used the maps to establish a corridor concept for the river, a vision of all the land that we hoped to protect. For hours we pored over satellite imagery and ranger reports identifying areas of urgent concern. Where were the new roads coming from? Where were the loggers hitting the hardest? We knew we had the devastating clearings by the Loreto to deal with, but we'd already put the lawyers and the police on that project; it was in process. There were reports of a new invasion near the Huáscar tributary, but those were still unconfirmed.

"Okay, so then tomorrow let's have the rangers go investigate," JJ said.

Roy made a note. "I'll coordinate with Ignacio and have them leave at dawn."

Mohsin caught my eyes across the table with a face that said, *Holy shit.*

I know, I told him without speaking a word, *this is wild.*

Our organization was becoming a real thing.

Do you remember Ignacio? Not Don Ignacio the shaman from the early years, but the younger Ignacio, the one who had been shot in the head by the Mashco Piro tribes? Well, he became a ranger. In those weeks when we were dedicating ourselves to forming a proper ranger force, he was among the best and brightest, the most daring and qualified. With a brand-new Junglekeepers shirt on, he began launching patrols. His superlative courage and deep local knowledge made him instantly one of our best. He was joined by a diverse crew of men and women from all over the Madre de Dios who became the first iterations of the Junglekeepers ranger team. Many of the people we hired used to be loggers or gold miners. Instead of cutting trees and working for terrible wages, suddenly they had respectable pay, uniforms, health insurance, a steady job, and a community. We were protecting large swaths of Las Piedras now, and the rangers' job was to be the eyes on the ground, living out in the wild, watching for loggers, miners, and roads—keeping the jungle safe.

After spending a lifetime reading about various conservation projects, I didn't want Junglekeepers to be like any of them. I wanted us to have a whole new take. I hated the colonialist conservation of the past, where foreign biologists would push out local people to designate national parks. I hated the idea that conservation was based on carbon, or anything quantifiable. To me it was all about protecting this vast wilderness, with all its unquantifiable species and its infinity of trees, and even the uncontacted tribes that lived out there somewhere.

We learned early on that it's all too easy to think of the people destroying the rainforest as bad or even evil. But I'd been in the Madre de Dios long enough to know otherwise. Pico used to be a logger. Hell, Santiago used to be a logger. Half the people I knew and loved in Peru used to be loggers. And they had all done it at the same time in their lives: when there was no other option.

Nobody wants to be a logger and risk their life for eighty soles, or about twenty dollars, a day. Just like no one wants to be a gold miner, up to your eyeballs in mud and mercury, literally murdering the Earth. And increasingly, I have seen that as time goes on, no one wants to be chasing animals through the jungle with a gun. All of these are essentially hunter-gatherer activities. There's no future in it. You have to get up and do it again tomorrow, and you might fail. And in the Amazon, your chances of being killed or maimed on the job are high. No, the people of the region were begging for another option.

JJ knew just about everyone in the region, and started calling landowners and arranging meetings. Often this meant long boat trips to remote camps far out in the jungle. One landowner told us why the loggers and invaders were coming in so freely.

He explained that he, like many landowners in the region, had inherited vast parcels of jungle from his father. The old generation was too old to be out hiking through the forest and fishing for a living. And the younger generation wanted to live in the city. When we would ask them what they wanted, it was simple: money, food, water, and Wi-Fi. They weren't interested in living days away from civilization in remote patches of the Amazonian wild.

Puerto Maldonado was growing. Many of these younger people were now in their thirties, forties, or fifties, and the vast acreage that they had inherited was largely useless to them. So what they would do is contract out the land to logging companies to make some money. Often after the loggers came in and ripped out the ironwood trees, the roads they left behind would be used by land-grabbers from other parts of Peru. The original owners usually had no idea. The invaders would slash down the old growth and establish farms. By the time anyone showed up with the police, it was far too late. The law in Peru is that if you establish a farm or dwelling with a roof for a certain amount of time, usually a year, without being removed, that land is yours. Even if it's not. Squatter's rights. That's what had happened on the Loreto. The loggers had made a road that the invaders had used to come in and burn everything down.

"Dis is how they do," JJ said to me one day while we were driving. "We are learning, no?"

I nodded as I drove the peke peke. Yeah, we were learning.

We were almost back at the station and the sky was pink. Macaws were flying over the canopy, and there were spider monkeys in the branches at the edge of the river. For a while we drove in silence. Our tiny boat was minuscule beneath the towering walls of green foliage that rose from the muscular red river. There are moments when the beauty of the jungle rushes up on you and lodges like a knot in your throat. When you suddenly realize how monstrous and powerful it is, how small you are, and how much you love it.

How could it be? That for the first time in a million years this great continent-sized jungle was in danger of being dismantled. The vast impenetrable wilderness, the very thing that had once defined this place, was now in the process of disappearing forever. How could it be that the great lupuna tree, with its overstory branches that had stood for a thousand years, would now certainly have been cut had we not been standing guard? Was it possible then, I wondered, that everything we had seen had been for a reason? That JJ and I had not only met in the right moment of our lives, but had been born at the exact moment in history when the jungle needed us?

As the frogs throbbed in the jungle twilight, I brought the boat around and JJ stepped off onto the shore. The sun was setting in the west.

THE
ANCIENT FOREST

HERE WAS ONCE A TINY BLACK SPIDER MONKEY WHO WAS born in the treetops. From the high branches like another world entire, nestled in her mother's fur, her first sunrise was reflected in her obsidian eyes. She clung to her mother, watching the sun cast light over the endless treetops, the warm breath of the trees smoking off the jungle.

She and her brothers and sisters and cousins lived in the great forest, traveling from tree to tree, watching for eagles, eating figs and other fruit. She rode on her mother's back, hung from her stomach, flew through the air between branches—through the emerald canopy of orchids and vines.

She clung to her mother when the gun fired and they fell.

Since the day her mother died, the little spider monkey lived in a mining camp with the dogs and chickens. All around the camp, the jungle had been cut and burned and destroyed. Even if she escaped, there was nowhere left to go. So at night she slept alone in the dark, in the dirt, under the floor. Her family was gone, her mother was gone. The forest was vanishing. She was barely alive and all alone, far from the branches and any of her kind.

When I found her, I dropped to my stomach, searching under the floorboards with a flashlight.

She was curled up like the orphan she was, her eyes bleary in the beam of my headlamp. I reached in and grabbed her with one hand. I inspected her and saw that she was healthy. I held her for a bit and her little moans sounded like crying. It made my heart hurt.

I could feel she was terrified, trembling, and uncomfortable.

I spoke to her for a time in broken spider monkey. I made sounds like what I had heard the monkeys in the trees make. This seemed to soothe her.

I let her crawl back into the darkness.

For a while, I was off doing human things: carrying gear, eating dinner, showering in the river.

But that night while I talked with the miners, I saw the reflection of the firelight in her eyes. I couldn't see anything else. She was jet-black—a starving shadow with sparkling eyes.

Once again I spoke soft, broken spider monkey.

For a while she just watched me, assessing.

I continued talking to her: "Oo-ah-ah-ah-oh-oh-ochh."

Slowly, she came out of the darkness.

She crept out of the night and climbed up my leg. When she reached my neck, she curled her tail around me, clutched me tight, and hugged me like her life depended on it. Like the touch of something warm and safe was the answer to a need more painful than hunger. I felt a lump in my throat as I stroked her black fur.

That night, she wouldn't let go. I brushed my teeth with her on my neck. I took my shirt off around her. I got into bed and slept the whole night, the little monkey clinging to me the entire time. In the morning, I woke on my back, the monkey snoring softly, several pellets of spider monkey poop on my chest. That day, she stayed perched there and refused to budge. I did my work, trekked the trails, and explored the forest—all with a wild-eyed little black being lodged on my shoulder.

Whenever she was hungry or scared, I'd hear the soft little staccato: "Oo-oo-ah-ah-ah-achhhoo."

When I spoke it back, she settled, pressing her ear to the skin of my neck. For a few days, I was her caretaker, her world.

We hiked in the forest together, her under my shirt, peering out, watching the world, never allowing her tail to slip. A spider monkey's tail is like a fifth limb, and ends in a long stretch of skin, like a ruler-length finger, that can grab and hold anything. This spider monkey held me with all she had.

I was all she had.

This little monkey was so incredibly starved for contact, for love, that after tasting it briefly in the afternoon, at night she'd risked darkness, dogs, and miners to come over to get more of the thing she needed most in the world: connection.

We think of humans as superior, but animals need affection, just as badly as we do; they love in ways we cannot understand. And in other ways that are universal: The sadness in her eyes was devastating. When I finally had to leave, she screamed like I was peeling her skin off.

Though I had to leave that day, I was determined to rescue her. And in the coming days I called the people who could help, a place outside Puerto Maldonado called Amazon Shelter. A little wildlife rescue run by a woman named Magali, who had dedicated her life to rescuing the orphans of the forest.

Over the years many orphaned animals have come into my life, each one giving me a unique glimpse into the world of their species. Spending time with Dharma taught me about elephants in ways I never could have imagined. Lulu the giant anteater, whom I raised when I was just nineteen, forced me to see the Amazon from an animal's perspective. Countless little spider monkeys, howler monkeys, snakes, hummingbirds, and a channel-billed toucan named Lucas came under my care over the years. Spending extended time with a new species and car-ing for it for days on end is a unique window into the inner workings, habits, personality, and aura of the animal. It is at odds with the fleeting, impersonal impressions we get when we see a passing eagle, or a fox darting in headlights. It's a deeply personal, intimate connection. That connection added across the years and multiplied by so many species is a summation of context that I carry with me every day. It alters how I walk through a forest, because as I do, I am seeing creatures that on some deeply personal level feel like friends.

We all know this to some degree. The fireflies we chased in the magic summer nights. The frogs and cicadas who sang us to sleep. Walking to school in last year's leaves. The birds and trees, the forest and streams—they are the backdrop and the sound-track, the substrate of our lives.

The Native people of the region speak of the animals with a kind of broad and ancient familiarity that I find comforting. *The jaguar, he always drinks like that. The anaconda, she never likes to leave the water. The kingfisher, he's always hunting for fish and chirping. The bear will never look you in the eyes. The mischievous grin of a weasel.* In this way each individual of the species becomes the manifestation of all of their kind—a fixture of the natural world that has persisted through all human generations. They are both comfort and fear, friend and foe, but undeniably the siblings of our past as a species. The swallows in the sky. The deer in the fields. Each is part of the fabric of our reality. Just as all fire is fire—an ever-present force in our universe that blos-soms into our reality, whether candle or campfire or volcano. But unlike fire, or the ocean, or the frigid mountain peaks, these species, like us, are a tentative and fleeting manifestation of life. A sacred lineage of ancient creation, a thing so much like our-selves, that must survive against the elements, evade predators, and in one way or another care for their young.

Perhaps it seems dramatic to consider that if you scaled our planet to the size of a basketball and wrapped it tightly in cellophane, the cellophane would still not be proportionally as thin as our atmosphere is. That the most prominent features of our Earth, from the Mariana Trench (the deepest point in the ocean) to Mount Everest (the highest point on land), would be too indistinct to feel, because at such a size, they'd have less texture than our fingertips. Earth, the size of a basketball, would feel smooth to the touch.

Maybe it is dramatic, or romantic, but it's how I've always thought of it: that in the trillions of frigid unknowable miles out beyond our Earth, in the limitless light-years of the known universe, our collective home is limited to the minuscule gaseous atmosphere that clings to Earth's crust. It's such a tiny, delicate thing. And in that way, how could we not look at the species we share it with as brethren?

Even to take a more Earthbound view, just looking at the destruction, all the plundered oceans, all the burned forest, the concrete-covered miles, the high-rise crowded coastlines. When you think of the ever-increasing number of iconic species orbiting the black-hole-finality of extinction, how could we not be stirred to action?

You can quantify animals, lump them in and call it all biodiversity, and make the case that they should be saved for their contributions to the ecosystems we depend on. You can justify them as crucial for our survival because they carry seeds and pollen—creating and maintaining healthy ecosystems. Because historically speaking, they created the living world our own ancestors grew up in, and without them we'd never be here.

But for me, I need no quantification.

For me, I have known enough of these wild others, these nonhuman beings, that when I look at the world, the forests, the oceans, the rivers, the sky, I feel a kinship with those wild heartbeats, and a duty to defend them from the recklessness of my own species.

I tell you the stories of these species so that you can see what I have seen, feel what I have felt. Because as Junglekeepers began to move forward, the responsibility we shouldered was tremendous. And the more forest we protected, the clearer the line became. On one side was the ancient, vibrant green world of the living, and on the other side a charred wasteland. Either we saved these forests, or they would be destroyed. It was no longer a projection, it was reality. The road and the chain saws and the bulldozers were coming—like one massive howling smog-breathing monster. A monster that would inevitably take everything.

That's why I'm writing this book, that's why I'm telling you this story. And that's why I want you to understand the severity of what we are facing as a global society, the insurmountable obstacles that stood before us as a team, and what made it possible for us to fight against such daunting odds.

≡

If there is anything that shows the true power and utility of Junglekeepers, we found it in 2024 when we discovered a part of the jungle that we came to call the Ancient Forest.

Almost a year after I first appeared on *Lex Fridman Podcast,* Lex himself came to visit.

Lex said he wanted to see the real thing. He said that ever since he had read *Mother of God,* something in him couldn't shake the craving to see truly deep jungle. He asked if we could plan an expedition like the ones JJ and I told stories about, a hardcore, all-out, real-deal jungle expedition.

And so we loaded our packs and traveled hours and hours upriver. Then the boat dropped us and left, and we plunged off into the unexplored shadows beneath the trees.

This is one of those episodes that deserves its own chapter. Because as soon as we set off, we were thrown into chaos. The topography in this part of the forest was different from anything JJ and I had anticipated. The three of us would spend the next few days following our compass bearing and hacking through some of the roughest terrain we'd ever seen.

But we also made a monumental discovery: This forest had never been touched.

Perhaps due to the impenetrably dense foliage, the savage inclines and slippery declines of the landscape, we quickly realized that no one had ever logged this area. With upturned eyes, we marveled at fully grown ancient mahogany trees, tremendous shihuahuacos, gargantuan lupunas. The trees here were so massive that we were almost constantly in a state of awe. It felt like the most sacred, untouched, hallowed part of the forest. JJ's senses were lighting up, you could see it in his eyes. Even though we were suffering through entire days of brutal, relentless hiking through the bowels of the jungle, he was beside himself with wonder.

"They neva get here, the madereros. One hundred percent. Dis is the original forest, the way it was on the day God made it. I mean, lookadis! If they could cut this they would." Then his eyes narrowed in a wondrous smile. "But no one ever came here. We are the first ones."

Our rapture at finding the wildest place we had ever seen was short-lived. On the third day of the expedition, as Lex and JJ and I were coming up against the limits of what our bodies could take, we came out onto a logging road.

I could take you through the horror we felt, but by now you know. We had thought this was the wildest, most untouched part of the jungle. Now we knew with certainty that it was about to be destroyed. It was the heart of the river, with the gun barrel of the road pointed right at it.

As soon as we discovered the logging road and the Ancient Forest, the expedition changed from one of adventure to one of urgency. We hiked faster and covered more distance. We rafted and camped and rafted again. We braved thunderstorms and traversed dozens of miles of winding tributaries until, two days later, we made our way back out onto the main Las Piedras River. The whole time, I could feel a metronome in my chest, the stopwatch countdown in my heartbeat—the clock was ticking.

The thought of such fantastic forest being destroyed was an all-consuming dread that ran like poison through my veins.

When we arrived back at the station, we slept like we hadn't slept in years. Then, the next morning, something incredible happened.

But in order to explain what that was, I first need to catch you up on the fact that in the previous few months we had been putting the finishing touches on the treehouse. It was complete. A towering, beautiful treetop hideaway outfitted with a bathroom—shower, running water, and toilet—and even a bedroom with air-conditioning. The idea was to move away from the swampy, mud-soaked adventures of old and create something of a higher caliber, something . . . elevated. We called it the Alta Sanctuary treehouse, and began offering it to clients willing to make the 140-stair climb up the spiral staircase for a chance to stay in the canopy of the Amazon.

The incredible thing that happened the day after we got back from our expedition was that Jay, one of the clients who were staying in the treehouse, wanted to hear our story.

So we told him. From the dehydration to the topography, and the stunning untouched Eden we had journeyed through. We also told him about the road and what we knew would inevitably come next. That entire forest that had been growing since the dawn of time was about to be dismantled before our eyes.

When we told him this, Jay listened intently. He was a long-time listener of Lex's podcast and had also read my book. He knew where we were coming from. And from our bug-bitten skin, hollow cheeks, and tired eyes, he could see what we'd been through.

He asked us how much we would need to protect this untouched concession. JJ called Roy back in Puerto and found out that the area in question was almost ten thousand acres. Based on our previous land acquisitions, it seemed reasonable to assume that the price of the land would be in the ballpark of $300,000.

Sitting there at the station, at 7:30 in the morning, Jay told us that he would be proud and honored to give us $150,000 toward the goal. He said we should use it as a matching donation. Use our publicity and take it to the people and raise the rest of the money.

Before the week was over, Roy had confirmed the legal information of the land. JJ had discovered that he actually knew the owner. Together they reached out. Before long they raced back to town to hold an emergency meeting with the loggers and landowners. Things were moving.

The following day, I went into the forest and did what I had done so many times before: I turned the camera on myself and spoke with all the passion I could. I told the story of the Ancient Forest and what we stood to lose. I explained to people that through the Junglekeepers donor program, if they shared the story and liked it and used the full extent of the internet, we could easily garner enough support. If one million people gave us ten dollars a month, we could save the whole river before the year was over. Imagine the heartbeats, imagine the endangered species, imagine the Ancient Forest, imagine the carbon we would keep in the ground.

JJ and Roy got a contract drawn up with our lawyers in

town: the back-end work. This is how real conservation gets done, lawyers and land acquisition, papers and meetings over coffee.

I posted the video the following morning, and it blew up immediately. The people who followed me really did care. After all, many of them had helped us save Pico's life. But now there were four or five times that many people. Stephane updated the website and made our own donation counter. That way, we could see a live feed of how the funding was coming in. Within forty-eight hours, we had almost reached $100,000. Within the first three days, we cruised past the additional $50,000 mark, matching Jay's $150,000 and securing the $300,000. Barely a week after we had identified the problem, we had told the world, raised the funds, and had an actionable plan in place.

We had what we needed to save the Ancient Forest.

═══

By the time the paperwork on the land came through, it was long after Lex had gone home. I remember calling him from the station and telling him that we'd won. The forest was safe. He was speechless. We had been so certain there was nothing we could do, and now we had not only discovered but also saved the most magnificent and wild place any of us had ever seen.

In the weeks to come, Roy and JJ would meet the owners. We'd begin working with the loggers to stop operations and shut down the road. Soon we'd block it off and knock down the bridge that had been built to make the road possible in the first place.

People might not root for you when you are just starting out, but as you begin to win, they will come out of the woodwork to support you. As 2024 progressed it seemed like each month something incredible was happening. We were riding a wave of enthusiasm from all over the world. Our support was at record levels, which meant we could work rapidly to confront loggers, collaborate with local law enforcement, and truly begin reining in the rampant deforestation that had for so long been the narrative.

It was beginning to feel like we had a chance, like we actually knew the game and what we were doing.

That is, until one day in October 2024 when everything changed. Our whole team was in Puerto Maldonado when we received the call. It was from one of our friends in the upriver Indigenous communities. What he said was confusing and distressing—a grenade that blew apart the day and changed everything we thought we knew. He said that there was an emergency unfolding and they needed our help.

The Mashco Piro had come out of the forest.

MASHCO

SOON WE WERE RIPPING UP THE DARK RIVER IN THE WARM night air. Ignacio was driving and I was at the front of the boat lighting the way. At times he didn't even need my light. The moon was out and brilliant. The clouds an abstract painting of glowing blue beauty. The stars were in the millions, arching across the sky in between the dream-state cloudscape. We looked up in wonder as the Tsuchinshan-ATLAS comet burned across the night. Its tail was a luminous whisper against the celestial desolation. Mohsin said it came into our view once every eighty thousand years. Stephane explained that the comet's passing would be a onetime event in human history. The comet held our gaze like a harbinger of the miraculous—a flash of the intangible truth buried deep within the human heart but out of reach to our mortal hands. The Milky Way arced in blue-sparkled

brilliance. Everything felt slightly elevated and hyper. I just remember looking up and knowing: *This is it.*

For the first several hours, the night was wild and crisp. The
comet in the Milky Way and the clouds glowing from the moonlight, the giant forest standing in savage immensity over us, black
against the sky. We talked endlessly. Full of excitement. What
could happen? What do we do if this or that happens? Ignacio
was a machine. I'd pass him a cigarette and give him a ten-minute
break once in a while, but he was eager to drive. We went faster
when he drove. He took the river like he was trying to win. As
clouds eclipsed the stars, I sat at the front of the boat with the
headlamp lighting the way, picking out logs and branches. As
the hours passed we gradually grew quiet.

Around 1 A.M. the rain started. Razor blades for the eyes.
Ignacio stood so he could see. I was in my raincoat but it didn't
make any difference, we were drenched. The rain was hitting
horizontal, like tiny, blinding machine-gun fire. But I could not
abandon my post—I was Ignacio's only light. With the rain the
clouds had thickened and the night was a void of inky blackness. So I had to be up in the frontmost spear of the boat. Mohsin and Stephane had their heads down and hoods on. The rain
came at first as a stern, steady drive that fell consistently, reasonably, for over an hour. But the lightning was putting on a fire
show in the sky. It cut horizontal; it even went up. The sky was
wild with flashing light and deep rolling thunder. My face hurt
from the raindrops and squinting, and I was starting to shiver
badly. I always forget how cold it can get on a boat in the Amazon in a storm. As the storm persisted past 2 A.M., I had been in
the wind and then the rain for hours and was edging toward
hypothermia.

Whenever the boat hit the river bottom, we'd dump out into
the water and push it free. At these times we'd have to push until

we found a channel where there was at least two feet of water for us to navigate. Then Ignacio would accelerate and we'd all pile back into the boat, soaking wet. My shoes were somewhere in the front of the boat under our gear, so when I jumped out I was barefoot. I thought of how bad it would be to cut my foot on a sharp stick—or worse, to step on a stingray—at a time like this. But onward we went. Through the deep, dark, rainy jungle. We did what we had to do. The shoes would never be worn again.

As the hours passed, the rain intensified. As we rounded one bend, the rain became an all-out downpour. With a hand to my brow, I kept the light out in front. My field of vision was like hyperspeed through outer space: all dark, with zooming white lights and spiraling insects. These would fly directly into my eyes. They burned and flailed under my lids and I had to rub my eyes and at the same time keep the light facing forward so we would not crash against a tree. I was the navigator, so it was my job to guide Ignacio. But the headlamp was illuminating the raindrops in the darkness so that most of the time I was blind. I had to use the reflection from caiman eyeshine along the edges of the river to guide us as we went. The rest was dead reckoning and hope.

There came a point when it was just about unbearable. I thought back to the expeditions with JJ and Pico and Chito in the old days. This was like that, but we'd never gone at night; it had never been this cold. We were driving through a storm of uncommon magnitude. The comet, the lightning, the intensity of this nocturnal odyssey—everything was swirling, racing, building.

It was approaching 3 A.M. when we reached La Cachuela falls. It's a place in the river where the current drops several feet. At that spot, the river is blocked by a perilous boundary of rocky clay, with only the one rushing waterfall as a channel. The only way to keep going is to somehow get over the rushing water. If you're going downriver, it's dangerous. If you're going upriver, it borders on madness. You have to drive the boat at full speed so the nose crashes into the waterfall and you jump a level of the river. If you take the falls badly, the boat flips, and everything gets dumped into the dark water. People die. It had happened many times in the past. For that reason, no one did the falls at night. Ever.

Ignacio never even lowered the speed. He came into view of the falls, and we exchanged a confirming nod, me on the nose of the boat using a headlamp to indicate right and left. He followed my directions and gunned it at full power. The boat smashed into the charging falls and leapt upward; I was sprayed in the face and lifted several feet into the air before crashing back down. In the back, Ignacio lifted the prop as the stern of the boat scraped over the rocks. We made it into the calm shallows above the falls.

Onward. I burned through two headlamps lighting the way. By 4 A.M. I was convulsively shivering and truly worried about whether I'd ever be warm again. I was wet to the bone, like a dog left out in the rain. We stopped on a muddy island in the middle of the river. Just stopped there. The climax of the rain had ebbed—now it was just pissing. For some time we just stood there, everyone too tired and wet and miserable to do anything productive. There was no way to get dry. Our tents would be soaked by the time we got them up. I lay under a plastic tarp on the floor of the boat with water dripping on me, but it was slightly less freezing than outside. I slept for twenty minutes, and when I woke the clouds were brighter. We could see. Howler monkeys were roaring somewhere in the jungle distance. A soft light was coming into the world.

Now, we thought, the sun would burn up the clouds and end this rain. But instead the clouds blackened and the thunder intensified. We came around the bend and upriver there was a whiteout of biblical rain. We kept riding straight into it. The rain sliced us like razors and the wind was pummeling us. Sheets of water fell one after the other. We did some whooping and hollering but realized that we were all beyond needing to rally. We just had to take it. We were doing what we had trained for, what we were made for. We were exactly where we should be and could endure any amount of discomfort needed to reach the destination in time. We gave it everything we had.

We slammed what is usually a two-day expedition in one night. We arrived in Puerto Nuevo at 9 A.M. to a warm welcome. Bacho, the one who had called, gave us big hugs. He was big, brawny, with large silver teeth and spiked hair. He was a village politician, an expert fisherman, an all-around Madre de Dios jungle wild man. I'd seen him many times on the river, fishing paco. He couldn't go near the river without swimming. A pure river otter, an animal at heart, both a product of and a testament to his environment.

"Welcome, welcome, it's good you came fast. Cómo estás, cachero?"

"Tengo mucho frio!" I said, convulsing.

He laughed loudly and clapped me on the back. "But you're here!"

The bad news hit quick: Despite our no-holds-barred, at-all-costs siege upriver, the Mashco had gone.

We were ragged and wet and exhausted. The folks at Puerto Nuevo gave us a room to stay in (the normal deal: four posts with a roof and a floor, no walls). There we put our tents on dry wood, where we'd be safe from the elements. I wasted little time in bedding down and conking out for the next several hours. It was the first time I'd truly stayed up all night since . . . I don't know when.

The whole next day it rained relentlessly. Puerto Nuevo was a community of fishermen, monkey eaters, basket weavers, and trackers. The community lived mostly off the things that they grew or hunted from the river and forest. Many of them worked for Junglekeepers as rangers. And we had become close with them because once every three months, the Junglekeepers directors and rangers would make the two-day journey upriver to visit and help them with the things they couldn't find in the surrounding jungle: medical supplies, education, and a plan for a future that included economic options that weren't logging, mining, or poaching. These were wild people who lived at the edge of the world. They were our friends. The grandmothers, the children, the shamans—they were all happy to see us. They were also all terrified.

The mood in the community of Puerto Nuevo was one of suppressed terror. Just days ago a tribe of Mashco Piro men had come out onto the beach, and no one knew what was going to happen next. The people of Puerto Nuevo had heard all the horror stories. Many of them had had arrows shot at them and narrowly escaped. Others had lost family to encounters with the Mashco. In 2013 the Mashco Piro had raided the community and frightened the people so badly that the government had sent the military to evacuate Puerto Nuevo.

This was the first time in more than ten years that a tribe had emerged. The situation was so serious that news had gotten through official channels outside the jungle. So the next day the Ministerio de Cultura arrived, the cultural ministry of Peru. It was a single boat with a few local men and one tiny little office guy named Palestino with beady eyes and spectacles. We knew he was going to be a problem. Also on the boat was the great, the legendary Rommel.

JJ had told me about Rommel for years. He was the one who could speak to the tribes. He knew many of them by face. They called him the grandfather. Abuelo. He had been all over the Madre de Dios, in Manu and Atalaya and Monte Salvado. He had seen the tribes many times. He was the most successful at communicating peacefully and clearly, and avoiding violent conflict.

On the afternoon of our second day in Puerto Nuevo, Rommel led an expedition of three boats carrying twenty people and at least ten shotguns upriver to see what evidence there was of the tribe's activity. The previous day had rained so much that the earth had been wiped clean, so any footprints we found on the beach today were fresh, there was no debating it. There they were. Rommel showed us a stick that had been stuck in the sand. This, he said, was their signal. If the stick was there to-morrow, then the tribe was still there. The stick was their warn-ing. If the stick was gone, it meant that they were gone.

Then a moment of panic. Someone saw something on the opposite side of the river. We all got into boats. Shotguns were loaded. On the opposite beach we stalked in slowly. Many of the communeros had their guns already to their shoulders. Rom-mel was in the front, scanning the ground. "They were just here," he said, "just now." He followed for some time and showed us where heavy front footsteps meant they had been ducking and running. "They're here. They're watching us."

It was late afternoon and in the dying light beneath a heavy sky, Rommel knelt to study the sand where there were fresh barefoot human tracks, only moments old. We all came in to see. No one spoke as we read the earth. The only sounds were wind and rounds sliding into shotguns. Rommel stood at the high point on the edge of the beach near a great black fallen tree. His eyes scanned the distance.

"NOMOLÉ!" he shouted softly.

"It's happening," Mohsin said. He was standing stock-still beside me with wide eyes. I felt my adrenaline simmering up my spine. We stood there frozen.

"Nomolé!" Rommel said again, holding up his hands. The sound of his voice echoed over the river. The severity of this wilderness was striking to behold; we were standing on the edge of the human presence on our planet, shouting out into the great beyond. We stood there with loaded shotguns on the sand beneath the tall river cane. The tribe didn't respond, but there was no arguing with the earth, they had been here just moments ago, which meant they could hear us now. They were watching.

Rommel stood brave, his hair dancing in the wind. His voice strong but gentle, "We do not want to hurt you, we do not want to fight, nomolé! We want to be friends with you, brothers, nomolé!"

Rommel's small stature looked wise and valiant in the savage wreckage of branches and blackened wood on the beach. The jungle stood implacable all around us. The shadows were full of hidden people. Our hearts throbbed with the anticipation of a moment that walked the razor's edge between centuries of human healing and all-out massacre. But after some time, and a short sermon from Rommel, he turned. "They won't come out, they are scared by us now. Let's go."

By that night, Stephane lost faith that anything else was going to happen. We discussed that we had probably missed them, and should head downriver at first light the next day. Mohsin agreed and we began shifting our conversation to the things we could get done back at the station. The Alta treehouse business stuff, helping JJ with the land deals. But we were done here. It was buggy, hot, cold, tough, and after all that effort we felt a little let down.

But the next morning we woke at five to Rommel suggesting we go check on the stick. If it was there, they'd be coming today. If it was gone, they'd be gone. Another expedition, men, guns, boats. And sure enough, the stick was gone. Which meant the tribe was gone. That was all we needed. We would go downriver after a quick breakfast.

While we packed and prepared to leave, Ignacio came to me. His eyes were severe.

"You are my boss, right? My director?"

"Sí. Yes, what about it?"

"I need to speak to you like a friend," he said, his eyes never wavering from mine.

I nodded for him to please spit it out.

"You can't leave. You would be an idiot to leave. The stick is gone but the footprints are still there. They are going to come. Maybe not today, maybe tomorrow. We came all this way, you'd be an idiot to come all this way and leave. They are going to come."

I had a hard time explaining this to the guys. Stephane had already switched gears, and felt that in this community everyone seemed to have a theory, it was all based on footprints and sticks and the wind—things that were hardly visible, let alone quantifiable data. Mohsin brought up that maybe they were keeping us here just to try to take us for a ride. I disagreed wholeheartedly with them both. All these years in the jungle had taught me that the locals are never wrong. From Don Santiago and the Floating Forest to countless times JJ and others had just *known* things.

"We stay. I'm staying. That's that." I told them they could figure out their own way down if they wanted to leave. Stephane's tent was already on the boat. There was some bickering, some feelings thrown around. Everyone was hot and tired and bug-bitten and raw. But stay we did, and in the coming hour we split up. If we had to spend the day, the guys figured they'd better use their cameras to document what they could of Native life.

I found a quiet place on a wood floor and opened my laptop and a book about the shaman Don Ignacio Duri. The buildings in Puerto Nuevo are all decks about a meter off the ground, with wooden boxes constituting rooms. The roofs are either corrugated steel or palm thatch. Few of these houses had working doors. I had just opened the book and the laptop, found a quiet place to write. I was working on the earlier chapters of this very book. The birds were singing. An hour passed, and then another. The world seemed peaceful. Then it happened for real.

"MASHCO!"

I don't know who called it, but I was on my feet and out the door.

As I ran, there was a dread quality to the moment. Terrified women were lifting children off their feet and running with them. Dogs and chickens were scrambling. Bacho met me somewhere, panting, his eyes wide. "Vamos!" We ran together across the small village, zipped through yuca plants and plantain trees. There is a haunting piece by composer Clint Mansell from the film *The Fountain* called "Death Is the Road to Awe," and it was ringing through me as I ran. Barefoot, we leapt through the trees and out to the bluff, and set our eyes on the far side of the river.

They came like shadows, melting from the sullen weight of the jungle and out onto the beach. Ghosts in the flesh that you could have dismissed as apparitions had it not been for the clouds of millions of green-and-white butterflies reacting as they came—lepidopteran confirmation of reality: The butterflies saw them too. Dark, wild-haired warriors with bows and arrows. They were crouched low, arrows nocked, ready. There was something ancient in how they moved, like cavemen, like early hominids glimpsed through a magic lens that could see into our collective past. The origin of our species that never left the green womb, the children that time forgot, now stepped out into the light a thousand years late. Their eyes as dark as night, sorrow-shaped and full of the horror of profound unknowing.

They were coming straight for us.

At first it was just four or five of them, off in the distance. But soon there were others coming from the trees. All of them were armed.

"Watch for arrows, and stay by a tree." Ignacio was breathing like a scared animal.

Shotgun shells clacked home as everyone loaded up. Some of the guns were homemade wooden rigs with pipe kits (which in a fight are only slightly better than muskets because you have to manually knock the hot shell out of the barrel by hand before reloading). Others had better guns: savage little folding-stock semiautomatic Magnum shotguns, nasty close-range metal fuckers. Everyone was watching everyone. I was scared. Stephane was already on the bluff when I found him, silent, shutter firing, ceaselessly capturing the images that would change everything. Mohsin dropped to one knee and started sniping visions of prehistoric men, images that could have been from ten thousand years ago. His entire photographic career in the Amazon had been leading to this moment. As I passed him I hugged him tight, my own eyes glued to the distance. I watched as the Mashco Piro came across the beach. They were barefoot and naked from head to toe, save for the rope they wore around their waists to tie their penises up. Distant Paleolithic figures had become visible people with features. I could see their faces and the fear, their wild hair and the yellow-and-red war paint on their fore-heads.

We stood quiet and waiting in the wind.

The Mashco men were moving closer.

When literally anything can happen next, you notice your instincts kick in. Your eyes trace escape routes and identify hiding places. You check the river and wonder if you could dive in and drift away before they got a clear shot at you. We watched them walk closer and every one of us was calculating how far those arrows could fly.

Soon they were directly opposite where we stood.

The moment of contact was approaching.

Rommel, the Native anthropologist, was already at the edge of the water. "Ay! NOMOLÉ!" Rommel was standing on the bank. Hobbitlike, wise and calm. His eyes squinted, his hands by his side. "HO! Nomolé!"

The tribe spoke. "Nomolé!"

Rommel replied, "Nomolé."

The air was thick with the smell of wet earth and iron. I was acutely aware that only a small stretch of river divided our two sapien tribes. Their tribe naked, our tribe clothed.

While only Rommel, our leader, spoke, the Mashco all spoke at the same time like a flock of birds. It sounded like twenty people all at once saying, "Teeshi tawi katana shashuha nani pashicano tashe peappedey hateiiyyyy!" None of it made sense to us.

Rommel spoke in Yine telling them to put down their weapons. We were all close to trees and the house, ready to take cover. Ignacio's eyes were burning as he scanned. The men we could see before us on the beach were only some of them. There were more of them standing in the forest where the shadows still clung to them. They didn't speak or look at one another, they were fixated on us. They were all fixated on Rommel. "Nomolé!" Every so often this refrain. "Brothers! Brothers! Put down your weapons. Please put down your weapons, brothers! Nomolé!"

Mohsin and I finally made eye contact, this was it. The tribesmen were close enough for us to see the whites of their eyes. Only men had come. Their hair was wild. They were tall and thin, not like the stout Peruvians beside us. Their skin was clear and healthy. They all wore bracelets and bands beneath the knees. Some had facial hair, others had nothing. Some looked forty, some were twelve. All of them had their balls showing. All of them were armed with massive bows with wide, bamboo-tipped arrows that could cut a man in half.

Rommel spoke with passion, projecting his voice across the river, begging the Mashco men to lay down their arms. Timidly, they listened, and when they had laid their weapons on the sand, they clapped their open hands, showing us their palms— empty.

Rommel nodded, *Good,* and took a step into the river.

The leader of the Mashco also took a few steps forward, entering the river to his knees.

Someone *clack-clacked* a shotgun beside me.

No one made a sound.

All eyes were on Rommel. He was peaceful, calm, and sage-like. Beside him a few of the other men were preparing a canoe filled with gifts of plantains and rope and sugarcane. Everything was building toward this moment of exchange. We were all busy watching him work in front of us on the river, so much so that there was panic when something happened from behind.

It was an ambush! We were surrounded! Suddenly all the men with guns rushed toward the jungle side. The Mashco across the river fled and became agitated. As I jogged with the gunmen we passed a little man with glasses who was wearing an official shirt. It was the guy from the Ministry of Culture, Palestino, and he had grabbed a kitchen knife and found a place to hide. I saw him do the sign of the cross and beg God aloud not to let him die.

I came up beside Bacho's brother, who spat and squinted, mouth open, gun to his shoulder, ready to brawl. An old man with a gun took position behind a tree. I took cover beside him. I had no weapon, but if this turned into a massacre, I wanted to see it coming as well as have the best chance to do what I had promised Katlin: protect Mohsin at all costs. We had all agreed long ago that if this day should ever come, my one job was to get Mohsin home to his son. Him being a father meant he had to always be in a position where no arrow could find him. We had never thought it would actually happen. Now that it had, I was on full alert.

This is how it happens, I thought. It would be only moments until the first arrow zipped out of the foliage and cut someone down. Then the shotguns would go wild. The tribe would scream a war cry from the opposite bank, lift their bows, and charge across the river. I found myself focusing on my breathing. If it went bad, it would go real bad. We had twenty men and six or seven guns. There were easily forty of the Mashco that we could see, and perhaps another forty we couldn't. If this turned into a battle, it would be a slaughter. For a long, terrible time, I stood on the balls of my feet, knees bent, ready to run. My heart slamming in my ribs.

But the commotion from behind was not an attack. Slowly we realized that the movement that had triggered the alarm was actually the unseen Mashco women. They were indeed behind us, but they were busy pillaging the farm. They were stealing bananas while the men made a commotion at the river.

A young man with a wide, friendly face and a kind smile

came to me. He said his name was George, and it struck me as odd that he seemed so calm. He said things were getting started on the river. Slightly dizzy, I followed him and returned to the bluff, where everyone was now trying to regain composure. The tribe had calmed. Rommel and another man named Linner were stepping into the river. Just thirty meters from where the tribe stood. They waded in.

Ignacio was standing with arms folded beside a tree. His eyes were a storm as he watched. This was exactly how he'd been shot. Doing exactly this—trying to help them. Now it was happening all over again. He lifted binoculars to his eyes. He looked scared and savage and full of seething emotion. Rommel was down below, waist-deep in the water, moving farther and farther from our side of the river, farther from the safety of the shotguns and nearer to the tribe, nearer to the abyss of possibility.

"Nomolé!" Rommel said, this time sternly. "Nomolé!" He walked calmly, guiding the boat with the offerings, keeping it strategically between himself and the tribe should he need a shield. "Nomolé!" He said it as if he needed to keep reminding them that he was a friend, and they should not kill him. As though they might forget in just a few minutes' time.

Everyone watched in tense anticipation. It was within the realm of possibility that the tribe would spook. That someone would fire an arrow that would zip right through him. Kill him right where he stood. The mortal weight of the moment held us all still. Rommel's bravery was breathtaking. He guided the canoe out into the center of the river, one small man before forty warriors.

Then, when he had gotten as close as he dared, he pushed the boat forward so it drifted toward the tribe. The water began to churn as they rushed forward. A dozen naked men stormed onto the boat like starving animals, each man clutching at plantains.

They fought and shoved and shouted as they removed every last one of the green gifts. For a horror-filled moment you could see the lack of organization, the every-man-for-himself desperation.

Then the whole dance began again. The tribe sent the boat back and began chattering, and a dominant man with a samurai mustache spoke powerfully and with grand gestures. More bananas were brought. The boat was loaded. Again, Rommel went out into the river, but this time the mood had become considerably calmer. He held the back of the boat as the tribe advanced. He spoke softly, often repeating the refrain: "No-molé!"

Again the tribe attacked the boat and snatched everything it contained: plantains and sugarcane and rope. As they did, Rommel stood there, not more than twelve feet from them. Calm. When all the cargo had been removed he spoke to them so softly we could not hear him. They were motioning to him. They wanted his clothes. He took off his shirt and threw it to them. One of the Mashco grabbed it out of the air and kept it for himself. Another came forward now, motioning to Rommel's shorts. These too he removed and threw over. Then he turned and came back to our side of the river.

For some time we watched them. The golden river flowed between us. A few dozen meters of water separating the Stone Age and the modern world. Terns flew through the air and the beach was brilliant with butterflies. We stood in solemn silence, confronted with the historic proportions of what we were seeing. First contact: the intersection of centuries, a group of well-meaning local Indigenous people exchanging the most basic gifts of food and rope with a people wholly untethered from the machinations of the modern world.

Soon the tribe was gesturing for more.

This time Ignacio made his way down beside Rommel. I was standing ten feet back near a papaya tree. Ignacio looked back at me with a scoundrel smile and took off his Junglekeepers shirt. It was the green long sleeve with a white logo that the rangers wore. He motioned to me, *Can I give this to them?*

I shrugged and motioned to Rommel, *He's the boss.*

This time it was Linner's turn to bring the boat out into the river and deliver the last of the plantains. He did this and once again the explosion of activity as the starving tribals clutched and fought over the big green bunches in the boat. They carried off the plantains.

Then Ignacio threw the shirt to Linner and he waded out and tossed it over. The tribe was now practically on our side of the river. One of them caught the shirt as it hit the water, lifted it, and wrung the water out of it. We all smiled. They smiled. It was a monster of a moment. Somehow both sides knew it was silly. Somehow the two tribes, theirs and ours, softened. Rommel would later confirm that this was the first time he'd seen these men, this particular clan, this tribe. The gifts we gave, the smiles we exchanged, seemed like small acts of atonement for a brutal past that none of us fully knew, a history of violence that had wrought the divide we were now reaching across.

FOR OVER THREE HOURS the people of Puerto Nuevo and the Mashco Piro exchanged words and gestures and gifts. In the last hour that the tribe was present, things calmed down. Rommel told them, "We have nothing left, you have all our plantains and sugarcane and rope. We have nothing left to give, so go now and be happy."

One of the Mashco warriors strode out onto the beach, lifted his longbow from the sand, and fit an arrow to the string. He walked proudly, and obviously, to the edge of the water, pulled back the string, and shot an arrow. It wasn't at anyone in particular. It wasn't a threat. Judging from his calm shoulders and narrowed eyes, it seemed like a playful bit of insolence.

For a long time I sat with Ignacio and Bacho on a bench beneath some palms by the river. It was an old canoe with two stumps under it. We watched the tribe walk along the opposite bank under the shadow of the cecropia trees. They had made their way to a farm on the other side in the jungle and found some plastic sacks and even a machete. "Hey, what are you doing with my machete!" Bacho boomed across the river. We were all laughing now. The naked man on the other side waved dismissively and brandished the blade, taunting. Bacho threw up his hands and laughed. "Take it! Bastards." We were all smiling now. No one had died. Ignacio stood up and spoke to the Mashco for some time. He danced and they danced. Two tribes across a river.

Back up at the bluff, Stephane was still shooting. Rommel was there too, still wearing a necklace they'd given him. Still answering questions as they came in.

"They want to know how to tell the difference between the bad people and the good. They want to know why some people cut down the trees. They hate when people cut down the trees. Especially the big ones. The trees are like gods to them. They want to know why we do it."

Rommel turned to me.

"How can I explain our world to them? Some call them Stone Age people but they're wrong. These are pre–Stone Age people. There are no stones here, so they never learned to shape stone. They don't have any concept of mining metal. Or building boats. Other tribes make clay pots, but not them. They drink water from the stream but have never seen it freeze or boil— they don't even know it can. Here," he said, "show them you mean no harm."

He broke off from speaking to me to answer a question a Mashco man shouted from across the river.

"They are curious about you," Rommel said.

"Me?"

Rommel smiled. "They said you look big and strong like a warrior, and they want to see you properly, come here."

I stepped out of the shade and into the sunlight. Rommel had one hand on my arm—he was presenting me. I didn't want to keep my shoulders square or look intimidating or warriorlike at all. If there was anything uniting us in the community with the Mashco Piro, it was the kinship of shared fears. So I held up my hands, palms out. I waved. On the other side of the river, several of the warriors held up their hands, waved. We lowered our hands. Then I did it again. It was exhilarating. Communicating across cultures and time and language with the simplest of human gestures: *Here are my empty hands, I have no weapons, I am a brother.* I said, "Nomolé!"

The last we saw of the tribe was like some mesmeric vision from another century—as though a wrinkle in time had momentarily folded us into a fleeting spectral aperture from another epoch entire. A few dozen naked warriors moved off along the beach. Bows and arrows in their hands, bare feet on the sand, plantains lashed to their muscular backs. The naked human form. An anachronistic vision of our own species, vanishing into the periphery of credible understanding. One by one they dissolved into the distance, swallowed by the green womb of the great jungle beyond.

=====

That night we met in the communal hut with Bacho and the rest of Puerto Nuevo. I explained that as directors of Junglekeepers, we were now willing and compelled to help them. We had seen the stark reality of the world in which their lives unfolded. We had seen their bravery and humanity as they risked their lives to give the gift of their own food, the most basic and meaningful offering, in the hopes the tribe would be peaceful.

But these people were scared. At any moment, the tribes could choose violence and massacre them all. There was simply no telling. "We need a safe house," Bacho said. "We need some kind of protection."

Mohsin and Stephane and I made eyes at one another. The tribes had been here for ages. Millennia. It was Puerto Nuevo that had come in and cut down the trees and made clearings and started firing the tchee-tchee-xu (fire sticks, guns) that the tribe hated so much. Indigenous or not, the people of Puerto Nuevo had been here only a few decades. They were on the Mashco's land.

We told the community leaders we would do all we could to help. They thanked us profusely. It was complicated in our hearts. Using our satphone, we called JJ and the team in Puerto Maldonado and they dispatched an entire boatload of rice and yuca and salt and sugar and tuna and various other items, including medical supplies and eighty gallons of gasoline. It would arrive in two days.

The following morning, amidst hugs and some final group photos, we boarded our boat and made our way downriver.

Later that day, some of the men from Puerto Nuevo who assumed the tribe had left went out fishing. As they were traveling upstream, the tribe attacked from both sides. The ambush had been orchestrated. Over a hundred of them running across the beach. Others were poised like snipers, hidden high in the jungle at the river's bend. Arrows filled the air. As he was piloting his friends away from the danger, one arrow hit George in the back just beside the spine and traveled through his body from just over his scapula to just behind his belly button—

collapsing his right lung. He fell as another friend took over driving at full speed. The tribe was charging behind them, running through the jungle and across the beaches, loosing arrows, in full war paint, red-and-yellow faces, howling, chasing, ready to kill.

THE
OVERSTORY

"**T**HE GOVERNMENT IS SENDING A HELICOPTER FROM CUSCO. It's going to land here in Puerto and then go straight out to Monte Salvado to get George."

I said nothing. I couldn't. My mind was too busy imagining poor George, whom we had just seen, lying there gasping, with an arrow through his chest. He and everyone else in Puerto Nuevo had been evacuated to Monte for safety. I couldn't fathom how he was still alive and felt certain that if the wound was as bad as they described it, he would die.

We were all back in Puerto Maldonado at the Junglekeepers office.

"Listen," JJ said, "there's something else. Something strange is happening. The Mashco are out in the river. After George was shot, when the others got away, they saw hundreds of them. They are out of the jungle. The river is very shallow. They are walking up. Out in the open. They are going toward Monte Salvado."

"What happens when they reach Monte?" I asked.

JJ's eyes went wide, exasperated at the thought of it. "I think you need to be ready."

"Ready for what?" I asked. It seemed like everything was

building, rushing, like a runaway train accelerating down a mountain.

"I think you gonna needa you tent."

"My tent? What?" I said, squinting.

Then JJ smiled. It was the smile of a friend you've known for twenty years. The one who's seen you do things so irresponsible and reckless that he had to save your life multiple times. The one you survived with. It's the smile of someone who knows your nature almost better than you do—and in that moment, you realize that's why you're friends in the first place. He knew before I knew. And when I saw that scoundrel spark in his black eyes, a grin spread across my face. There are those among us who experience an almost pathological joy at fighting against stacked odds, enduring harsh elements, and cheating death. JJ knew exactly where this all was heading.

Then his phone rang again. This time he rushed inside and I followed.

It was at that moment that something incredible happened.

I was surrounded by a flurry of activity and felt like I was watching a movie of my own life. There we were in the Junglekeepers office. The registered, official place where our organization held its headquarters. JJ, with glasses on, was bent over, scribbling notes regarding the rescue helicopter. Stephane was running inventory on the supplies that we were going to send to the communities to make up for what the tribe had taken. Mohsin was hurrying back and forth with the ranger coordinator carrying sacks of rice. Roy was sitting in another room between two lawyers who were preparing the paperwork on yet another tremendous concession—the owner, they would later tell us, was willing to forgo logging and sell us the land, happy to be paid for doing nothing. Loggers from all over the region were lining up to ask for jobs as rangers.

≡

Somewhere along the way our vision for protecting the forest had graduated from a distant idea to a present reality. Where we once had a vague and undefined dream, we now had a definitive and attainable goal: to save the Las Piedras watershed. The discovery work was done, the strategies crafted, the targets set, and now it was on for real. The time of talk had long ago passed—we had entered the phase of implementation.

If you quantify the land encompassed by the river's watershed between the Madre de Dios Territorial Reserve and the destroyed farmland that exists below Lucerna, the sum is an area on the order of 300,000 to 350,000 acres, depending on how you add it. Either way, somehow, and almost without noticing, we had gone from hopeful wannabes to undeniable practitioners. By the end of 2024 we were protecting more than 110,000 acres of rainforest. An area that is so great in size, it can be difficult to imagine. To give you an idea, that's half the size of Singapore. It's almost eight times the area of Manhattan Island. It's a quarter of the size of Sequoia National Park.

How the hell did we get here?

At what point does the foal graduate from faltering steps to effortless gallop? It's something that happens almost unconsciously, the result of repetition and absolute necessity.

How many swamps had JJ and I waded through, only to come back empty-handed? How many times had we thought we had taken flight, only to crash down and have to rebuild from scratch? The old days had seemed so directionless, the horizon so hidden. I remember the nights with Don Santiago and the old jungle stories. I still leaf through journal pages that I penned while on solos deep in the wilderness, littered with crushed mosquitoes and raindrop spots. I recall the times drinking ayahuasca with Don Ignacio. My time wandering the forests of India with Dharma. I remember thinking, *What is any of this for?*

And that's the thing. Looking back now, it's clear to me that the greatest burden, the most daunting and dispiriting obstacle I ever faced, had been never knowing if I was on the right path. All that pressure and depression, all the existential dread—it had all come from the same source. I was a kid in school terrified I had been born in the wrong time. Even when I got to the Amazon, the feeling persisted. Was it my destiny to watch the most beautiful things on Earth destroyed? Was there really nothing we could do to save the Ancient Forest and the animals of the Amazon? Have we really been thrust into consciousness at a time when the world is dying?

The truth, speaking plainly, is that I wasn't always motivated by inspiration and certainty; I acted out of fear and doubt. I went to the Amazon because deep down I knew that I could never do anything else. The same darkness that chased me and kept me up at night is the exact thing that had me running toward the light. It's like pulling the cord on the peke peke motor: You gotta do it or you'll die. It's the same thing that has kept soldiers running across battlefields and tigers racing at full speed behind their prey. It's what kept me going long enough to find my way.

The stoics had it right: I've suffered far more in anticipation than I ever did in reality. What I interpreted as depression was actually a white-hot yearning to see the fruition of my dreams. So many people told me that the discomfort I was feeling could be fixed with pills. And maybe they were right. But the restlessness and disassociation we feel in modern times is often nothing simpler and more tremendous than our soul clawing at the cage. We are all eager to transform, to break free of the chrysalis and enter the arena.

I've always found great meaning in the idea that the master

has failed more times than the beginner has even tried. Maybe because I've failed so many times. And maybe because now, somehow, over the years, I can see I have begun to make progress in traversing the distance between the two. Each year we find larger anacondas and learn more about their biology. Last year my observations from the field resulted in numerous scientific publications. One paper, in the journal *Check List,* established our river as one of the most diverse in the world. I was even included as co-author on a paper describing the hunting habits of lowland anacondas in the *Journal of Natural History.* Each year, we continue to protect more forest; each year, we save more acres. And although I failed out of school and will probably never have a PhD, I'm penning the final words of my third book. The mission we are on has been shared in photos and videos and documentaries—the story is reaching the world.

Each day my inboxes are full of messages from kids worldwide who ask questions like "How can I get out there and help?," "How did you get started?," and "How do I get your job?"

The last one always makes me smile. If they only knew.

If there's any common thread in the thousands of messages that I now receive, it is a growing concern for the future of our natural world. We've all been emotionally brutalized by images of ocean fisheries collapsing, the coral reefs bleaching, the rainforest being dismantled, and the climate in chaos.

After nearly twenty years in Amazonia, I can tell you that the stakes are high. It is true that we've lost nearly 20 percent of the basin's original area. Scientists are warning that we may be approaching a tipping point. If too much more of Amazonia is cut, it could disrupt the moisture cycle and trigger a kind of basin-wide drying that would be catastrophic, and from which there is no going back.

It's a terrifying thing to consider. The environmental issues we face today are more urgent and all-encompassing than anything we've faced before. We *have* to fix it. And so, from what I've seen, there is no question that we are alive at the most important time in history. Either we save the natural treasures that make our world what it is, or we curse all future generations with the repercussions of our greed. But contained in these elevated stakes is the opportunity for a redefining of our species.

Can we peel back the quotidian veil and consider the full and unflinching view of what we face? We are, for the first time in history, confronted with a planetary problem. A question so grave that it requires the attention of everyone.

While popular culture and the news seem increasingly seduced by the idea of life outside of Earth, I cannot help but double down on the simple, irrefutable truth: Our Earth is the one place in all the frigid darkness of the universe where we know for certain that life exists. It is the only planet on which we have existed; it contains all of our past and all of our present, and for that reason, it is the one onto which I project all of our future hope. How could anyone endure watching it be dismantled? How can we not see the destruction we wage on the face of this Earth as self-inflicted wounds?

The same questions that haunted me as a child now motivate me. I've learned that hopelessness is a poison peddled by the darkness. Look around. There is a kind of dreadful doubt that has pervaded in the recession of religious belief, leaving many with the message that makes the miracles of life look like a bad joke. Even human art and love and compassion are reduced to little more than the blind instinctual functions of biological entities. The high philosophers of the sapiens ride through space on a rock where everything has been carefully curated to our exact specifications, and they dare to doubt?

They question whether we are alone in the universe while we are surrounded by our wild brethren. And in the face of the hip, cynical atheism that has pervaded the present, I resist. I've seen too many people working to pass on the light. There are people all over the globe working to save species. Helping to fix habitats in peril. There are doctors and scientists and teachers and parents, and all kinds of people dedicated to making the world better. What I've seen is that it doesn't take traveling to far-flung countries to rescue exotic species—it's what happens in our own homes, in our own backyards. It's people voting for leaders who care about the environment. It's planting trees, saving old ones. It's making our backyards wildlife friendly—being allies to the wild things of this world. It's being allies to one another. There are shock waves from the brilliance of our ever-expanding compassion that grow to encompass our own two-legged kind as well as the four-legged, the scaled, the feathered and finned. I think of all the animals I have known, great and small, from turtles to toucans, anteaters to elephants. It takes assuming our role and realizing our power to step into the destiny we were made for.

We are the keepers of this world. It's up to us. Because the problem is us. But we are also the solution. It's as simple and as complex as whether or not we can stop our own species from cutting trees, plundering the oceans, covering paradise in cement. We are indeed at a critical time, but we were made for critical times. We as humans are given the mind of a philosopher, the body of a warrior, and the heart of a hero, but without a way to use these gifts, you'll be a caged wolf. Growing more disoriented and savage by the day, not even knowing the limitless potential of your powers—that you could run and hunt and live with such vitality that you'd be capable of racing along the rocky peaks of mountains so high you could touch heaven.

If you need proof of this power, just look at JJ, who has spanned the whole spectrum. When it comes to the jungle, he has become the master. The guy who started out as another naked Amazonian child, barefoot in the village, swimming in the rivers—he decided early who he was. He saw the jungle gradually being degraded and decided to take a stand. And through the years, he stood by the little research station and never left. Now he owns and operates the Alta Sanctuary, the world's tallest treehouse. There are dozens of ex-loggers and gold miners and poachers who work there, who all have stable, sustainable jobs. And although there's now a fancy staff and clean trails, it retains its authenticity and remains nestled in a vast landscape that is still 99.99 percent untouched. Lucerna and the logging boats have done some damage, but the truth is that if we saved it now, it would still mostly be in its primordial state.

At the end of 2024, not long after we saw the Mashco, we got news that JJ had been selected as one of *Time* magazine's 100 climate leaders of the year. It came out of nowhere, a glowing international recognition of his mission as an Indigenous leader and a resounding confirmation of his life's work saving the Amazon through ecotourism and his organization, Junglekeepers. Keep at something long enough and the world will notice; throw a stone into the lake and the universe ripples.

And that's the truth at the end of the tunnel: It really is all up to you.

Today there are thousands of people in the Junglekeepers donor program. People from all over the world who care about the fate of the wildest place on Earth. The fact is that now we've found a way to bridge the gap between faraway species and ecosystems and the people across the globe who want to save them. Most of our donors can afford to part with the price of an expensive coffee once a month. Five dollars from enough people, and we could save the river tomorrow. That makes each single

small donor just as crucial as the larger donors, because whatever the size of the donation, it comes down to individual
responsibility—whether you're like Jay, who gave us half of
what we needed to save the Ancient Forest, or you're like the
many smaller donors who are critical to the mission.

One mother told me that her family donates five dollars a
month, that she has two jobs, but that she wants her kids to
know they are part of saving something special, that they can
make a difference. She said they watch our wildlife videos on
social media.

We've found a way to bridge the gap between donors around
the globe and local people in the Amazon. We've seen that loggers aren't evil, they just need better jobs. If we improve the
lives of the people with no other options, we can move the nee-
dle and show that the narrative of conservation can be rewritten
from one of loss and tragedy to one of innovation and light. It's
only possible because of all the people who support us.

Today our mission is clear and definable: Protect this one
thing. This one glowing emerald of a river basin that contains so
much life, so many tribes and trees, and all those millions of
heartbeats. It's a mission with a start and a finish. The question
is no longer "Can we save the river?" but instead "Can we do it
in time?"

Between Alto Purús National Park, the Tambopata National
Reserve, Manu National Park, and the Madre de Dios Territorial Reserve, the Las Piedras River runs like a golden thread.
The connective tissue of it all, the heart of the most biodiverse
terrestrial habitat on Earth. So many years in, we are finally on
the playing field, in the big leagues. We have a real chance of
saving this river, these animals, these trees, these tribes.

Junglekeepers is now protecting a significant portion of the
total area we need to save. At 110,000 acres, we are roughly one-

third of the way to our goal of protecting the original growth
of the Las Piedras River basin. *One-third* of the way. If we can
make it that far, how can we logically argue that this isn't something we can do? Whether or not you can chisel through granite
depends entirely on whether you continue to swing the ham-
mer.

===

"I need to be on that chopper."

"I know," JJ said.

We knew the tribe was marching up the river. We knew that
Monte Salvado would evacuate its women and children. We
knew that Rommel and a few men would stay back to guard the
village. There was no doubt that come war or come talk, something incredible was about to take place out in the jungle. For a
long moment we stood there, each forming sentences that never
emerged.

"Let's go!" said Stephane, who had dispatched the supplies
to meet us at the airfield.

"Be careful," JJ said, "take care a-you-self."

We hugged tightly. One more look square in the eyes.

As Stephane and Mohsin and I piled into the pickup and
drove off, JJ was already back on the phone, talking to the police about a possible invasion by the narcos up past the Ancient
Forest.

When we arrived at the airport, the security guard was wearing camo and holding a gun. Leaders from the communities
were already there, waiting to see George arrive. The ambulance was flashing on the tarmac. I was praying he was still alive.
That he would live.

We felt the low thunder of the helicopter before we could
see it.

"What are you gonna do?" Mohsin asked.

We could see the helicopter now, coming low over the jungle.

"I don't know." It seemed like madness to voluntarily go. But then it seemed like madness not to. Maybe there would be a massacre. Maybe the Mashco would be reasonable. There was no way to know. Either way, an interaction between human tribes of a kind that is rare on this Earth was drawing nearer. Either way, I was the director of Junglekeepers and we were sending food and support to the communities. If there was an interaction of any kind, I would be the only person present with a professional camera. The only one capable of representing the story to the world. The tribes had asked Rommel why our people cut the ancient trees. The tribes had no idea of the annihilation that was coming for them. After all the massacres of Indigenous cultures over the last several centuries, now the last truly free people on Earth are unknowingly tied to the tracks with the freight train of civilization charging toward them. I was scared, but at the same time, if it really happened, it was my *job* to see it. And by now, if shit did hit the fan, I knew I could run into the forest and survive for days if I had to. Twenty years of experience and a machete—I had everything I needed. The rest was in my bag. I was ready. It would be madness to miss it.

Soon the deafening *wap! wap! wap!* of the chopper setting down. The stretcher carrying George was rushed into the ambulance, which went racing off. As it did, I spoke to the security guard at the gate. He had already been told we would be there. He knew we were sending supplies. He asked me if I was going to accompany the supplies out to Monte Salvado. I told him I was and asked him how long it would take to get there. He said he didn't know, maybe an hour.

My God, I thought. A four-day peke peke ride by river, an hour by chopper. Everything was moving so fast.

I was signed in and brought past the gate. I looked official in my camo pants, Junglekeepers shirt, and black hat with sunglasses. There was no time for goodbyes. In the backpack on my shoulder were my journal, cans of tuna, my camera, a change of clothes, a tent, and a bedsheet.

As the helicopter team worked to load supplies onto the open chopper, I was trying to think, *Am I the kind of person who would gamble everything to learn what I don't know?* After all these years of chasing adventure . . . there it was.

To one side, the insane gusting energy of the helicopter— a flying machine ready to take me into the deepest jungle on Earth. Where a historic battle was about to take place. The rotor was spinning. I knew if I got on, there was no going back.

To the other side, my friends were off in the distance behind the chain-link fence at the edge of the airfield. I couldn't speak to them, I couldn't ask their counsel. That time had passed. I was beyond the gate. And even if I could, I knew what they would say. They'd convince me to stay, forbid me to go. I saw Mohsin shake his head, a look of dread bordering on horror on his face: *Don't do this.* But I couldn't say a thing. We had come too far and it all felt so final. I was separating from them. It felt immense, like this one moment was a dizzying precipice, a one-way door, a defining moment in my life. If I got on that helicopter, there was no going back.

For a moment a lump formed in my throat and a flurry of fear rose up my body. It was followed by a deep sense of admiration and love. Somehow this team had come together to create a kind of task force capable of doing things I had never dreamed possible.

In the coming days Mohsin would continue to photograph

and strategize with the coordinators. Roy would be running the lawyers and slogging through negotiations, signing documents that would save vast tracts of forest. Stephane, like some kind of coding superhero, would be building the systems that allowed us to reach millions and function as a single entity—and somehow keep it all organized, focused, and under control. Then there was JJ, the rarest of species. Without him none of this would have been possible. He had given us the keys to the Amazon, to adventure, to our dreams. And now we were doing it. We were really doing it. It was no longer a dream or a joke, this was the real thing. In that moment it dawned on me the incalculable odds involved in bringing this unlikely crew together. These people, this team—each had followed their own unlikely path. Each was the only one who could do the job they were doing. And together we had the chance to pull something priceless from the flames, saving it for the world, for the animals, for every unborn child in generations to come who will look out into the blindness of his or her future, and want with the fire of their being to be part of healing the wounds of this planet.

I looked at the chopper and I knew what I had to do. I was stepping into something I'd been moving toward for decades. And I knew that the moment my feet left the tarmac and touched the stairs of the helicopter, I would be thrown headlong into the adventure my whole life had been preparing me for. I knew how high the stakes were, but also that if I'd learned anything, diving in headfirst was the only way. As I climbed the stairs I felt a kind of blazing entropic acceleration. There comes a point when you have to make a fundamental decision about who you are.

The helicopter's high-frequency turbine sound was climbing. I stopped at the top of the stairs and held my hand up long enough for Mohsin and Stephane to see a final goodbye. They raised their hands in acknowledgment.

I went in and found a seat, the turbine spooling to incredible speed, going faster and faster until the deep thudding shook the air. I put a headset on and reset my sunglasses. The wind began to batter us. Everything was swirling. We lifted off from the ground, and then we were rushing through the air. Cruising across the Madre de Dios River and then over the breathtaking infinity of unbroken green.

It was a cargo helicopter with open-air, porthole windows. When the crew saw me looking out, one of them beckoned me to the door. With sign language, he showed me to hold on tight to the pole. Then he threw open the door. And we were blasted with air. The helicopter was cruising above the canopy of the forest—it couldn't have been more than one hundred feet above the trees.

It was difficult to breathe with so much rushing air. It was difficult to believe my eyes as the jungle that I had looked up at for almost twenty years now sped below me. I had never seen the jungle like this. I was looking down on great kapok trees. I saw troops of howler monkeys and spider monkeys swinging lower to take cover. I saw macaws fleeing over the green. I was clutching tight to the pole because nothing else was holding me inside the chopper.

As we went, I was humbled. The jungle is more immense than I ever could've imagined. More deep and complex and fantastic. With a smile, I realized that I was glad some of my most ambitious plans for solo expeditions had never been executed. This jungle was so damn big, so beyond the comprehension of a human mind.

When we hit the Las Piedras, the helicopter banked left and flew up along the channel. I recognized beaches that I had camped on. Places that had become the center of my reality that I was seeing from a whole new perspective. It was so exciting, so beautiful and crisp and stunning, that I tried to soak in every moment, and held a long inward smile. No, I wasn't born in the wrong time at all.

The helicopter was racing low over the endlessness of Amazonia—so unbroken and grand that my eyes could see only green as we thundered toward the wild horizon.

AFTERWORD

L AST WEEK, NARCO-TRAFFICKERS TRIED TO ASSASSINATE JJ.
In the months since I finished this book, a storm of change
has hit the river. Before then, our movement had spent several
years picking up galloping momentum—a stirring hope that
the dream of saving this river was actually possible. The public
support, the large donors, the ranger program, our acreage going
from 50,000 acres to 117,000—it was all miraculous. That all
ended one day with the sound of a gunshot.

Over the last few months, narco-traffickers have flooded
into the Las Piedras basin. They have identified our river as a
place where they can grow coca and remain hidden from the
law. They are a different breed than the loggers. The loggers are
usually friendly locals who are happy to be approached, negoti-
ated with, and ultimately persuaded to join our team. The narcos are different. They are accustomed to brutal violence, and
they need the cover of remote wilderness, far from the reach of
law enforcement. Somehow they've settled on our river as an
option. Many of them are connected to the people from Lucerna who moved in on that road and undoubtedly told their
friends and relatives that on this river, you can simply take land,
clear forest, make farms—farms that produce cocaine. That
there are no laws. No consequences. So we have gone from

studying the trees and butterflies to fighting a drug war. The funding that was allowing us to protect land is now being sucked away by the security we need. It's become very dangerous. People are dying. A few members of our own local conservation team have now been murdered.

Several weeks ago, when the police intercepted intelligence that the narcos knew about Junglekeepers, it was concerning. Even more concerning, they discovered, on a confiscated phone, a conversation where the narcos specifically identified JJ and me, and advised all who worked with them to take us out if the opportunity presented itself. We officially had a hit out on us. We all took it seriously, but we had no idea how focused and severe the threat really was.

On June 23, JJ was supposed to leave the station and meet our car in Lucerna. He got held up with work and decided to stay in the jungle another day. So he sent word ahead to the car to go back to town and pick up some rangers. As our driver, Percy was driving alone along the long, lonely Lucerna road, a team of men stopped him by barricading the road with a tree. They put a pistol through the open window against his head and asked if JJ and I were in the back. Where is Juan Julio? Where is the gringo? When he told them he had no idea who we were and that we weren't with him, they pulled him out onto the road at gunpoint. They roughed him up and took his license and his phone. They told him we'd been lucky. Next time we wouldn't be. Thank God they didn't hurt him.

But when Percy got back to town and told us what had happened, the story shook us all to our core: If JJ had gotten in the car that day, like he was supposed to, he would have been murdered.

It's a new reality that none of us had been prepared for. We are taking every precaution we can while continuing to fight to protect this river, but now the stakes have changed. It's not just the tribes and the trees and the wild and the sky, but our own lives that are in the balance. We are now actively being hunted. And if history has taught us anything, it's that the assassination of environmental leaders is far too common in Amazonia and rainforests across the world.

I wanted you to know. I thought everyone should know. We've come into hard times. This is the defining moment, the third act. And as the narcos clear forest and blaze new roads, we are faced with the obstacle that they are better armed and willing to do things we would never dream of to accomplish their goals. There is talk on the river that they've been using machine guns against the Mashco Piro they encounter. There is talk on the river that more of them are coming. We are working with police and the government, but the reality is the roads they are blazing are moving quickly through the heart of the land that we are working so hard to save, the heart of the corridor. This is the endgame. Either we save the forest now, or everything we have worked for will be erased. The next year or two will tell.

ACKNOWLEDGMENTS

═══

H OW DO I THANK THE INCREDIBLE PEOPLE WHO MADE ALL THIS possible? Is there a way to thank parents who understood their child's wild heart and never wavered in their support of it? Ed and Lenore, you have made this life an adventurous miracle. To my sister, Michelle, my best friend, who edits and carefully critiques all of my writing, thank you for helping me shape this wild story into a book that makes sense.

To my agent and friend Lindsay Edgecombe: You were the first to believe in me, and I'll never forget it. Just look how far we've come! Three books in, and here's to so many future adventures!

Thank you to Linda Carbone for working with me on the proposals for both this book and *Mother of God*. Your guidance and care made my career as a writer possible.

Thank you to Matthew Burdette, Derek Reed, Rachel Tockstein, Steven Boriack, Claire Hendrix, Ashley Shoemaker, and everyone at Penguin Random House and Convergent for believing in this book and this story, and so passionately helping to bring it to the world.

A tremendous thanks to Dax Dasilva and Age of Union for supporting our work in the Amazon. Dax, you know that we would not be here without you. Thank you for believing in me when no one else did, and allowing us to save so many millions of heartbeats. The work you are doing not just with Junglekeepers but with conservation around the globe is inspiring. I am so proud and encouraged by the hope and progress that you and Age of Union have made possible.

Thank you to Rebecca Foon and Guillaume Brun for helping us establish Junglekeepers as a Peruvian NGO. And thank you to Dina Tsouluhas for your unending dedication to this ranger program and saving this river.

Thank you to Vanessa for saving our asses so many times. Thank you to Eric and Bronwyn for helping us land the punches at the crucial time that made our success on the river and the creation of this book possible. Thank you to Jay for making it possible to save the Ancient Forest. Thank you to Lex Fridman and Joe Rogan, Julian Dorey, and Danny Jones: You guys were kind enough to help us get the message of this story to millions. Thank you so, so much to Vajra Olana Kingsley, my love, for helping me survive the edits of this book.

Thank you to so many people who have donated to Junglekeepers and allow us to notch wins toward saving this incredible wild.

Thank you to the people of Peru, my adopted home: Te amo mucho!

PAUL ROSOLIE is a naturalist, explorer, author, and award-winning wildlife filmmaker. For more than fifteen years, he has specialized in protecting threatened ecosystems and species in countries ranging from Brazil and Peru to India and Indonesia. He is the founder of Junglekeepers, an organization that focuses on protecting threatened habitats in western Amazonia. To date, Junglekeepers has protected more than 117,000 acres of primary forest.

Instagram: @paulrosolie

YouTube: @junglekeeper

X: @paulrosolie

Facebook.com/paulrosolie

TikTok: @junglekeeper

ABOUT THE TYPE

This book was set in Bembo, a typeface based on an old-style Roman face that was used for Cardinal Pietro Bembo's tract *De Aetna* in 1495. Bembo was cut by Francesco Griffo (1450–1518) in the early sixteenth century for Italian Renaissance printer and publisher Aldus Manutius (1449–1515). The Lanston Monotype Company of Philadelphia brought the well-proportioned letterforms of Bembo to the United States in the 1930s.